THE SACRED JOURNEY

Books by AHMAD KAMAL

The Seven Questions of Timur (1938)

Land Without Laughter (1940)

Full Fathom Five (1948)

One Dog Man (1950)

The Excommunicated (1952)

The Sacred Journey (1961)

THE SACRED JOURNEY

Being

Pilgrimage to Makkah

The Traditions, Dogma, and Islamic Ritual that govern the
lives and the destiny of more than five hundred million
who call themselves Muslim: one seventh of Mankind.

by

AHMAD KAMAL

DUELL, SLOAN AND PEARCE
New York

This volume
And all that I attempt
I dedicate to my son
TURAN MIRZA KAMAL

The endorsement of His Eminence

Al Haj al Mufti Muhammad Amin al Husseini

May God increase the thawab of the honorable author, Ahmad Kamal, and reward him and all who serve the cause of Islam and the Muslims, for God will not fail to reward the Believers.

Beirut, Lebanon
June 20, 1960

PREFACE

By

His Eminence, Grand Imam Al Shaykh Muhammad Ibn
Muhammad Mahdi Al Khalisi, Head of Jami'at Madinat
al 'Ilm, Al Kadhimiyyah, Baghdad, Iraq.

In the Name of God, the Beneficent, the Merciful.

Praise unto Him who unifies the Muslims; those who profess His
Oneness, believe in His Book, and have faith in His Messenger.
Praise unto Him who unifies the Muslims as groups on Fridays, at
their Feasts, on their Pilgrimages and at their prayer-time when all
face Makkah. I confess that God is the only God and has no equal.
All His creatures on earth and in heaven manifest the miracle of
His unity. I confess that Muhammad is God's Servant and Messenger. I believe God's message and His glorious and eternal miracles as related in the Quran and as given in His Laws. All of these
revelations contain the surest guide for Man in his development;
they at the same time reject all evil which falls to the human race
or to the individual. God's miracles are the more evident as science
and technology advance. This we observe time and time again.
Each day we behold a new and magnificent miracle in the Prophet's
message. As God has blessed Ibrahim and his family, may God
bless His Prophet, the Prophet's next of kin and first supporters.
God is glorious and to Him be Praise.

As Islam and Muslims are my constant preoccupation, I am
perplexed and surprised by how the two contradict one another—
for they are intended to be one. In Islam I see the most elevated
philosophy, the most accurate doctrine, and the most beneficial

ix

guide to human progress. Islam, more than any other doctrine,
Law, or order known to Man, is a path toward knowledge, unity,
happiness, brotherhood, discipline, morality, modesty, gentleness,
self-respect, security, justice, righteousness, progress, and peace.
However, when I study the present situation of the Muslims, I see
that they are far from living according to the tenets of their religion. They are degenerate, ignorant, weak, poor, miserable,
divided, and confused. Even in their homelands Muslims are
humiliated. Among them justice is not practiced and they are
misguided, lacking leadership.

How is this gulf between Islam's precepts and the conduct of
Muslims to be explained? Muslims do not know the Laws of their
own religion; this is the worst. They are unaware of the worldly
and heavenly blessings which stem from their faith; a few writers
and learned men have examined this subject. This conflict between
Islamic precepts and Muslim behavior has commanded my attention and I have been most anxious that it be a topic for our writers.

It was the will of God that Ahmad Kamal, of Jami'at al Islam,
international Muslim rescue organization, fill this need.

Here in Baghdad we two entered into a thorough discussion on
the Laws of Islam and the matter of Pilgrimage; we counted its
blessings and advantages, one of which is to unify Muslims. We
were not particularly pleased with the books available on the Pilgrimage: some written according to Abu Hanifah, others according
to Shafe'i or Malik or Ibn Hanbal. We reviewed books written
according to the Shi'ah way. We examined volumes prepared according to each of the Four Schools—all were incomplete and
inadequate. Then, after deliberation, we parted.

In the middle of the month Shawwal I received *The Sacred
Journey*. I asked Mr. Hussein 'Auni 'Ata to translate it for me; it
contains many concepts which I had always wished that Muslim
writers would bring forward. I thanked God for inspiring this
author to examine these issues. Together we can now work for the
enlightenment of all Muslims.

I will touch upon the main features of the volume. It is an ex-
cellent work and will be treasured by all of discriminating taste.
While reading it I recalled the popular proverb: "Honey is one of
God's soldiers." Than spiritual honey, to sweeten the soul and

comfort the body, what could be better! Read this book: it de-
scribes the holy places in such a manner that,.forgetting yourself,
you will feel that you have been transported there. When the ap-
pointments are described, you will be there; when the Haram is
mentioned, you will see yourself there, inside it; and when the
Ka'bah is portrayed it is with your eyes that you will see it. When
the author mentions the Tawaf, "The Wandering," you will
visualize yourself going around the House. When you are taken
to Ibrahim's or Isma'il's shrines, you will not doubt that you have
visited both places and prayed there. And when you are between
Safa and Marwah, it will be you who pray there. The descriptions
are so vivid that you will feel that you are present, seeing all, as
you are guided from one place to another, hearing the prayers of
the pilgrims and following their sacred journey.

By reading this book you will become acquainted with all aspects
of Pilgrimage. It provides excellent advice as to food, drink, and
dress; at the same time you learn how to manage most effectively
with the people of Makkah and Madinah. Similarly accurate is
the description of the Prophet's tomb.

The narrative is not narrowly limited to the sites of the Pilgrimage. We are reminded of the hundred and eighty million
Muslims who suffer under the heavy yoke of alien repression. Many
of these Muslims may not practice their religion and are prevented
from fulfilling the duty of Pilgrimage. We must pray for these
deprived ones and labor to free them.

That it combines the Shi'ah and Sunni ways is the most important feature of Ahmad Kamal's book. The difference between
these two sects, as you will realize, is not wider than the inconse-
quential space between Shafe'i and Hanafi. Muslims are called
upon to unite, leaving trivial differences behind—particularly urgent
in this age.

This volume includes the laws pertaining to Pilgrimage, and
whenever the author approaches a facet or aspect of the Pilgrimage
he provides an insight into the origin and the rituals. In brief,
within these pages you will find the complete ceremony of Pilgrimage, its laws and observances, and implicit therein, an appeal
to Muslims to unite and thrust out of bondage, with a warning
against discord and its perils.

I wish the author every success. May God reward him for this worthy effort. I wish all good and blessings to the translator and the publisher. To all Muslims, and particularly to all pilgrims, may this book serve its good purpose.

Baghdad, 1952

AUTHOR'S NOTE

THE SACRED JOURNEY, now to appear in an English edition, took form during my own Pilgrimage to Makkah and 'Arafat and was completed in Bandung, Indonesia, then my home, eight years ago. I wrote a *manasik* which abandoned schism and returned to the fundamentals of Islamic tradition and faith; sectarianism wherever encountered has been a blight. The manuscript was submitted at my request to *Madinat al 'Ilm*, Al Kadhimiyyah, Baghdad, a Shi'ah Muslim stronghold and center of learning. His Eminence Al Iman al Shaykh Muhammad Ibn Muhammad Mahdi al Khalisi al Kebir, head of this great institution and spiritual mentor for a vast following of Muslims in the Arab East as well as Iran and Afghanistan, had for half a century been one of the foremost exponents of Islamic unity.

His Eminence Al Khalisi ordered the manuscript translated into Arabic, and the book was printed on the presses of his foundation at Al Kadhimiyyah. For a Sunni Muslim author to be sponsored and published by leading Shi'ah Muslims was something of a precedent and an omen.

The Sacred Journey was circulated widely in the Arab world and was successful. The book was accepted by Hanafi and Maliki, Shafe'i and Hanbali—by Shi'ah and by Sunni—and was very well received in Makkah, the Sacred City, where it was made available to arriving pilgrims as a guide to the rites before them and as an admonition against disunity, which pleased and honored me.

The Baghdad edition, intended for a very wide Arabic-speaking audience, was more nearly an educational than a commercial enterprise and is entirely out of print.

The acceptance enjoyed by the volume was underscored when the proofs of this new edition received the formal endorsement of

His Eminence Grand Mufti Al Haj Amin al Husseini—soldier, statesman, and foremost Sunni religious figure. Storm center of controversy, asbestos giant in a world of flames, right or wrong for four decades unremitting in his struggle to assist his people toward an Islamic Renaissance, immovable and uncompromising at the Treaty Table, Guardian of Islam, he approved *The Sacred Journey* and affixed his signature.

This English edition in no way differs from the *manasik* published at Al Kadhimiyyah. Bound together with the English is the complete Arabic original, reset in Beirut in a beautiful and easily read typeface, providing, I believe, a valuable reference work for all who engage in the study of either language or who seek to understand the East and Islam, the latter an inspiration and driving force for a great segment of mankind.

Transliteration of Arabic into English has led to sufficient dispute over the years. Arabic, unlike English, is for the most part written without vowels. The name Muhammad in the Arabic is spelled *MHMD*. Makkah is *MKH*. This sort of abbreviation, projected infinitely, provides ample opportunity for argument on transliteration. The method I have employed is a close guide to correct pronunciation and has the acceptance of competent European linguists and scholars. To be completely consistent is an impossibility as is evidenced in Scripture. In this text, whenever there has been any possibility of confusion, I have elected in favor of clarity.

To Shaykh al Hajj Muhammad Mahdi Amir, Makkah, Saudi Arabia, and Asad Muhammad Alkalali, of Tjeribon, West Java, I must express my indebtedness; the former was my guide during Pilgrimage, the latter is an Arab classicist. Both provided essential guidance throughout the preparation of this manuscript. I also tender my warmest thanks to Dr. Pangkat Harahap, who scrupulously and patiently corrected the manuscript and the proofs. Finally, I must thank Mr. B. Rogard, Mr. J. R. Price, and Dr. Paul Linebarger for their tireless insistence that the English text see publication—and their efforts to this end.

Dr. Ahmad Ould N'gawa of the Wolof nation, Senegal, Africa, will not witness the publication of this edition, nor will Zahidallah Bey Agish, Siberian Tatar, deceased President of *Jami'at al Islam*. They were convinced that wide publication of *The Sacred Journey* would strengthen them in their struggle to save their peoples and win the understanding of men of whatever persuasion. Humanitarian endeavor their vocation, their lives were consecrated to the emancipation of the enslaved and the restoration of dignity to the humiliated. The African met death in Portuguese Angola recently, while on a rescue mission. Death came to Zahidallah Bey more quietly, in California, just before this volume went to press. I honor them *in memoriam*.

I dedicate this book, and all that I attempt, to my son Turan Mirza Kamal.

AHMAD KAMAL

Madrid, Spain, 1961

CONTENTS

xvii

PART 2

THE SACRED JOURNEY TO MADINAH AND JERUSALEM

PART I

THE SACRED JOURNEY TO MAKKAH

CHAPTER 1

MAKKAH: THE HOLIEST OF THE CITIES OF ISLAM

IT IS TOLD that after Adam and Eve were expelled from Paradise, Adam, heartsick, prayed beside a temple which was the duplicate of another temple in Paradise, perpendicularly overhead, where angels worship. The stone walls of the original edifice echoed the first prayers uttered by mankind.

The first House of Worship founded for men was that at Bakkah; Blessed, and of guidance for all beings. In it are signs evident, even the place of Ibrahim. Whoever enters it attains security. Pilgrimage thereto is a duty men owe to God—those who can afford the journey. But if any disbelieve, God does not stand in need of any of His creatures. [Quran 3:96-97]

Visited by the progeny of Adam until the Deluge, when it disappeared and they were overwhelmed and destroyed, later rebuilt on the same site by the Prophet Ibrahim and his son Isma'il, today the Holy Ka'bah stands in massive, severe beauty: a simple cube-like edifice of stone and mortar veiled in blue-black cloth which is lettered in gold.

Twelve meters in length, ten meters wide, fifteen meters high, the Holy Ka'bah—also known as Al Bayt al-'Atiq, "The Most Ancient House"—is in a great mosque courtyard which may be entered through any one of twenty-four gates.

During the Pilgrimage great rivers of humanity flood into Arabia

3

from every point of the compass, arriving by land, sea, and air, overflowing the approaches to Makkah, then inundating the sacred city Makkah al-Mukarramah, Makkah the Noble, forbidden to all who are not Muslim. Night and day the dark-draped Ka'bah is the center about which a vast, surging current of Faithful perform the ritual circling, again surrounded, wave upon wave, by a sea of exhausted pilgrims lying upon the ground or seated or standing in attitudes of devotion and prayer.

After the opening of the Pilgrimage, at Makkah, the multitude departs from the city en masse, journeying through the wastes to 'Arafat.

'Arafat, the place of "Recognition" or "Knowing," is a naked stone mountain in a wide and barren valley. There is a legend that when Adam and Eve were banished from Paradise they were separated. Two hundred years they fruitlessly searched the earth for each other, alone and despairing—until the Angel Jibra'il descended and led Adam to Eve. And here, on the desert mountain, they came together again and *knew* each other.

And there is a tale that in Ibrahim's time the Angel Jibra'il, having initiated the prophet into all the rites of the Pilgrimage, here questioned him. And Ibrahim *knew*.

At the close of the ceremonies at 'Arafat the great host, often five hundred thousand strong, thrusts mightily through the desolation, pausing in the night for prayers at Muzdalifah, an isolated oratory. Then, rising from its devotions, it forges on to Mina where the faith of the Prophet Ibrahim and his son Isma'il is believed to have been tested: where the distraught father prepared to offer up his son as a blood sacrifice to God, and where Satan, tempting the youth to revolt against his father, was stoned by Isma'il.

These are the scenes of the Pilgrimage. These are the holy places. The holiest of all is in Makkah—there, in the center of the sacred, forbidden city, is the terrestrial heart of Islam. We have been instructed to pray five times each day, and we have been told that it is better for us to offer up our prayers in unison, in congregation, than to worship in solitude. From Capetown to Arctic Siberia, from Mindanao and the islands of the South Pacific, then back across all Asia and Europe to Finland, southward again to Africa's Atlantic shores, east to west, north and south, each day one-seventh of mankind faces toward Makkah and the Ka'bah and unites in prayer.

The inviolable territory which encloses the holy places and the city of Makkah, surrounded on all sides by a terrible labyrinth of narrow, rock-strewn valleys and exposed passes, itself desert, has since the dawn of recorded time been the focus of trade and pilgrim caravan routes which cross the most inhospitable terrain on earth.

Makkah is founded not only in a desert waste, but also on soil which is said to be sterile. The heat is almost unbearable and its toll of pilgrim lives, and those of the natives of Makkah, has been terrible. In the Holy Quran we read the Prophet Ibrahim's supplication:

O our Lord! I have made some of my offspring to dwell in a valley without cultivation, by Thy Sacred House, in order, O our Lord, that they may establish regular prayer. So make the hearts of some among men yearn toward them, and provide them with fruits that they may be thankful. [Quran 14:37]

Seventy-three kilometers from its burning, oppressive port on the coast of the Red Sea, Makkah lies in a long, irregular hollow among naked, mountainous hills so precipitous that in ancient times it was unnecessary to protect the city with a wall, but only to dam the valley at three exposed points with fortified gates which led into the city. Today the gates—which once were closed against

Muhammad ﷺ by the pagan Quraysh—remain in name alone, and storeyed habitations and ruins cling to the boulder-strewn hillsides.

A broad, twining thoroughfare follows the irregular floor of the valley of Makkah, dividing it and the city longitudinally; this main artery is intersected beside the great mosque by a broad way which crosses the valley from hill-flank to hill-flank, cutting through the busiest market place. Roofed to protect pilgrims and Makkans from the indescribable heat of the summer sun, this latter is the sacred course between Safa and Marwah. Here trod Hajar, mother of Isma'il, in desperate search for water for her infant son, before there was a Makkah. Now the way is lined with shops filled with tons of rosaries of amber and rare and fragrant woods, with Qurans so tiny that a full, illuminated page is smaller than a woman's thumbnail and must be read with a powerful magnifying glass, with food and drink and footwear, umbrellas to turn not rain but sun, semiprecious stones and incense and musk and civet and heavy perfumes, attar and rosewater and Coca-Cola, Taif grapes and ripe Taif melons, primitive lithographs of Makkah and the holy scene—wares holy and wares profane to tempt the appetite of the solid tide of pilgrims which thrusts to and fro between Safa and Marwah in performance of the rite called sa'y.

And yet Makkah is not so much a geographic location, or Pilgrimage a ritual, as it is a frame of mind. Pilgrims will discover in Makkah only what they take to Makkah. We are not to come here in search of inspiration, but because we are inspired. Pilgrimage is a declaration of Belief, not a search for it.

Islam rests upon five pillars:

The first pillar is Faith and the Declaration of Faith: "There is no deity except God! And Muhammad is the Messenger of God!"

The second pillar of Islam is Prayer; there are things to be done for this world and for the world after this.

The giving of alms is the third pillar, and the observance of the periods of fasting and abstinence is the fourth.

Pilgrimage, Hajj, is the fifth pillar of Islam.

The Hajj is an immense congress of Faithful from all the corners of this earth, that Muslims of every race and complexion may worship in unison and come to know the power which springs from unified belief and concerted action. In our being called to gather in the holy places we have been granted an unparalleled opportunity to discover our potential might, spiritual and physical. Nowhere else is there such a yearly congress. No other people are privileged to know such oneness of being, such singleness of purpose.

Today Islam is opening its eyes after a sleep which has lasted almost a thousand years. An annual average of sixty thousand non-Arab Faithful made Hajj in the years between World Wars I and II. Eighty thousand pilgrims came to Makkah in 1941. One hundred and fifty thousand came in 1946. Two hundred and thirty thousand pilgrims gathered in Makkah and at 'Arafat in 1950.

Five hundred thousand pilgrims fulfilled the Pilgrimage in 1952. In 1960 there were seven hundred and fifty thousand pilgrims.

The giant is stirring. Waking to the new world, we must labor on this earth to make it a place of opportunity and joy and liberty for all mankind—as men certain of remaining here forever. And we must prepare for the world to come—as men certain of death on the morrow.

CHAPTER 2

PREPARATION FOR PILGRIMAGE

FOREMOST AMONG THE requisites of the Pilgrimage is that the pilgrim be able to afford the rite; we are not to make Hajj if it brings hardship to those dependent upon us.

TRADE

It is lawful for pilgrims to bring with them merchandise and trade goods from whose legitimate profit they may defray the cost of the voyage from and to their homelands and the expenses of the Hajj itself. This is in the interest of the trader and the mass of pilgrims who might otherwise be greatly inconvenienced for the necessities of life.

PROVISIONS

There are many nations in Islam and each has its own appetite and diet. It will be prudent if pilgrims not financially prepared to bear great expense for daily requirements bring with them staple foods; this is wise, too, from a standpoint of physical well-being. The demands of the Pilgrimage upon the pilgrims are severe, and digestive upsets are to be guarded against. In any case, the pilgrim must be equipped to bear expenses precisely twice those included in the most liberal estimates of the cost of the Makkan journey.

PILGRIM GUIDES

Whether pilgrims travel to Makkah alone or with companions, on arrival in the Hejaz the Arab authorities make certain that all are placed in the keeping of established, organized guides recognized by the government. These guides are called Mutawwifin or Mashayikh al-Hajj.

As it is inevitable that pilgrims will be grouped under such leadership during the Pilgrimage, probably it is best that the pilgrim join the group of one such guide from the start, in the pilgrim's country of origin. These pilgrim guides are to be found in every land where Muslims dwell—except those areas under alien rule or domination.

The Shaykh al-Hajj makes a profession of escorting pilgrims to Makkah and guiding them through the ceremonies. But these guides are mortal. There are many who are capable and sincere, there are others who are neither. The pilgrim starting from his or her home region with a group under its own Shaykh al-Hajj can make the choice. And the guide who must return with his pilgrims at the conclusion of the Pilgrimage, a man resident in the land from which he plans to escort other pilgrims to the Hejaz in following years, is likely to protect his reputation. Enquire into the character of a Shaykh al-Hajj by consulting those who made the journey under his guidance in past seasons.

The Shaykh al-Hajj is responsible for the care of those pilgrims brought by him from foreign lands or placed in his keeping by the Arabian officials in the Hejaz—a procedure governed by the pilgrims' land of origin and tongue and pertaining only to those who arrive unescorted. Each Shaykh al-Hajj provides shelter in Jeddah and Makkah and during the ritual journeying to 'Arafat and Mina. He provides transportation and directs his followers in the duties of Pilgrimage and leads them in the ceremonies. The devoted Shaykh al-Hajj assists his pilgrims in their dealings with the natives of Makkah and is an intermediary in all their affairs, whether private, mercantile, or official.

On the arrival at Jeddah the Shaykh al-Hajj must see that each person's baggage is cleared through Customs and transported to prearranged lodging. The Shaykh al-Hajj must tend to passport matters and obtain the "Way Card," which identifies the pilgrim after the surrender of his or her documents; all passports and travel papers are held by the authorities in Jeddah until the close of the Pilgrimage.

The sincere pilgrim guide protects his followers from rapacious shopkeepers, bargains on their behalf, and acts as their interpreter. He is father, brother, servant, and guard, and has been called the camel of the pilgrim. His responsibility does not end until the last of his party has completed the Pilgrimage and is embarked on the vessel, aircraft, or other means of transport which is to bear them homeward.

PRAYER

There can be no advice concerning, or discussion of, a man's spiritual qualifications or preparation for Pilgrimage. This is an affair between each pilgrim and God—but all creation sings praise of God and bows down before God; man and angel, the beast and the forest, animate and inanimate, each in its appointed way, the very mountains casting their shadows right and left in adoration and prostration, free from pride. [*Quran* 16:48-49]

And we read:

See you not that it is God whose praises all beings in the heavens and on earth do celebrate, and the birds with wings out-spread! Each one knows its own prayer and praise. And God knows well all that they do. [*Quran* 24:41]

We have been commanded to face toward Makkah five times daily in formal prayer. The time of the first prayer is daybreak, by the Arabs called *subh*; the second prayer is at noon, *dhuhr*, when the sun is just past its meridian; the third, *'asr*, midway between noon and nightfall; the fourth, *maghrib*, at sundown; and the fifth prayer, *'isha*, which is read in the night.

Each period of formal worship has prayers of fixed length: of a certain number of obeisances or *rak'ah*. Some are prayers and obeisances which are appointed; these are obligatory and are called *fardh*. Other prayers and obeisances were observed by the Prophet

Muhammad ﷺ ; these are traditional and are called *sunnah*.

When at home, or when remaining or intending to remain in one place for several days, we are instructed to omit no part of these prayers, *fardh* or *sunnah*, obligatory or traditional.

The morning prayer has two *rak'ah* which are *sunnah* and two *fardh*. The midday prayer is of four *sunnah* and four *fardh*. The afternoon devotions are the same. The evening prayer has three *rak'ah fardh* and two *sunnah*. The night prayer is of four *sunnah*, four *fardh*, then again two *sunnah*—by many Muslims followed with an additional *rak'ah* called *witr*, voluntary prayer, read before sleep.

But when we must journey great distances, as to Makkah, we are granted a release from the performance of the traditional prayers and obeisances and may shorten those prayers which are obligatory to two *rak'ah* in place of four. This applies only to prayer of four *fardh rak'ah*, not to those of three *rak'ah* or two, which may not be abbreviated.

Thus, during the journey to Makkah and throughout the Hajj (unless the pilgrim arrives at Makkah very early, or must remain in one place for a number of days), two *rak'ah* will be read at daybreak, *subh*. Two *rak'ah* will be read for the midday devotions, *dhuhr*, and two for the afternoon devotions, *'asr*; these will be read together. For the sundown prayer, *maghrib*, there will be three *rak'ah*, and two *rak'ah* for the night prayer, *'isha*; *maghrib* and *'isha* are read together.

Pray in solitude if you must, but know that no man may stand alone in this world. A man alone, laboring or worshiping, is a feeble thing. A nation alone awaits destruction or enslavement. Great numbers of men united in prayer or the struggle for right inspire awe and command respect; this will be witnessed during the Pilgrimage.

Islam has been divided by trifles, by age-old political arguments which our predecessors in their ignorance allowed to become articles of Faith. They and we have behaved like madmen—and have been punished. Most of the peoples of Islam are under foreign rule or suffering from the after effects of alien domination. In Soviet territory alone more than thirty-four million Turkic Muslims and forty million Chinese Muslims fear to worship openly; these figures do not include the lesser nations under that same rule.

If there is one of us who is a slave, none of us are free.

So long as we remain intolerant of one another and will not recognize that Hanafi and Maliki, Shafe'i and Hanbali—Shi'ah and Sunni—are nothing and *Islam* everything, none of us deserve to be free.

We have been told to perform the ritual prayers together. Shades of understanding are of no importance. We must approach God

each by the path he knows best, but we may not deny our brothers
the right to walk other, parallel paths.

Worship, shoulder to shoulder. All of our religion is in the
Quran. Our Faith is Islam. Our God is the God of Adam.

*To each is a goal to which he turns; then strive together toward
all that is good. Wherever ye are, God will bring you together:
for God hath Power over all things. And from whatever place
ye cometh forth, turn thy face in the direction of the Sacred
Mosque; and that is the Truth from thy Lord. And God is not
unmindful of what ye do.* [Quran 2:148-149]

THE EMBARKING

It is written that as the Deluge approached and the fountains of the earth gushed forth, Noah spoke to those who were to be saved, saying: "Embark ye on the Ark, In the Name of God be its course and its mooring! For my Lord is, be sure, Oft-Forgiving, Most Merciful." [*Quran 11:41*]

And so, today, departing from their homes and embarking for Jeddah, and frequently throughout the voyage, the pilgrims read: "In the Name of God be the course and the mooring..."

CHAPTER 3

IHRAM AND THE SACRED GARMENTS
OF THE HAJJ

THE FIRST of the principal ceremonies of the Pilgrimage is the putting off of conventional garments to don those of Ihram, the traditional habit which distinguishes pilgrims from all others but permits no distinction one from another. All, high-born and humble, wear identical robes and are reminded that in the eyes of God all men are created equal—and that on the Day of Judgement all will be accountable.

Ihram is a state of many sacred prohibitions.

On taking this garb the pilgrim enters into a period of peace and self-denial. Violence in any form is banned. The pilgrim must abstain from luxuries and gratification of the senses, however legitimate, until the rites of the Pilgrimage have been observed and Ihram put aside. Jewelry or other personal adornment is forbidden; so, too, is perfume or scent. It is forbidden for a pilgrim in Ihram to uproot any growing thing or to cut down a tree within the Sanctuary of Makkah. Sexual intercourse must cease temporarily and the sexual impulse is to be sublimated.

During the days in Ihram there may be no wrangling or argument, no rudeness, no discussion of the opposite sex, and no hunting. Bodily, the pilgrim is to be devoted to the acts of Pilgrimage; intellectually, he or she is to be concerned with prayer, aspirations, praise of God, and self-examination.

For Hajj are the months well known. If any one undertakes that duty therein, let there be no obscenity, nor wickedness, nor wrangling, in the Hajj. And whatever good ye do, God knoweth it.

*And take a provision for the journey, but the best of provisions
is right conduct. So fear Me, O ye who are wise!* [Quran 2:196]

O ye who believe! God will make a trial of you in a little matter
of game well within reach of your hands and your lances, that He
may test who feareth Him unseen; any who transgress thereafter
will have a grievous penalty.

O ye who believe! Kill not game while in the Sacred Precincts
or in pilgrim garb. If any of you do this intentionally, his expiation
is: an offering, made to the Ka'bah, of an animal equivalent to the
one he killed, as adjudged by two just men among you; or the
feeding of the indigent; or its equivalent in fasts: that he may taste
of the penalty of his deed. God will forgive what is past; for repeti-
tion God will exact from him a penalty. For God is Exalted and
Lord of Retribution.

Lawful to you is the pursuit of water game and its use for food,
for the benefit of yourselves and those who travel, but forbidden
is the pursuit of land game as long as ye are in the Sacred Precincts
or in pilgrim garb. And fear God, to Whom ye shall be gathered
back.

God made the Ka'bah, the Sacred House, an asylum of security
for men, as also the Sacred Months, the animals for offerings, and
the garlands that mark them, that ye might know that God hath
knowledge of what is in the heavens and on earth and that God
is well-acquainted with all things.

Know ye that God is strict in punishment and that God is Oft-
Forgiving, Most Merciful.

[Quran 5:97–100]

THE PERIOD OF IHRAM

Ihram's garments are worn during—

(I) The pilgrims' arrival at Makkah for the first tawaf and sa'y,
the initial rituals by and circuits of the Holy Ka'bah and the visiting of the hills Safa and Marwah, traversing the distance between
them seven times.

(II) The stand before the stone mountain 'Arafat on the ninth day of the Pilgrimage Month; then, that night, at the gathering of pebbles and the pause in the darkness for prayer at Muzdalifah, a sacred spot in the wilderness between 'Arafat and the Valley of Mina.

(III) Then, on the tenth day, the casting of stones at the Jamrat al-'Aqabah, the largest of the three crude stone-and-mortar monuments marking the places in Mina where Satan appeared to Isma'il, son of the Prophet Ibrahim.

(IV) And the offering of the blood sacrifice at Mina.

Ihram for Male Pilgrims   For men the Ihram dress is comprised of two large pieces of white fabric, without design, decoration, or seam. Many pilgrims prefer white cotton towelling; this is better than lighter cloth as a protection both from the killing heat of the summer and against the sudden, blade-like winds when Pilgrimage must be made during

the winter. Before the time of Muhammad ﷺ the Hajj ceremonies took place at a fixed time in the autumn. In pagan years the lunar months were kept to their solar setting by the insertion of extra days, a practice abandoned by the Prophet. Today the year is lunar and the time of Pilgrimage changes, passing through every season; pilgrims must remember this and prepare themselves accordingly.

In ancient, pagan times pilgrims approaching the Holy Ka'bah removed all of their clothing as a sign of humility. Naked, they performed the ritual tawaf, kissed the Black Stone, and otherwise

did as we do now. Until the time of the Prophet Muhammad ﷺ, it had been the custom to go, naked, in the dark before dawn to the Ka'bah for the rites of absolution. The Prophet did not approve of this nudity, nor of the loud manner in which the worship was performed. He introduced the Ihram dress we wear today and the more subdued manner in which we pray, but the rite is an ancient rite.

One length of the Ihram cloth is worn over the shoulders, covering the upper half of the body. The second length is worn wrapped about the waist and secured with a belt; it should reach to the ankles. Each piece of cloth should measure approximately two and a half meters in length and one and a half meters in breadth. No other garment is to be worn over this or beneath it, but it is common usage to wear a money-pouch on a shoulder sling or a moneybelt; one of these is requisite as the Ihram robes should have no pockets.

Men may not cover their heads during the Pilgrimage, nor are the feet to be shod in other except sandals which do not cover the backs of the heels.

Ihram for Female Pilgrims　　　Women do not wear the Ihram garments which are worn by men. They may keep to their customary dress, garbing themselves in plain, fresh clothing at the time of entering into Ihram. Though female pilgrims are not to veil their faces during the Pilgrimage, their hair is to be covered. Women's garments should reach to their ankles and the sleeves to their wrists; the neck-line should be high, revealing none of the breast.

Female pilgrims who are menstruating at the time they take Ihram, or who menstruate during the days they are in Ihram, should not perform any of the daily prayers or other ritual *rak'ah* until their menses have left them; but they may read all other forms of prayer—except those requiring obeisances.

No woman is to make Pilgrimage unless she is accompanied by her husband or, if she is unwed, by two male members of her immediate family, both of whom must be of such close relationship as to preclude sexual interest or eventual marriage. And no man is to approach his wife sexually, or woman to encourage her husband to enter her, during Ihram.

During periods of prayer only male pilgrims may worship aloud or recite audibly. Female pilgrims may not lift their voices or conduct themselves in such a manner as to attract attention; scrupulously they must avoid distracting males from their devotions.

Physical Preliminaries to the Taking of Ihram　　　Before entering Ihram each pilgrim, male and female, should trim the fingernails and remove underarm and pubic hair. Women should shampoo the head; men should shampoo or shave the head, for to trim the nails, clip the hair or beard, or shave the face is not again permissible until all the rites for which the particular Ihram is taken have been fulfilled.

And complete the Hajj, or 'Umrah, in the service of God. But if ye are prevented, send an offering for sacrifice, such as ye may find; and do not shave your heads until the offering reaches the place of sacrifice. And if any of you is ill, or has an ailment of the scalp (necessitating shaving), in compensation either fast, or feed the poor, or offer sacrifice; and when ye are in peaceful conditions, if any one wishes to continue the 'Umrah on to the Hajj, he must make an offering such as he can afford. But if he cannot afford it, he should fast three days during the Hajj and seven days on his return, making ten days in all. This is for those whose household is not by the Sacred Mosque. And fear God, and know that God is strict in punishment. [Quran 2:195]

THE FORMS OF IHRAM

There are *kinds* of Ihram, the selection of which is a matter of personal volition.

I. 'Umrah: The Lesser Pilgrimage Whatever the season, anyone visiting Makkah for the first time, or returning to Makkah after a long absence, or wishing to perform a meritorious act is obliged to wear the robes of Ihram and make the sacred visitation of the holy places in Makkah to read Praise and honor God. This is 'Umrah. The Ihram taken for 'Umrah is put aside after the visit to the Holy Ka'bah for prayer and tawaf—the ritual circling—and the performance of sa'y, the ritual going to and fro between Safa and Marwah.

'Umrah is complete in itself. 'Umrah is the Lesser Pilgrimage, it is *not* Hajj, the Greater Pilgrimage; and those who observe it may not call themselves "Hajji" unless they complete the rites of the Hajj, which may be accomplished only at the appointed time.

The months Shawwal, Dhu-al-Qa'dah, and Dhu-al-Hijjah are set apart for the Hajj, the Greater Pilgrimage. The first rites may be performed as early as the opening of the month Shawwal with a definite approach to Makkah, while the chief rites may not be observed until the eighth, ninth, and tenth days of Dhu-al-Hijjah, the last of the Arab year, when the pilgrim concourse reaches its height for the essential ceremonies.

II. Tamattu': The Performance of 'Umrah and Hajj Together   Ihram for Tamattu', generally referred to as Tamattu' with 'Umrah, may be taken by pilgrims arriving early for the Hajj. After entrance to Makkah and completion of the initial tawaf and sa'y, the robes of this Ihram, together with Ihram's prohibitions, may be put aside for the interim period and accustomed garb and normal pleasures and activity resumed. We are told that pilgrims availing themselves of this convenience should make a sacrifice. Those who cannot offer a blood sacrifice should fast three days during the Pilgrimage and another seven days after its completion.

Unlike the Ihram of 'Umrah which ends with the ritual visitation of the Holy Ka'bah and the hills Safa and Marwah, for those pilgrims wearing the Ihram of Tamattu' these observances are but the opening scene of a vast and earth-shaking event: the approaching Hajj. Tamattu' is the performance of 'Umrah and Hajj together. Laid aside after the opening rites in Makkah, this Ihram must be resumed before the advent of the important days of the Pilgrimage Month, Dhu-al-Hijjah.

The ceremony observed on the resumption of Ihram is the same as that followed when Ihram is first taken.

III. Hajj: The Greater Pilgrimage   Today it is general practice for the pilgrim to include 'Umrah when taking Ihram for Hajj: this is achieved by the simple measure of including 'Umrah in the *Niyat*, or Intention, voiced at the taking of Ihram for Hajj. The preparation for taking Ihram for Hajj is in no way different from that of other Ihrams, but Ihram for Hajj— or 'Umrah with Hajj—may not be put aside until all the rites and ceremonies of the Greater Pilgrimage have been fulfilled; only in this aspect does the Ihram for Hajj differ from that for Tamattu'.

Having taken Ihram, the pilgrim must observe all of Ihram's restrictions and prohibitions.

Having undertaken the Hajj, pilgrims must strive to fulfill all the observances and obligations contingent upon the completion of the rite.

If physically prevented, either by illness or injury, pilgrims may after the stand at 'Arafat—for there is no Pilgrimage without 'Arafat—make a symbolic completion of the Hajj rituals by sending a sacrificial offering to the Valley of Mina. A blood sacrifice would have been offered had the ailing supplicant been present; thus, those absent, whatever the cause, must make a vicarious offering, possibly sending a sacrificial animal to the site of the sacrifice. When the animal can be assumed to have reached Mina, the Ihram may be ritually terminated and ordinary dress resumed.

Fasting and alms-giving are acceptable in lieu of a blood sacrifice.

Ihram is a time of forbearance and patience. Ihram is an experience in brotherhood, an admonition for past disunity, and a promise and a demonstration of what Islam can become when we are unified. And Ihram is a warning of the privation and humiliation and destruction before us, before Islam itself, unless Muslims learn to think, act, and strive together in tolerance and self-denial—and even, if we must, self-sacrifice—for the glory of God and the betterment of all men.

THE RITUAL OF ENTERING INTO IHRAM

Pilgrims approaching Makkah from the north, by sea, should change to the garments of Ihram when their ship is opposite the small port of Rabigh.

Those who come overland from the north, via Madinah, should enter Ihram at Abiar 'Ali—in the time of the Prophet named Dhu-al-Hulaifah.

Arriving from the south, by sea or land, pilgrims should perform the rite and change dress at Yulamlam.

Faithful traveling overland from the east, from Nejd and Hassa, should enter Ihram at Qarn—in Muhammad's ﷺ time called Qarn al-Manazil or Wadi Mihrim.

Pilgrims journeying by land from 'Iraq are to change their garb at Dhat-'Irq.

Natives of Makkah enter Ihram in Makkah itself.

It is not obligatory that the change into Ihram be made at these places, but it is preferred. The world has changed, and today the many pilgrims who arrive by air will find it inconvenient to change clothing while airborne; it is better that they put on the robes of Ihram at the last landing place before Jeddah or after arrival at Jeddah.

Wudhu: The　　　　　The ceremony observed at entering Ihram
Ritual Ablutions　　　begins with the ritual ablutions. On removing
　　　　　　　　　　ordinary garb in preparation for Ihram, it is better to bathe entirely; if this is not possible, the pilgrim should make the ritual ablutions as if for prayer.

Many Muslims are accustomed to making their ablutions in silence, omitting almost all the prayers which should accompany or follow the actions; but if the pilgrim desires to perform the ablutions in the manner of the Prophet Muhammad ﷺ , he should say, in a low or inaudible voice:

I intend to perform the wudhu, for prayer . . .

Then wash the hands, rinsing them three times, saying, in the same manner as before:

In the Name of God, the Compassionate, the Merciful. Praise unto God, who sent down water for purification and made Islam to be a light . . .

Then rinse the mouth three times, saying:

O God, make my heart radiant with the Quran and let me be one of those who pray . . .

Then bathe the nostrils, three times, saying:

O God, grant that I may know the aromas and fragrance of Paradise . . .

Then wash the face, three times, saying:

O God, make my face white—and shining, on the day when faces shall be white—and faces shall be blackened . . .

Next, three times bathe and rinse the right arm, saying:

O God, give me my book in my right hand and reckon me with an easy reckoning . . .

Now bathe and rinse the left arm, saying:

O, God, do not give me my book in my left hand, nor behind my back, and do not reckon me with a severe reckoning . . .

Drawing the right hand over the crown of the head, front to back, say:

O God, shade me under the shadow of Thy Throne on the day when there shall be no shade but Thy shade . . .

Rinsing the ears, say:

O God, make me to be of those who hear what is said and obey what is best . . .

Rinsing the neck, say:

O God, free me from the Fire!

Lastly, bathe the feet, the right foot first, saying:

O God, make my feet firm upon the way to Paradise on the day when feet shall slip from it. O God, receive my good works and forgive my sins and my transgressions . . .

Closing the *wudhu*, say:

I testify that there is no deity except God, alone! He has no companion. I implore His forgiveness and turn to Him in repentance.

I testify that there is no deity except God! And I testify that Muhammad is His servant and His Messenger!

Tayammum: The "Dry" or Substitute Ablution   When it is not possible to obtain water, Muslims may perform an acceptable ablution with dust or sand—a symbolic purification. This is *tayammum*.

Strike the palms of the hands on any dry, clean surface which contains dust. The ground is best, but if there exists reason to doubt its purity, the pilgrim may use a wall or a blanket which holds some dust. Then wipe the face with both hands. Strike the surface again and wipe the right hand and arm as high as the elbow. Strike the surface a third time and stroke the left hand and arm similarly. This completes the ritual.

O Ye who believe! Approach not prayers with a mind befogged, until ye can comprehend all that ye say; nor in a state of ceremonial impurity, until after bathing your whole body if ye are ill, or on a journey, or one of you cometh from the offices of nature, or have been in contact with women, and ye find no water, then take for yourselves clean sand or earth and rub therewith your faces and hands—for God doth blot out sins and forgive again and again! [Quran 4:42]

It is not required that we perform ablutions before each of our prayers if we are conscious of having avoided every kind of impurity since the last ritual ablution. This is true, too, when putting on the garments of Ihram—provided that water is not to be had.

Salat (Formal, Ritual Prayer)— at Entering Ihram   After bathing and making ready, then donning the garments of Ihram, each pilgrim should read formal prayer of two *rak'ah*. These *rak'ah* may be brief. For example:

Quran 1. AL-FATIHAH—

In the Name of God, the Compassionate, the Merciful . . .

Praise be to God, Lord of the Worlds!
The Compassionate, the Merciful!
Master of the Day of Judgement!
Thee do we worship,
And Thine aid we entreat.
Show us the straight way,
The way of those on whom
Thou hast bestowed Thy Grace;
Not of those with whom
Thou art wrathful—
Nor those who go astray. Amen.

The above may be followed with the verses:

Quran 110. AL-NASR—

In the Name of God, the Compassionate, the Merciful . . .

When comes the help of God, and victory,
And thou dost see the people
Enter God's Religion in throngs,
Celebrate then the praises of thy Lord,
And pray for His Forgiveness—
For He is Oft-Relenting.

Quran 113. AL-FALAQ—

In the Name of God, the Compassionate, the Merciful . . .

Say: I seek refuge
With the Lord of the Dawn,
From the mischief of created things;
And from the mischief of darkness
When it overspreads;
And from the mischief of those
Who blow on knots;
And from the mischief of the envious
Practicing envy.

Du'a (Prayer of Supplication and Praise) During Ihram   At the close of formal, ritual prayer there comes a time for supplication and praise. The following *du'a* should be read at this time and after every period of prayer.

O God, Thou art Peace,
From Thee, Peace—and to Thee
Returneth Peace.
Let us live, our Lord, in Peace,
And accept us in Thy Paradise,
The Mansion of Peace.
Thou art Glorious and Most High,
To Thee belongeth Greatness and Honor!
We hear and we obey!
Thy forgiveness, our God, and to Thee
We return again.

Niyat for Ihram:
The Declaration
of Intent

Those pilgrims taking Ihram should make verbal declaration of intent. Still in an attitude of prayer, pilgrims intending to make 'Umrah will address their Creator, saying:

O God, I intend to make 'Umrah
And I am taking Ihram for it.
Make it easy for me—
And receive it from me.

Pilgrims taking Ihram for Hajj will employ the same phrases, but will add the necessary words. Remember, the Ihram of Hajj cannot be put aside—unless from the beginning the pilgrim declares that the Hajj being performed is that of 'Tamattu', the "interrupted Ihram"—until the full rites of the Pilgrimage have been concluded. This does not mean that a pilgrim must wear soiled Ihram robes; we may change our robes and bathe as often as we desire, donning fresh garments if they are to be had, but we may *not* resume our accustomed garb.

TALBYAH: THE CALL, THE ACKNOWLEDGING

Talbyah is the most frequently uttered of all the formula prayers of the Pilgrimage. Immediately after declaration of intent, as above, each pilgrim will say:

What is Thy Command? I am here, O God, for 'Umrah—

Or—

What is Thy Command? I am here, O God, for Hajj—

Or—

What is Thy Command? I am here, O God, for 'Umrah and Hajj—

Follow the above with talbyah:

What is Thy Command? I am here, O God!
What is Thy Command? I am here!
What is Thy Command? I am here!

Thou art without companion!
What is Thy Command? I am here!
Praise and blessings are Thine, and Dominion!
Thou art without companion!

We must repeat this formula countless times throughout the Pilgrimage. We must repeat it when traveling, when ascending, when descending, when hearing another pilgrim utter these words, when waking and before sleeping, and before addressing anyone. If we come upon men disputing we must tell it to them—and occasionally we must add:

O God, shower Thy Blessings upon Muhammad,
And the family of Muhammad,
As Thou didst shower Thy Mercy upon Ibrahim,
And the family of Ibrahim;
Thou art Praised, Glorious!
O God, beatify Muhammad,
And the family of Muhammad,
As Thou hast beatified Ibrahim,
And the family of Ibrahim;
Thou art Praised, Glorious!

CHAPTER 4

JEDDAH—AND THE APPROACH
TO MAKKAH

Wheresoever ye turn, there is the face of God!

PILGRIMS coming from far lands by surface or by air, on nearing
Jeddah, are to read:

My Lord! Let my entrance be
By the Gate of Truth—
And let my exit be
By the Gate of Truth—
And grant me from Thy Presence
A helping power. [Quran 17:80]

The principal landing place in the Hejaz for pilgrims, Jeddah
is built on the crumbling, rotten coral shore of a shallow shelf of
the Red Sea. Even the sea is heated by the fierce temperatures, and
an unbelievably oppressive blanket of humidity lies over the city.

Disembarked and through Customs, pilgrims who have come
from their home country escorted by their own Mutawwif or
Shaykh al-Hajj are taken to their temporary quarters in the port
city. This is likewise true for pilgrims who form the party of a
Shaykh who has preceded them to Jeddah and Makkah, perhaps
by an earlier boat, in order to put everything in a state of readiness
for their reception; for now they will be welcomed by their Shaykh
or his wakil in Jeddah. A resident of Jeddah, the wakil is the
Shaykh's agent and assistant in that city and in the Shaykh's
absence acts as his delegate—receiving and sheltering pilgrims,
tending to their needs, obtaining travel documents, and otherwise
serving them.

Pilgrims who arrive independently and are not part of a party under the guidance of a recognized Mutawwif or Shaykh al-Hajj are by the authorities of the Hejaz taken to a receiving center and thence delivered into the charge of the Shaykh into whose province the individual pilgrim naturally gravitates. All pilgrim guides belong to closed Makkan guilds, each guild organized to cater only to pilgrims of a particular nation or area whose languages or dialects the guild members speak and with whose peculiarities they are familiar—knowledge which is a two-edged blade, bleeding the unwary at least as often as it protects them.

The inhabitants of Makkah are mortals in no way different from the pilgrims who flood into Arabia except that the city's merchants, and much of the populace, are there not to make Hajj but to exploit it. Dwelling in close proximity to the Holy Ka'bah has not transformed them into angels. Makkah has been a place of constant pilgrimage for thousands of years and a great temptation has been put before these people; even their thinking is affected. Among them are good and bad, rich and poor, but almost all have come to consider pilgrims their legitimate prey—to be charged, or from whom are exacted, exorbitant sums for the most basic daily requirements. Aside from income derived from the Hejaz' oil deposits, a government monopoly, the entire revenue payable to the household of the king, the private and national economy is based on gain taken during the annual Pilgrimage season.

Pilgrims who bring with them merchandise to sell and finance their Hajj should tend to their trading sensibly. "It is no crime in you to seek the bounty of your Lord." [*Quran* 2:198]

Yourself trade honorably and take a fair profit for your goods—and guard against being victimized.

There is nothing in Jeddah of religious significance to Muslims. The city, on its present site, is not even of any particular antiquity; its importance lies in the fact that it is the seaport-gateway to Makkah.

The Way to Makkah   Pilgrims are transported from Jeddah to Makkah by lorry, bus, truck, automobile, and by camel and donkey. Some Muslims prefer to travel by camel as this was the means of transport in the time of the Prophet. Whatever the conveyance, the awed voices of massed pilgrims reading talbyah as they set forth on the last stage of the holy journey to the holy city evoke an enchantment which descends upon the desert road. This, the reading of prayer and praise, the worship of God, is the only *sihr halal*, the only *lawful magic*, in Islam.

We have been told to read talbyah constantly during the final stages of the approach to Makkah.

The distance from Jeddah to Makkah can be covered in well under two hours by car, but some among the pilgrim horde will be seen making their way afoot—just as they may have crossed the African Continent, from Sierra Leone and the Gold Coast and the Congo. A few years ago, before Pilgrimage from China and Central Asia was banned, pilgrims came afoot from as far away as Kansu, China, some requiring two and three years to complete the almost inconceivable journey.

We are not required to mortify ourselves in the name of religion, nor is poverty an excuse; Pilgrimage is a duty men owe God, but only those who can afford the expense. Whoever uses all his substance to perform Hajj, depriving his family of necessities, or saddling his children with debt, in coming to Makkah may be committing an evil act.

The way to Makkah is all desert with a few small, isolated gardens beside the burning road. The paved highway passes below rugged hills littered with boulders and crowned jaggedly with the ruins of fortifications and watchtowers built in the time of Turk rule to fend off Bedawi attacks on the pilgrim caravans.

The first halt, where all pilgrims are inspected by Arab police, is at Um al-Salam, a hut-like barrack and guard post in the waste.

The second halt, again for scrutiny by the police, is at Bahrah, where there is a grimy coffeehouse beside the guard station.

Al-Shemisi, Once Al-Hudaybiyah, and the Treaty of God's Good Pleasure   The third halt is at Al-Shemisi, once Al-Hudaybiyah, the barrier point beyond which no non-Muslim may pass and the entrance to sacred ground. Read talbyah! Here, near this paved highway, was signed the Treaty of God's Good Pleasure.

It is told that while dwelling in Madinah, in the sixth year of his exile from Makkah, which still was the stronghold of the

idolatrous and hostile Quraysh, the Prophet Muhammad ﷺ had a dream in which he saw himself, unopposed, re-entering the city of his birth. Waking, he resolved to attempt the Pilgrimage, even in the face of his foes. The pagan Quraysh were at war with the Prophet and had even attacked Madinah, but by Arab custom warfare and violence of any kind were prohibited during the sacred months of the Hajj.

Accompanied by between fourteen and fifteen hundred of his

companions and followers, Muhammad ﷺ led the way toward Makkah. All were unarmed; the Quraysh were to be given no excuse, valid or pretended, for violence in the sacred territory. But the Muslims had not reckoned on the bitterness of the Quraysh.

In the six years which had passed since Muhhamad ﷺ, himself of the Quraysh, had been compelled to depart from Makkah to save his life and protect the lives of his followers, the Makkans had seen their power threatened. Islam's moral and spiritual force had been reflected in its powers of organization and resistance. Repeatedly the Prophet and his Muslims had thwarted or thrown back attacks by superior numbers sent against them by Makkah.

As the pilgrims led by Muhammad ﷺ approached the Valley of Ibrahim they were met by a sympathizer who warned that the alarmed Quraysh had put on their armor and their leopard pelts— their insignia of valor—and had vowed to prevent the Prophet from setting foot on Makkan soil; violating all Arab tradition, weaponed horsemen had ridden to oppose the pilgrims from Madinah and force them to abandon all hope of performing the rites of the Hajj.

Taking evasive action, Muhammad ﷺ led a forced march through a wasteland from which the pilgrim column at last emerged exhausted—at Al-Hudaybiyah. Tents were pitched on the present border of the Sanctuary, and surrounded by his people and their camels and the sacrificial animals brought from Madinah, the Prophet attempted to enter into negotiation with the Quraysh who had closed the gates of Makkah against his coming.

Muhammad ﷺ sent a courier to tell the Makkans that he

and his followers came but as pilgrims, but when the courier attempted to deliver the message, the Makkans hamstrung his camel with their swords, dismounting the rider and maltreating him. He returned to the camp at Al-Hudaybiyah, followed by an envoy from the Quraysh who threatened the Prophet and the Madinah Muslims, all of whom were in Ihram.

A second envoy from Makkah was angrily reminded by the pilgrims of the respect due their leader. On his return to the waiting Quraysh, their envoy reported: "I have seen Caesar and Khusru in their pomp, but never have I seen a man honored as Muhammad is honored by his comrades!"

A band of mounted Makkans attempted to raid the Muslim camp and were captured and brought before Muhammad ﷺ who forgave them on their promise to abandon hostilities. Then, at last, proper envoys came from the Quraysh, and after some negotiation the trouble ended with the truce known as the Treaty of Hudaybiyah, or the Treaty of God's Good Pleasure, Bai'at al-Ridhwan. It stipulated that there was to be peace between the signatories for ten years. Deserters from the pagan Quraysh to the Muslims during the period of the truce were to be returned; not so deserters from the Muslims to the Quraysh. Tribes wishing to share in the treaty as allies of either faction could be accepted. Lastly, Muhammad ﷺ and his party must turn back to Madinah without visiting Makkah and the Ka'bah—but they could return and enter Makkah the following year provided they came unarmed.

The item referring to the desertion of Muslims and Quraysh to each other's camps was strenuously objected to by the followers of the Prophet and there was general dismay. This truce, however, was to prove the greatest victory yet achieved by the Muslims. Converts to Islam who were sent back to Makkah would be agents for the Faith in the enemy stronghold. And warfare between the followers of Muhammad ﷺ and the idolatrous Quraysh had been a barrier to the spread of the new religion. Now, men of the opposing factions could meet in peace and argue their beliefs.

Muhammad ﷺ traveled to Al-Hudaybiyah with less than fifteen hundred followers. The following year he returned to

Makkah for three days, during which he and all of his company performed the Lesser Pilgrimage, 'Umrah, departing again in peace.

Faithfully the Muslims kept to the terms of the treaty—until one of the tribes in the Makkan alliance broke the truce with an attack. Then, only two years after the signing, the Prophet marched against Makkah with an army of ten thousand. The city was stormed and taken, the idols removed and smashed, and the Holy Ka'bah restored to the pure faith of Adam and Ibrahim.

The Treaty of God's Good Pleasure, at its writing considered to have marked the defeat of the Muslims, had opened Makkah to them and assured the unaware but waiting world of the coming rise of Islam.

Here, at Al-Shemisi, Al-Hudaybiyah, where all this was made possible, pilgrims enter upon sacred ground. Beyond this line no man of another religious belief may put his foot. This is forbidden land; constantly read talbyah.

The following guard station is at Um al-Dud, seven kilometers before Makkah.

The Final Ap-   The next and last halt is at the gates of
proach to Makkah Makkah.
—and Du'a
                    As they make the final approach to Makkah
pilgrims should read:

O God, in it let there be a place for me—
And lawful provision.

Then, passing through the gates and into the city, read:

O God, this Sanctuary is Thy Sacred Place!
And this city is Thy City!
And this slave is Thy Slave!

I come with many sins,
From a far land,
And I petition with the petition
Of those who are compelled,
And fearful of Thy punishment.

And I beseech Thee to forgive me,
And accept me with Thy complete forgiveness,
And admit me into Thy spacious Heavens—

O God, this Sanctuary is Thy Sacred Place!
And that of Thy Messenger!
Forbid my flesh, my blood, and my bones
To the Fire!
And Peace and Blessings upon our Prince,
And his family and his companions.

MAKKAH

O God, have mercy when I fall in death
and am lonely in my grave,
And when I stand between Thy Hands,
For I have been a stranger in this world.

CHAPTER 5

MAKKAH THE NOBLE

What is Thy Command? I am here, O God!
What is Thy Command? I am here!
What is Thy Command? I am here!
Thou art without companion!
What is Thy Command? I am here!
Praise and Blessings are Thine, and Dominion!
Thou art without companion!

THE ENTERING into Makkah is a profound emotional experience. Men know not why they gather before ancient things rather than the new. Perhaps it is because that which is ancient has proved its quality, and that which is new, like ourselves, has not. Our ancestors' ancestors, since the dawn of Time, have worshiped before the Holy Ka'bah; and unless the godless prevail, our children's children will worship here until the end of Time.

Makkah is not a place: it is the Beginning, the Present, and Forever, and whoever enters Makkah feels this and is shaken.

Most pilgrims come here gratefully to discharge a duty owed to God. But ever since the beginning men have come to the Ka'bah to seek refuge with God, bodily refuge from harm at a foe's hand, or sanctuary where the confused heart can find a way and the wounded soul be healed. Today, again, there are pilgrims for whom Makkah and the holy places are a haven after savage trials and relentless persecution—pilgrims escaped from Muslim lands under foreign, atheistic rule. Countless devout Muslims trapped in nations now Soviet, forbidden by the Communists to worship God

or perform the Pilgrimage, have perished attempting to cross closed
frontiers and come here. A few thousands, survivors, have made
Jeddah and Makkah their house of exile, taking some solace from
their nearness to the holy places.

On passing into the city conduct yourselves with restraint.
Makkans with containers of water from the well Zamzam will
offer you to drink. If you accept, give a gift of money in return,
and remember that that which is holy cannot be bought. You are
not here to worship things, but to worship God. The water is from
a holy place, but in itself it is not divine: it is water. Makkah is a
city of this earth, peopled by men. The sacred Ka'bah is made of
mountain-stone and mortar and its covering kiswah ' was woven
and ornamented by mortal hands. The only deity in Makkah
is God.

Inside the gates of Makkah, arriving pilgrims are questioned by
the authorities and delegates of the Pilgrimage Committee, Lujnat
al-Hajj, who request the name of the Mutawwif or Shaykh al-Hajj.
If the pilgrim guide is not accompanying his party and is not at
the gates to receive them, the officials now direct whoever is in
charge of their transport to the quarter where he will be found.

Then, later, dwelling place located and effects cared for, rested
and refreshed, bodily clean and mentally prepared, each pilgrim
will turn his or her footsteps toward the Sacred House, Al Bayt
al-Haram, the great mosque, where in the open courtyard, under
the sky, waits the Ka'bah.

In the center of the valley and city of Makkah, the Bayt
al-Haram's outer walls on all sides are flanked and pressed upon
by the bazaars, shops, and in some parts by the Makkans' tall
houses whose upper levels overlook the vast inner courtyard and
the Ka'bah. The nearest surrounding houses are towered above by
others ranked on rising ground behind. And still other dwellings
on the rock-strewn heights gaze down over the intervening roof-
tops: all windows oriented, like eyes turned in answer to a sudden
call, to keep constant watch on the guardian mosque and its
treasure.

Day and night, whatever the hour, whatever the season or temperature, there is never a time when the Ka'bah is deserted. Blind-
ing, stifling midday and dark of the moon, men or shadows, always
there are figures making the ritual circling—and then traveling the

Mas'a, the sacred course between Safa and Marwah, just outside the great mosque's walls.

It is best that newly arrived pilgrims renew their ablutions before approaching the Bayt al-Haram. Adjoining the mosque are places to perform the ablutions—one just within the Gate of Peace, or Greeting, Bab al-Salam; another at the Gate of 'Umrah, Bab al-'Umrah—but during the height of the Pilgrimage the throng will be too great. If water is not to be had in the pilgrims' own Makkan lodging, it may be bought from any of the coffeehouses surrounding the mosque or on the streets and lanes which converge on it. Also, there are places for ablutions in the streets called Ajiad and Suq al-Saghir.

Pilgrims must not separate from their party in impatience to present themselves at the holy places. As many as half a million pilgrims, most of whom speak little or no Arabic, will be in the rivers of humanity thrusting through Makkah's inadequate streets, through the heat and dust. By day the incandescent sun will be overhead, and at night the stone walls of the tall houses will exhale a furnace-breath. Many pilgrims will be dazed with fatigue and heat shock and all but overcome with religious emotion. There will be Indonesians—Javanese and Sundanese and Sumatrans and Dyaks; pilgrims from Burma, Malaya, and Thailand; from Mindanao in the Pacific; Iranians and Turks and Kurds; Indians, Afghans, and Pakistanis; Berber and Riff and Tuareg; pilgrims from Senegal and Nairobi, and men and women of the nations and races of the length and breadth of Africa. There will be displaced Tatars from the groups now in Germany and Finland.

Before—and again one day, God willing—pilgrims came from Albania and Bosnia and Hertzgovina, from Poland and the Caucasus and Crimea, from Turkistan and Kazan and Siberia, from China, and from all the other lands where, today, Pilgrimage is banned. (Some of these peoples, like the Crimeans, have been annihilated and never will be seen in Makkah again; the others dwell in slavery. There will be times during the Hajj when we may pray for them.)

There will be tribes and races and complexions, every skin hue from Siberian white to African ebony, and every dialect and tongue. Guard against becoming lost. Guard against becoming separated from your companions. And as a precautionary measure

learn the names of your leaders and guides and write these on a
piece of paper to be kept on your person at all times. Include the
address of your lodgings, and do the same for those of your party
who cannot write. Then, if all these measures fail and you are lost,
keep your wits. The Hejaz sun is deadly. Avoid the crush and thrust
of the pilgrims and find a sheltered place from which the passers-by
can be observed. When you see a pilgrim who appears to be of
your race, speak to him. If he is from your country his Shaykh or
Mutawwif will be under the same Shaykh al-Mashayikh or Shaykh
al-Mutawwifin as your leader and will be in a position to restore
you to your group.

When you are ready, go to the Bayt al-Haram with your companions. Pilgrims unaccustomed to the terrible heat which en-
velopes Makkah and all the Hejaz when the sun stands high will
be wise to delay until nightfall their approach to the mosque.

AL BAYT AL-HARAM: THE SACRED HOUSE,
THE GREAT MOSQUE AT MAKKAH

In pagan times the dwellings of tribal leaders and nobles encom-
passed the Holy Ka'bah. The twenty-four entrances of today's
great mosque and courtyard are said to be the sites of the passages
between the original dwellings. In that age the sanctum included
but a small open area around the Holy Ka'bah, without walls or
colonnades, and no part of it was shielded from the blazing sun.
With the growth and spread of Islam the early Khalifs bought and
demolished the surrounding habitations to clear a place for the
increase of worshipers inundating the holy site. Later, other rulers
of Makkah widened the area about the Ka'bah and added the
colonnades and sheltered expanse around the now vast mosque
courtyard.

There are, as was remarked earlier, twenty-four gates through
which the Bayt al-Haram may be entered, but it is best for the
pilgrim to enter by the Bab al-Salam.

Women who are menstruating should, if there is sufficient time,
wait until their menses have passed before performing the first rites
at the Ka'bah. If there is no time, if the Hajj ceremonies are about
to begin, they may proceed regardless—omitting, however, all

prayers of obeisance. And tradition tells us that those of sufficient means should later make a sacrificial offering.

Entering the Bab al-Salam, read:

O God, Thou art Peace,
From Thee, Peace—and to Thee returneth Peace.
Let us live, our Lord, in Peace;
O God, open the doors of Thy Mercy and Forgiveness,
And grant that I may enter through the portals of Thy Paradise.
In God's Name! And Praise unto God!
And Blessings and Peace
To the Messenger of God,
On whom be Peace and Blessings!

And now the eyes of the pilgrim will behold the Holy Ka'bah. Master the emotions. This is an hour for awareness and conscious reverence. This is one of the great experiences of life. Read:

There is no deity except God!
There is no deity except God!
There is no deity except God!
God is Most Great!
God is Most Great!
God is Most Great!
I take refuge with the Lord of this House,
Against disbelief and poverty,
And the torments of the grave,
And the burden of the bowed-down heart.
And God bless and grant peace to our Master,
Muhammad—and his family and companions.

O God, increase the dignity of this Thy House,
And its honor, and its renown,
And its authority, and its prestige,
And its majesty, and its eminence,
And its Truth.
And increase, O our Lord, the dignity,
And the honor, and the renown,
Of those who glorify this House,
And who honor it ...

THE HOLY KA'BAH

Shrouded from top to base in rich brocaded drapery, which more than midway from the ground is adorned with a broad band of quotations from the Holy Quran embroidered in gold, open to the wind and sky, at night illuminated by lamps and the lightning which so frequently glowers over Arabia, dampened by the heavy dewfall and parched by the blazing Arabian sun, the Ka'bah stands in majesty in the center of the immense courtyard.

During the Pilgrimage the courtyard is solid with massed thousands, the Ka'bah the axis of an inexorable current of worshipers engaged in the rite of tawaf. As pilgrims complete the seven ritual circuits and fall away, some with children clinging to the parents' Ihram robes or sleeping, exhausted, in their arms, the spaces are filled by new tens of thousands arrived from Jeddah and the outer world. But there is a measurable lull from midnight to an hour before dawn and those who are well advised will wait until this time to perform their tawaf, especially during the years when the Pilgrimage falls in the hottest months.

Outside the stream of those who perform tawaf, standing apart from the Ka'bah—but within the limited marble-and-stone paved area which encompasses the Most Ancient House and indicates the boundaries of the original place of worship—are the sheltered well Zamzam; the Place of Ibrahim, covered by a domed kiosk; the spired mimbar from which the Friday sermons are read; and the archway which marks the accepted approach to the sacred enclosure.

Du'a Read on Passing Under the Arch Before the Sacred Enclosure The whole of the mosque courtyard is floored with loose amber-hued gravel intersected by nine broad paths of cut stone—one of great breadth—which radiate from the Ka'bah. Crossing toward the sacred enclosure by the path which leads diagonally from the Bab al-Salam, as pilgrims pass under the archway they should read:

Say: O my Lord! Let my entry be
By the Gate of Truth,
And let my exit be,

By the Gate of Truth,
And grant me from Thy Presence,
A helping power.

And Say: Truth has come—
And falsehood perished: for untruth
Is bound to perish. [*Quran* 17:80–81]

To the left of the archway, between it and the two-storeyed building housing the well Zamzam, is kept the railed staircase which is used to mount to the elevated threshold of the Ka'bah. Of thirteen steps—for the Ka'bah's threshold is two meters above ground level—the stairs are moved forward and into place only when the gold and silver doors are to be unlocked; otherwise the staircase would impede the way of those engaged in tawaf.

Directly in front of the pilgrim approaching through the archway is the Place of Ibrahim, the Maqam Ibrahim: the stone, today sheltered, on which the Prophet Ibrahim is said to have stood while building the Ka'bah and where he worshiped. Beyond the Maqam Ibrahim, separated from it by the wide marble-floored area of the rite of tawaf, is the veiled Ka'bah and the rich curtain which conceals its doors.

Mounted in massive silver and set in the south-east corner of the Ka'bah is the sacred Black Stone, Al Hajar al-Aswad, received by the Prophet Isma'il from the Angel Jibra'il during the rebuilding of the ancient edifice. The stone will not be seen at once: fixed in the corner at a height convenient to the hand or lips of those who pass during the ritual circling, screened from view by the stream of Faithful, its position will be made evident by the knot of fervent, straining pilgrims gathered there to honor and ecstatically kiss or touch the Black Stone.

To the right of the Maqam Ibrahim, standing parallel, is the high and ornate pulpit, the mimbar.

Beyond, shielding the lower section of the Ka'bah's northerly face and within the area circled during tawaf, is a massive stone wall built in the form of a half-circle; this is Al Hatim. Shoulder-high, the wall encloses a place of prayer, Al Hijr, and it is told that here, beneath the worn marble floor, are buried seventy prophets, among them Isma'il. Here, too, it is told, lies the Prophet Isma'il's mother, Hajar.

And the Prophet Muhammad ﷺ was sleeping here on the night of the twenty-seventh of Rajab, a year before his Flight from Makkah to Madinah, when the Angel Jibra'il descended with the heavenly steed Al Buraq. From this spot, whether in the flesh or in spirit, Muhammad ﷺ began the miraculous night journey, Al Isra', to Jerusalem and the ascent, Al Mi'raj, through the seven heavens to the presence of God—returning before daybreak.

If during the journey to Makkah the pilgrim omitted any of the five daily prayers, it is better that they be read now, before beginning Tawaf al-Qudum—the first of the three tawafs of the Hajj.

CHAPTER 6

TAWAF: THE RITUAL CIRCLING
OF THE HOLY KA'BAH

IN PARADISE, it is told, angels worship God by circling another
Ka'bah and reading His praise. And for many thousands of years
men have been circling the terrestrial counterpart in the same
manner, performing an identical rite, even when in the long darkness of the Time of Ignorance the sacred places were perverted to
idol worship.

The Holy Ka'bah and the Black Stone have known the footfall
of the Faithful, then the footfall of the pagan; the first Believer's
tawaf of fervent prayer and praise, then the idolater's blind tawaf
and fevered incantations.

The Prophet Muhammad ﷺ smashed the many idols and
restored the sacred places to their ancient purpose, the glorification

of the One God. Then Muhammad ﷺ received the divine
revelation which from that moment forth barred pagans from the
Sacred Mosque [Quran 9:29]. Since that time no unbeliever has
knowingly been allowed to approach Makkah.

Respect this place for its antiquity and all that has transpired
here, but do not forget that the Holy Ka'bah, a House of God
in the days of the Prophet Ibrahim, was to become a house of idols

long before Muhammad ﷺ was born. In the beginning, pilgrims
returning from Makkah carried away bits of stone of the Ka'bah.
Such fragments and relics were borne wherever the possessors wan-
dered and provided a sacred point about which worship could be
read and tawaf performed, according to the Arab custom. That
soon the more ignorant would begin to credit their stones with
miraculous powers was but one step from the keeping of relics. The

next step was the worshiping of the stones themselves instead of
what they signified. Then such stones were placed in the hollowed-
out bodies or heads of graven images, investing the images with
a "soul" or "divinity." Thereafter men gathered and worshiped
idols. It is recorded that three hundred and sixty false gods were
smashed by Muhammad ﷺ, when he made Makkah clean again.

Today we venerate Makkah, the Ka'bah, the Black Stone, the
well Zamzam and its waters, the Place of Ibrahim—the holy places
—for their history and associations, but *not* for themselves. God
and God alone is the object of our worship; remember this.

When the pilgrim is ready to begin tawaf, he or she should go
to a point opposite the Black Stone. By now there will have been
momentary breaks in the stream of pilgrims making tawaf and
those thronging about the sacred corner and it will have been
glimpsed—the Black Stone, completely sheathed in silver except
for a protruding opening large enough for a pilgrim to insert the
face and kiss or touch the stone.

Niyat for Tawaf: Do not interrupt others at their devotions.
Declaration   Do not jostle or thrust. Once a place has been
of Intent   found begin, saying:

In the Name of God, the Compassionate, the Merciful.
O God, I desire to perform tawaf
Around Thy House, the Holy.
Make it easy for me,
And receive from me,
The seven circuits.

Concluding, declare whether this tawaf is that of 'Umrah, or
Hajj, or 'Umrah with Hajj, just as the Intention was announced
at the taking of Ihram.

Male pilgrims will wear the upper half of their Ihram robes over
the left shoulder and under the right arm, as did the Prophet
Muhammad ﷺ .

The weak and the halt of either sex may hire bearers and a litter
and be borne the seven circuits. The Prophet Muhammad ﷺ

is said to have performed tawaf on camelback on at least one occasion; no longer is this permissible, but bearers will be found.

The Opening   Traditionally, tawaf is begun by touching or
of Tawaf   kissing the Black Stone; if, however, during the
Hajj the press of pilgrims is too great and the sacred stone cannot be approached without adding to the existing confusion, from a short distance make a gesture of simulated touching, afterward passing the hand over the face, saying:

> *In the Name of God! God is Most Great!*
> *And unto God, Praise!*
> *O God, by my belief in Thee,*
> *And believing Thy Book,*
> *And fulfilling Thy Command,*
> *And following the Traditions*
> *Of Thy Prophet, Muhammad—*
> *On whom be Peace and Blessings . . .*

With these words the tawaf has begun. Leaving the Ka'bah's Black Corner, the pilgrim will join the current which flows counterclockwise around the Most Ancient House, passing the threshold and on toward the Iraq Corner, then past the low wall, Al Hatim, and the enclosed place of worship, Al Hijr; then past the Damascus Corner and the Yemen Corner to complete the circuit with the return to the sacred Black Stone, Al Hajar al-Aswad.

The Yemen Corner holds another stone which is bound in straps of silver. It was the Prophet's habit to touch this corner as he passed during his tawaf. Today, during the height of the Pilgrimage, to approach it may be most difficult and the actual contact may be omitted, but whenever passing between the Yemen Corner and the Black Corner the pilgrim should read:

> *Our Lord, grant us good in this world,*
> *And good in the Hereafter,*
> *And save us from the torments of the Fire.*
> *And allow us to enter Paradise*
> *In the company of the virtuous,*
> *O Glorious, O All-Forgiving,*
> *O Lord of the Universe!*

And whenever passing the Black Stone, either touching it or lifting the right hand in a gesture of touching, read:

In the Name of God! God is Most Great!
And unto God, Praise!

During the first three circuits of the Holy Ka'bah all male pilgrims will travel part of the distance at a hastened pace, following the lead of their Mutawwif or Shaykh. Female pilgrims are not to hasten, but are to continue their tawaf at an unchanging, even gait.

THE FIRST CIRCUIT

The pilgrim guide will lead his party in prayer during each of the seven circuits. During the first circuit he will read aloud—and his followers are to repeat after him:

Praise be to God, and unto God, Praise!
There is no deity except God!
And God is Most Great!
There is no power nor strength
Except that from God, the Most High, Most Mighty!
Blessings and Peace to the Messenger of God,
On whom be Peace and Blessings.

O God, by my belief in Thee,
And believing Thy Book,
And fulfilling Thy Command,
And following the Traditions
Of Thy Prophet, Muhammad—
On whom be Peace and Blessings . . .

O God, truly I ask Thy forgiveness,
And health, and everlasting soundness
In Religion,
In this world and in the Hereafter,
And that I be granted Paradise,
And freed from the Fire.

THE SECOND CIRCUIT

During the second circuit of the Ka'bah the pilgrim guide will read—and his followers are to repeat after him:

O God, this House is Thy House,
And this Sanctuary is Thy Sanctuary,
And this Security is Thy security,
And this slave is Thy Slave.
I am Thy Slave and the son [or daughter] of Thy Slave.
And in this place of those who taketh refuge with Thee,
    from the Fire,
Forbid our flesh and our bodies to the Fire.

O God, make us to love the Faith,
And adorn it in our hearts,
And make us abhor disbelief,
And wickedness, and transgression,
And make us to be among those who are guided.

O God, protect us from Thy punishment
On the Day when You resurrect Your slaves.
O God, grant that we may be of those who
Unexamined, enter Paradise!

THE THIRD CIRCUIT

During the third circuit the pilgrim guide will read—and his followers are to repeat after him:

O God, truly I take refuge in Thee,
From doubt, and idolatory, and discord,
And hypocrisy, and immorality,
And the evil eye.
And the perversion that is the worship
Of worldly things:
Wealth, family, or offspring.

O God, truly I ask that Thou art pleased
With me, and grant me Paradise.
And I take refuge in Thee,

From *Thy displeasure, and the Fire.*
O God, truly I take refuge in Thee,
From the examination in the grave.
And I take refuge in Thee,
From the trials of life,
And Death.

THE FOURTH CIRCUIT

During the fourth circuit the pilgrim guide will read—and his followers are to repeat after him:

O God, make this Pilgrimage to be accepted,
And this endeavor rewarded,
And my sins forgiven,
And my good deeds approved—
Merchandise that shall not perish;
O Thou who knoweth all that is in our hearts.
Take me, O God, out of Darkness and into light!

O God, truly I ask Thee that I be
Worthy of Thy Mercy,
And that my deeds make certain
My forgiveness, and absolution,
And redemption from all sin—
And that I be rewarded for all acts
Of piety, and gain Paradise,
And escape the Fire.

Lord, make me content
With what Thou hast bestowed upon me.
And with whatever Thou bestoweth
Let me be blessed.
And concerning that which I lack—
Let my compensation be Thy Favor!

THE FIFTH CIRCUIT

During the fifth circuit the pilgrim guide will read—and his followers are to repeat after him:

O God, shade me in the shadow of Thy Throne
On the Day when there shall be no shadow,
And no face, except Thine.
And may I be offered a drink from the well
Of Thy Prophet, our Master Muhammad,
On whom be Peace and Blessings;
A drink so pleasant that it will quench
Our thirst for all Eternity.

O God, truly I ask Thee the best of that
Which Thy Prophet, our Master Muhammad,
On whom be Peace and Blessings,
Asked of Thee.
And I take refuge in Thee from the evils
From which Thy Prophet, our Master Muhammad,
On whom be Peace and Blessings,
Took refuge in Thee.

O God, truly I beseech Thee to grant me
Paradise, and its delights,
And whatever may bring it nearer to me,
By word, or act, or deed.
And I take refuge in Thee from the Fire,
And from all that draws it nearer to me,
By word, or act, or deed.

THE SIXTH CIRCUIT

During the sixth circuit the pilgrim guide will read—and his followers are to repeat after him:

O God, Thou hast many claims on me
For what is between Thee and me,
And there are many claims against me
In my relation to the world of Thy Creation.

O God, release me of that owed to Thee
And bear for me that which is between me
And Thy Creation.

Make me content with what Thou hast made lawful,
Instead of that which is forbidden by Thee;
Submissive to Thee,
Instead of disobedient to Thee,
Knowing Thy Favor above all others,
O Most Forgiving!

O God, verily Thy House is Glorious,
Thy countenance, Benign,
And Thou art Clement, and Giving,
Noble and Oft-Forgiving—
So forgive me.

THE SEVENTH CIRCUIT

During the seventh and last circuit of the Holy Ka'bah the pilgrim guide will read—and his followers are to repeat after him:

O God, I ask of Thee:
Perfect Faith and true conviction,
And Thy boundless bounty,
And a God-fearing heart,

And a tongue praising Thy Name,
And lawful joys,
And lasting repentance,
And repentance before death,
And tranquillity in death,
And forgiveness and mercy after death,
And pardon on the Day of Reckoning,
And that I be rewarded with Paradise,
And salvation from the Fire,
By Thy Mercy, O Glorious, O Oft-Forgiving!

Lord, increase my understanding,
And let me be among the virtuous.

Any pilgrim who cannot follow the pilgrim guide's words, unable to hear because of the tumult or separated from him by the crowding, and who is not able to recall the lines on these pages, may with perfect confidence substitute any prayer and praise God in whatever language. There are many races of men and many languages—and One God, and the contents of all hearts and the meanings of all tongues are known unto Him.

AL-MULTAZAM: THE PLACE OF HOLDING

Separating themselves from those still engaged in the performance of tawaf, pilgrims who have completed the seven circuits should go to the wall of the Ka'bah at the Place of Holding, Al-Multazam, between the elevated gold and silver doors and the sacred Black Stone. If there is no standing place beside the wall, the pilgrim may face the Place of Holding from a short distance, as from the outer boundary of the circling worshipers. It is convenient to stand near the Place of Ibrahim, Maqam Ibrahim, which is almost directly opposite the elevated threshold of the Holy Ka'bah.

Du'a Read at
Al-Multazam
Facing the Most Ancient House, close within its shadow, or from a distance, the pilgrim will lift both hands, palms front. Arms high, hands pressed to the sacred wall, or holding to the brocade kiswah, or clinging to the sacred threshold—or, from the medium distance, arms outstretched in an attitude of holding—read:

O God, Lord of this Ancient House,
Free our necks and those of our
Fathers, and mothers,
And brothers, and children,
From the Fire.

O Thou who art Beneficent,
And Benign, and Most Gracious,
And Favor-Granting, and Oft-Bestowing,
And Best.

O God, let the consequences of all our works
Be for good; and keep from us
The afflictions of this world,
And the torments of the Last Day.

O God, I am Thy Slave and the son [or daughter]
    Of Thy Slave,
Standing beneath Thy Door,
At Thy Threshold, humbly before Thee,
Hoping for Thy Favor and fearing
Thy Punishment, O Eternally Beneficent!

O God, truly I ask Thee to raise
My praises of Thee, and to relieve me
Of my burden, and to make successful
My affairs, and to purify
My heart, and to let there be light
In my grave—and forgive my sins!
And I beseech of Thee high places
In Paradise.
Amen.

The Place of Ibrahim: Maqam Ibrahim   At the conclusion of the above petition the pilgrim must read two *rak'ah*; for these prayers it will be best to go to the kiosk which covers the Place of Ibrahim and secure a place inside. Four of its six pillars stand at the corners of the stone on which the Prophet Ibrahim is said to have stood and where he prayed, now enclosed by an ornamental grill. The space between the two pillars nearest the archway—through which the sacred enclosure was first approached—is open; awaiting an opportunity, any may enter.

For the first *rak'ah* it is better to follow AL-FATIHAH with:

Quran 109. AL-KAFIRUN—

In the Name of God, the Compassionate, the Merciful ...

Say: O ye unbelievers—
I worship not
That which ye worship!
And ye will not worship

That which I worship.
And I shall never worship
That which ye have been
Wont to worship!
Nor will ye worship
That which I worship;
To you be your religion
And to me, mine!

For the second *rak'ah* read:

Quran 112. AL-IKHLAS—

In the Name of God, the Compassionate, the Merciful . . .

Say: He is God, Alone,
God, to whom all resort!
He begetteth not, nor is He begotten,
And there is none like unto Him!

Rising to the feet, read:

O God, truly Thou knowest that which I
Keep secret—and what I reveal,
So hear my appeal for forgiveness.
And as Thou knowest my need,
So grant me what I ask;
And as Thou knowest what is in my soul,
So forgive my sins.

O God, truly I ask Thee
For Faith which will content my heart,
And true conviction,
That I may realize that naught can befall me,
Except what Thou hast decreed for me,
Apportioned at Thy pleasure.

Thou art my Master in this world
And in the Hereafter.
Make me to die a Muslim,
And make me to join with those who are virtuous.

O God, *let it not transpire that in this place*
Any of our sins go unforgiven,
Or that any anxiety go undispelled by Thee,
Or any need go unheeded or unrequited by Thee;
And make our affairs to prosper,
And lighten our breasts,
And illuminate our hearts,
And place the seal of virtue on our every action.

O God, *make us to die as Muslims,*
And make us to live as Muslims,
And make us to join with those who are virtuous,
Without affliction,
And not with those who are tempted.

Al-Hijr: The
Enclosed Place
of Prayer
Al-Hijr, the semicircular enclosure between the 'Iraq Corner and the Damascus Corner, may now be visited by those who desire to offer up prayer near that wall of the Ka'bah and by the large slabs set in the floor and said to mark the graves of Hajar and Isma'il.

Here, as was told before, slept Muhammad ﷺ on the night of his miraculous journey.

Read two *rak'ah*, then read whatever prayer or praise, formal or spontaneous, comes to the lips.

All prayer is good—and no prayer is adequate. It is what lies within the heart that matters. It is not our words, but what remains unspoken for lack of words, that God hears.

Pray for those who have gone before and those who are yet to follow. Pray for loved ones. And pray aloud for those who must themselves pray in silence, secretly: pray for the Muslims in bondage.

The above concludes the Tawaf al-Qudum, the initial ritual within the Sacred Mosque. There will be two more tawafs before the pilgrim, Hajj fulfilled, departs from Makkah for the homeward journey; the second tawaf, Tawaf Ifadhah, after the return from 'Arafat, and then the Farewell Tawaf, Tawaf al-Wada'.

Pilgrims making 'Umrah after the Pilgrimage will perform another tawaf, for 'Umrah, before the Farewell Tawaf.

But now, before departing from the Holy Ka'bah, go to the well

Zamzam and drink of its waters; refresh and fortify yourself for the trial immediately to follow. Slightly brackish, tepid despite the depths from which it is drawn by the well-keepers' buckets, water from this well—discovered to them by the Angel Jibra'il—quenched the thirst of Hajar and Isma'il when, mother and child, they were abandoned in this barren, furnace valley—before there was a Makkah.

The mortar joining the stones of the Ka'bah was mixed with water from this well. Muhammad the child, Muhammad the man,

and Muhammad the Prophet ﷺ drank of these ancient waters. It was his habit to drink from Zamzam at the close of his tawaf, preparing himself for the rite of sa'y.

Departure from the Ka'bah and the Sacred Mosque   Departing from the Bayt al-Haram, the Sacred Mosque, by the Gate of Purity, Bab al-Safa, read:

> *Verily! Safa and Marwah*
> *Are among the Symbols of God—*
> *So if those who make Pilgrimage*
> *To the House, or make 'Umrah,*
> *Go around them both,*
> *It is allowed to them.*
> *And if anyone obeyeth his own*
> *Impulse to good—*
> *God is Grateful, All-Knowing!* [*Quran* 2:158]

Emerging to the outer street, turn to the right and, reading talbyah, continue until the steps of Al-Safa have been reached—seventy-six paces from the gate through which the pilgrim exited from the mosque.

Pilgrims must make sa'y immediately after completing tawaf—including whatever spontaneous praise or supplication may well from the worshipers' own hearts, for these become a part of the ritual of tawaf and the time devoted to such prayer is not unwonted delay—and drinking from the well Zamzam.

CHAPTER 7

AL-SAFA AND AL-MARWAH—AND
THE RITE OF SA'Y

IT IS NARRATED in an ancient tale of forgotten authorship and unknown authority that after putting Chaldea, the land of his fathers, forever behind him, Ibrahim went on a journey into Egypt. With him he took his wife, Sarah.

Sarah, it is told, was of a loveliness beyond all describing; and rumors of the foreign woman's beauty reached the palace. Now, the Pharaoh Salatis was a tyrant over his land, possessing himself of whatever he saw and coveted. No man's wife was safe from him and none dared refuse him. The most exquisite women of Egypt were numbered among his female slaves.

So it came to pass that one day Ibrahim's wife was brought before the Pharaoh; for, having listened to the rumors, Salatis desired to behold the foreign woman. It is written that all he had heard of her was true.

Left alone with the tyrant and terrified by his gaze and the illicit thing he asked of her, Sarah begged for his mercy—pleading that she be allowed to return to her husband inviolate. Unhearing, speaking softly in her ear, Salatis attempted to possess Ibrahim's wife.

Unable to deny her body to the Egyptian, the despairing woman sank down in an attitude of prayer. Salatis, half-angered and half-amused by the device which in her helplessness she had employed to frustrate him, watched her a moment. Then, suddenly impatient, for Sarah's grace and comeliness were such that even at prayer she aroused him, he approached the wife of Ibrahim intending to seduce her while she was at her devotions—and was struck down by a convulsive weakness which left him in momentary agony. Three times he attempted to make her his—and three times collapsed. Then, retreating in awe, the Egyptian understood that the woman he coveted had been taken under divine protection.

In another version of the legend it is recounted that Ibrahim was kept in an adjoining room during the attempted seduction of his wife. The masonry wall separating the two chambers slowly became transparent to Ibrahim's eyes and seeing, but unseen, he was witness to all that transpired.

Releasing Sarah to return to her husband, the Pharaoh Salatis made her a gift of one of the most lovely of his female slaves as a remembrance.

Hurriedly departing from Egypt, Ibrahim took his wife and her slave to Canaan and there they settled.

Now, Sarah had not yet borne Ishaq; long unable to conceive of Ibrahim, she had come to think of herself as barren. And, that her husband might beget a son, for he often prayed for one, Sarah presented him with her female slave, Hajar.

Again Ibrahim prayed; and this time his prayer was answered. Hajar conceived and bore a male child which they named Isma'il.

In the beginning Sarah was fond of her husband's son by the lovely slave, but when she observed Ibrahim fondling and caressing the tiny boy and treating Hajar with gentleness and affection, Sarah became jealous. Her jealousy grew and increased until Sarah's life was poisoned by it and made unbearable—and she came to detest the child and to hate the slave-mother.

Transformed, Sarah demanded of Ibrahim that he take Hajar and the boy into the wilderness and there abandon them.

Asking divine guidance, after a time Ibrahim the Prophet set out with Hajar—for whom life had also been made unbearable, by Sarah—and traveled southward out of Canaan and through the wasteland until the present site of Makkah had been reached. Here, in what was then called the Valley of Thirst, Wadi al-'Atash, he put the mother and child down, leaving the frightened woman his depleted provisions, himself turning homeward.

Departing from the arid, suffocating valley, Ibrahim paused on a rise and looked below for a final glimpse of the two—and beheld Hajar running after him, calling his name. Coming up to him she tearfully asked if he truly intended to forsake her and the child in this burning desolation. He nodded, in his prophetic wisdom convinced that in this place no harm could come to either; this was ground on which the original Ka'bah had stood, before the Flood. (Some commentators contend that in the Prophet Ibrahim's time evidences or ruins of the pre-Deluge Ka'bah yet remained and that it was to these he referred when, out of the Valley of Thirst, Hajar and his son left behind, Ibrahim offered up the supplication to be found on page 5.)

Abandoned, Hajar became fearful for the life of her child. Leaving the boy-child close beside where the Holy Ka'bah stands today, she went in search of water; there was a small rise in the land and she went up on it and besought God's aid. This is the hill Al-Safa.

THE ORIGIN OF SA'Y

Looking to the north, Hajar sighted what appeared to be a small lake. Descending from Al-Safa, running and walking in turn, she hurried toward the lake—but it disappeared as she approached. Wearily she mounted another low hill, searching for the vanished water. The eminence on which she stood is Al-Marwah.

Looking back in the direction whence she had come, Hajar beheld still another small lake. Descending again, again running and walking, she made her way back to Al-Safa. In near-panic she did this seven times, going from hill crest to hill crest, through almost insupportable heat—and through the mirage.

At her seventh disappointment Hajar looked hopelessly toward the spot where she had left her son and saw a figure standing by the child. She hastened toward the stranger, then slowed, for as she drew near she recognized him to be the Angel Jibra'il. The Angel Jibra'il struck the earth and water bubbled forth: the beginning of the well Zamzam.

Another version of the same tale has it that when, overcome by anxiety, Hajar looked toward the place where she had put down her child she beheld that water was gushing from the earth and flowing in all directions. Returned to the side of the infant Isma'il, Hajar found that the spring welled from a shallow hole gouged in the earth by the child's feet. Seeing the precious liquid escaping into the surrounding sands, Hajar cried: "Zumi Ya Mubarakah!

Come together O waters of Divine Providence!" and a pool formed. And this was Zamzam's beginning.

Hajar dwelt by this sacred pool, caring for her son; trusting in the God she had invoked in her fear and thirst—and who had answered her.

Then one day a wandering tribe from the Yemen happened to pass and found Hajar and the small Isma'il and the well where no water had been before. Halting, they asked leave to share the water, pitching their tents near the pool.

Some narrators tell that once each year Ibrahim journeyed from Canaan to the Valley of Thirst to see that all was well with his family, but never dismounted, having at Sarah's insistence taken an oath never to leave his camel's back during his visits to Hajar and their son.

Other chroniclers write that many years had elapsed and that Isma'il had grown and wed, taking a wife from the tribe which had settled beside the well Zamzam, before the Prophet Ibrahim returned to the Valley of Thirst in hope of finding some trace of the two he had abandoned to God's mercy.

Hajar was dead and Isma'il was absent, hunting; the valley could not be cultivated and its inhabitants lived by the chase. Without divulging his identity, the old man sought out his son's wife. Isma'il's wife complained of her life with her hunter husband and did not offer the stranger any hospitality. Departing, the Prophet Ibrahim left word with the young woman to tell her husband that their threshold was not good.

Returned from the hunt, Isma'il heard the old stranger's words and sensed that it was his father who had come and gone away again—and understanding the message, he put from him his wife and took another. This was to happen again the following year, with the same consequences. But when the Prophet Ibrahim made the wearying journey from Canaan for the third time, once again to ask concerning his son, again absent, Isma'il's young bride greeted the old man and invited him into her house, apologizing for its humbleness but full of praise for Isma'il.

When Ibrahim declined to dismount and enter, remaining on his camel, unwilling to enter the house of the son he had deserted until he heard a welcome from Isma'il's own lips, the young wife carried meat, bread, and milk out to him, handing them up.

Before departing, the Prophet Ibrahim spoke to his son's wife and told her to tell her husband that their threshold was good and should be made secure.

And when Isma'il heard these words he understood and valued his bride.

Then, later, in Canaan, the Prophet Ibrahim received the divine command which sent him once more to the barren valley where his hunter son dwelt, there to build a place of worship: to restore the Holy Ka'bah, gone since the time of the Prophet Noah and the Deluge. And Ibrahim obeyed, rejoicing.

Father and son, side by side, Ibrahim and Isma'il labored in the blazing sun and raised up the edifice. And when it was completed Ibrahim climbed to the top and called unto all mankind, summoning them to prayer.

Sa'y is the ritual in the observance of which pilgrims go between Safa and Marwah seven times, as did Hajar when in search of water for her child. The Prophet Ibrahim received the rite from God that he might pass it on to all men:

And Behold! We gave to Ibrahim the site of the House, and said: "Associate not aught with Me! And sanctify My House for those who circle it, or stand, or bow, or touch their foreheads to the ground. And proclaim the Pilgrimage among men: they will come to thee on foot and on lean camels, arriving from every deep defile; that they may bear witness of the benefits for them, and celebrate the Name of God on the known days, over the animals He has provided for them; then eat ye thereof and feed the distressed, the poor. Then let them purify themselves, perform their vows, and again go round the Ancient House." [Quran 22:26–29]

In pagan times, during the Jahiliyah, long after the Prophet Ibrahim, idols were placed on both Al-Safa and Al-Marwah, male on the former and female on Al-Marwah, declared to have been turned to stone for committing adultery with one another. In the performance of sa'y, pagan pilgrims would touch the male idol at the start of the ritual, then go to Al-Marwah and touch the female idol, then back again, to and fro, seven times.

After the fall of Makkah to Muhammad ﷺ and his Muslim forces, all the images and idols in the city were removed and shattered; but later there was some argument among Muhammad's followers, one faction contending that as it had been a pagan rite sa'y should be discontinued. The opposing faction argued that sa'y had been adopted by the idolaters from the earlier, pure Faith of Adam and Ibrahim. The dispute was settled when the Prophet received the divine revelation (to be found on page 55) read by each pilgrim on emerging from the Bayt al-Haram's Gate of Purity on the way to Al-Safa.

THE RITE OF SA'Y: THE GOING BETWEEN AL-SAFA AND AL-MARWAH

Male pilgrims arriving from the Sacred Mosque, their tawaf completed, are to mount to the top of the broad steps on Al-Safa. Female pilgrims should not ascend to the top when the steps are crowded, but may begin their sa'y from below.

As at tawaf, those incapable of performing sa'y on foot may hire a litter; unlike tawaf, for the performance of sa'y any available conveyance may be employed. But know that for the able-bodied of either sex to employ transport between Al-Safa and Al-Marwah or otherwise evade the obligations and observances of the Pilgrimage is to reduce the sacred observance to a farce.

The pilgrim will discover desert royalty bringing their women to perform sa'y in closed limousines, windows black-draped so that none in Makkah's teeming, medieval streets may glimpse their wives' features; armed Arab soldiers and police riding the bumpers and fenders and walking ahead of the nobles' creeping automobiles with rods and switches and whips, above the Law, forcing and lashing a path through the pilgrim sea. Their Hajj is empty and their sa'y ridiculous.

It is not ritual that is Religion, nor words and prayers that are Faith. Belief cannot be measured by how many *rak'ah* a Muslim reads, nor by the dust clinging to the forehead. It is not enough to be devout with an obvious devotion. Pilgrimage is not a proof.

Ritual is meaningless unless there is understanding. Prayer is valid only when it wells up from the heart to the lips. Obeisances have value only when there is true humility. Pilgrimage attains its final stature or purpose only when there is brotherhood among Muslims, and humanity.

NIYAT FOR SA'Y: DECLARATION OF INTENT

Facing in the direction of the Holy Ka'bah the pilgrim will read:

In the Name of God!
O God, I desire to make sa'y
Between Al-Safa and Al-Marwah,
Seven times . . .

Here declare whether this sa'y is for 'Umrah, or sa'y for Hajj, or for 'Umrah with Hajj, just as the Intention was expressed at the taking of Ihram and before the Tawaf Al-Qudum. Then, doing as the pilgrims about you, or following the lead of your guide, lift both hands high, putting them forth in a gesture of reaching toward the Holy Ka'bah, reading:

God is Most Great!
God is Most Great!
God is Most Great!
And unto God, Praise!

Descending from Al-Safa the pilgrim will now start toward Al-Marwah, about four hundred and five meters distant, following the Sacred Way, the Mas'a, through Makkah, past the Bayt al-Haram. Green pillars mark the limits of the area where those performing sa'y are to increase their pace: an interval of about forty meters.

It is likely that the heat will be all but insupportable. During much of the Pilgrimage a dust pall will hang over Makkah and hang thickest over the Mas'a. There will be enormous throngs thrusting relentlessly in opposite directions, forcing through each other's ranks, the Nejdi Arabs marching in groups with locked arms sweeping others before them, massed thousands without order or plan except to attain one or the other of the sacred hills; until by day and by night the Mas'a takes on the aspect of a pre-Carthage battlefield with countless white-robed combatants surging in incoherent struggle in the heat and dust, the sa'y becoming more nearly a conflict than a religious rite.

This, too, is a symbol and a warning to Muslims to emerge from the past and abandon the primitive individualism which already at the close of the medieval period had begun to weaken Islamic nations and ultimately led to their downfall. In the future the conduct of pilgrims at sa'y will be an accurate measure of our people's progress toward the dignity of social discipline and devotion to the common good beyond that pertaining to the individual, or the family, or the tribe, or any single nation.

When sa'y becomes orderly again—and with intelligent supervision it could so become within an hour; or, of itself, within a quarter of a century, if all Muslims are granted adequate educational opportunity—it will be an indication that Islam is about to rise again as a light for all mankind. And the earth will tremble beneath the feet of the godless and those who oppress.

Du'a Read Atop Al-Safa and Al-Marwah   Avoid the turbulent main current of the human tide. Keep to the outer edges of the Sacred Way. And read Praise. Follow the prayers of the Mutawwif or Shaykh al-Hajj—or, if this becomes impossible, recite the Names of God or any prayer of praise in any tongue.

Attaining the steps of Al-Marwah and mounting them, turn and face the Ka'bah, again putting forth the arms in a gesture of reaching or touching, and again read:

> *In the Name of God!*
> *God is Most Great!*
> *God is Most Great!*
> *God is Most Great!*
> *And unto God, Praise!*

These words and gestures will be repeated each time the pilgrim completes a trip between the two hills: a total of seven times. On completing the seventh trip, on the steps of Al-Marwah, read:

> *Our Lord, accept our prayers,*
> *And forgive us, and make us obedient to Thee,*
> *And grateful to Thee;*
> *And make us not to look to any except Thee!*
> *Make us to die as Believers,*
> *Our Islam perfect,*
> *Knowing Thy approval.*

O God, by Thy Mercy,
Grant that I may avoid evil
Throughout the span Thou grantest me life;
And, by Thy Mercy, may I never concern myself
With that which concerns me not.
And bestow upon me true vision,
That I may do all that pleaseth Thee,
O Most Merciful of those who show mercy!

The above prayer concludes the sa'y. If this sa'y was for 'Umrah or for Tamattu' with 'Umrah, there remains but to cut the hair and put aside the robes of Ihram. 'Umrah has been fulfilled by those who came only to visit and honor the holy places and fulfill the vows of 'Umrah. The cutting of the hair need only be a token gesture: we may clip a few hairs or a lock of hair—and this is all that is required of female pilgrims—but it is considered better for men to shave the head.

THE CLOSING OF IHRAM FOR THOSE WHO PERFORM ONLY 'UMRAH

Those pilgrims who have come early to Makkah to wait in the sacred environment perhaps some weeks for the approaching Hajj, and who therefore took Ihram for Tamattu' with 'Umrah, are with the putting off of their robes likewise released from the prohibitions and abstinences of Ihram but will resume all these when taking Ihram for the days of the Hajj.

On laying aside the robes of Ihram a sacrifice should be offered.

If the tawaf and sa'y just completed was that of Hajj, or 'Umrah and Hajj, the pilgrim cannot put off the Ihram or cut the hair until the termination of the rites of the Pilgrimage on the tenth day of the month Dhu-al-Hijjah.

Pilgrims who have taken Ihram for Hajj, or 'Umrah and Hajj, need not perform another sa'y. But pilgrims who took Ihram for Tamattu' with 'Umrah will make another sa'y on completing the tawaf read after the return from 'Arafat: the Tawaf Ifadah.

If the Pilgrimage has begun or is about to begin, the pilgrim should at the close of the sa'y return to his or her lodging to rest and prepare for the rigors of the ceremonies to follow.

Constantly read talbyah.

THE PILGRIMAGE

God is the light of the heavens and the earth.
The parable of His Light is as if there were a Niche,
And within it a Lamp:
The Lamp enclosed in Glass:
The glass as it were a brilliant Star:
Lit from a blessed Tree, an Olive,
Neither of the East, nor of the West,
Whose Oil would burn bright,
Though no fire kindled it:
Light upon Light!
God doth guide whom He will to His Light:
God doth set forth Parables for men:
And God Knoweth all things! [*Quran* 24:35]

CHAPTER 8

PILGRIMAGE: HAJJ

SUDDENLY, on the sixth, seventh, and eighth days of the month Dhu-al-Hijjah, Makkah changes.

Already the Shaykhs have sent their agents and servants ahead to make ready tents and provisions for the pilgrim horde to follow. And Bedawi shepherds have slowly brought vast numbers of sheep down from the high wadis to the east of Makkah, all to perish in blood sacrifice. These wait at 'Arafat and Mina, in the desert, while in the transformed holy city motor transport and camel caravan angrily commingle and tangle in the choked, dust-filled streets as a vast exodus begins—pilgrims and pilgrim transport preparing for the Hajj rites to be performed in the Valley of 'Arafat, about twenty-two kilometers distant.

The Departure from Makkah for 'Arafat   Pilgrims who desire to follow the traditions, doing as Muhammad ﷺ did on his Farewell Pilgrimage, his final Hajj before death, must depart from Makkah before the sun passes its meridian on the eighth day. This is *not* to be attempted during the years when the Pilgrimage takes place in the hot months, and pilgrims journeying afoot must not ignore this warning! Instead, it will better to depart from Makkah after sundown. God does not want human sacrifices, and the toll will be great without any pilgrim deliberately seeking death.

Even while late-arriving pilgrims enter Makkah by the Jeddah Gate and hasten to perform their initial tawaf and sa'y, the exodus toward 'Arafat begins. Makkah shudders and beneath a vast pall of dust disgorges what amounts to its entire population into the desert—even the Makkan shopkeepers board up their stalls and with their wares ride along on the pilgrim flood.

During periods of great heat this march takes place in the night. Then, frequently, summer lightning spasmodically lights the scene, highlighting the heavy clouds of dust drifting over a land on which time has wrought no more change than it has upon the sea.

The great host, its disordered ranks at times numbering half a million human beings, winds across a desolate, blasted landscape, crossing the Wadi al-Nar, Valley of Fire, day and night a place of suffocating heat whatever the season. The very earth and stones beside the way are of the hue and dull glitter of ash and slag from some unearthly furnace. In the year of the Prophet's birth the Abyssinian Abrahah Al-Ashram declared that he would destroy Makkah and raze the Ka'bah and marched against the holy city with a large expedition which included war elephants. Here in the Valley of Fire his entire army was destroyed, mysteriously struck down by small pebbles rained upon it by vast flights of birds—a parable which has been interpreted to mean smallpox.

As pilgrims make this march, they must read talbyah constantly.

During his Farewell Pilgrimage the Prophet slept the night to the ninth day of Dhu-al-Hijjah at Mina, on the way to 'Arafat.

It had been in Mina that Muhammad ﷺ was first publicly acknowledged: by twelve persons and in the following year by twenty. On the morning of the ninth day, after sunrise, he departed from the tiny sun-tortured settlement and continued on his way.

Again: During the hot months pilgrims are advised not to do as the Prophet Muhammad ﷺ did, but to complete the march to 'Arafat during the night.

Passing, or departing from, Mina, read:

O God, to Thee I turn,
Praying to approach Thy Noble Countenance;
Make my sins to be forgiven,
And my Hajj acceptable,
And have mercy on me,
And do not disappoint me,
For Thou hast Power over all things.

Du'a Read on Passing, or Departing from, Mina

'ARAFAT

At the entrance to the Valley of 'Arafat pilgrims pause at the lonely mosque named Masjid Namirah. Those who are making the journey in accordance with the Traditions will arrive at this point during the morning hours. It is better to remain here until noon and then to bathe in preparation for 'Arafat. After bathing, pilgrims should enter the mosque—or approach as near to it as the throng will permit—and, following the Imam, pray both *dhuhr* and *'asr*—two *rak'ah* each. Then, reading talbyah, depart, continuing toward the mountain 'Arafat, an up-jutting of naked stone in the heart of a broad, barren valley. Crossing a low rise in the land, pilgrims who arrive from Makkah by night discover the Valley of 'Arafat by its hundreds of thousands of fires and candle-lanterns glowing through decorated tent panels. Occasional primus lanterns suspended in the open from long poles glare whitely in the immense encampment, and heat-lightning frequently shudders on the mountaintops. Sheep bleat in the darkness and men read zikr.

This is the site where, banished from Paradise, lost in the wilderness and wastes of a strange world, Adam and Eve found one another after two centuries' separation.

As the eyes first behold 'Arafat, approaching pilgrims should read:

O God, forgive me and aid me in my
  repentance,
And grant me all that I beseech of Thee,
And wherever I turn let me meet good works.
God be Praised! Praise unto God!
There is no deity except God!
And God is Most Great!

*Du'a Read
on Entering
the Valley
of 'Arafat*

Read talbyah constantly and, when reaching the foot of the mountain 'Arafat, read Praise.

WUQUF: THE RITE OF STANDING

All pilgrims must be in the Valley of 'Arafat by high noon on the ninth day of Dhu-al-Hijjah. When the sun passes its meridian, the ritual of Standing, Wuquf, begins. *This is the Hajj.* These are the supreme hours.

The soul-shaken pilgrim entering the Sanctuary of Makkah and for the first time beholding the Holy Ka'bah and the Black Stone knows a humility and an exaltation which are but a prologue for 'Arafat. Here, by the mountain, the pilgrim will pass what should be, spiritually and intellectually, the noblest hours of life. The tents of the Faithful will cover the undulating valley as far as the eye can see. This immense congregation with the sacred mountain at its center is the heart of Islam. This is the day of true brotherhood, the day when God is revealed to His servants.

We are promised that in these hours by 'Arafat, God will send down His forgiveness and mercy to those who are deserving and they will feel His presence.

This is the day of brotherhood and heartbreak—heartbreak that we have not yet learned to cling to this solidarity where we dwell and labor in valleys and on mountains far from 'Arafat.

This is the day of promise: the guarantee of what Islam shall be when Muslims everywhere achieve the oneness today known only at 'Arafat.

Du'a Read at 'Arafat   Facing the mountain, at high noon all pilgrims rise to their feet and declare their repentance. There are formal prayers which have been prepared for this time, but no man can put into words what is hidden in another's heart. Speak to God in your own tongue if you will, aloud; the sound ascends from the multitude like a vast music, chord upon chord. Read Praise. Glorify God and be humble. And those pilgrims physically capable should so remain, standing, at wuquf, until the sun passes below the horizon.

Read:

There is no deity except God, the One, without companion!
For Him is the Kingdom and the Praise.
He maketh to live, and to die,
And He liveth—but dieth not!
And in His hand is goodness,
And He is All-Powerful!

Our Lord, Thou hast granted that we may stand here,
And brought us here,
And gave us a favorable wind,
Until Thou hadst delivered us by Thy benignity,
Into the presence of Thy House,
And the Stand at this great and sacred place,
Following the path of Thy Friend,
And following the footprints of Thy Chosen
From all Thy creatures,
Our Prince, Muhammad,
Upon whom be Peace and Blessings.

Truly, in Thee there is for every guest, hospitality,
And for all who come, a reward;
And for every visitor, Thy bounty,
And for every petitioner, a gift,
And for all who hope, fulfillment,
And for the supplicant, a requiting,
And for all who implore a place near Thee, a favor.

We stand at this great and sacred place hoping for Thy favor.
Do not make us to be disappointed, O our God!
Our hope is in Thee, O our Master, O our King!
O Thou to whom all things do submit,
Because of Thy Glory—
And before Whom all faces are anxious,
Knowing Thy Supremacy!

Our Lord, to Thee we approach,
Dismounted in Thy open place;
And to Thee alone do we look,
And for Thy favor we pray,
And for Thy beneficence we make petition,
And for Thy compassion we hope,
And from Thy punishment we ask pity,
And to Thy Sacred House we make Pilgrimage.

O Thou, Keeper of all that is needed by Thy supplicants,
And Who knoweth the thoughts of the silent;
O Thou, than whom there is no other lord to be worshiped,

And no deity to be looked to,
And beyond whom there is no other creator to be feared,
And no vizir to hear an appeal,
And no chamberlain to be bribed;
Who respondeth not except with bounty and excellence,
And to the needs of mankind—
Provideth but with charity;
O Thou, before Whom voices cry in languages,
Beseeching Thee to hear their wants,
Tears pouring down, weeping and sighing,
Importuning Thee and petitioning.

And I seek of Thee, Our Lord, Thy forgiveness,
And that Thou art pleased with me,
After which there can be no anger;
And guidance, after which there can be no error;
And a good end,
And liberation from the Fire,
And reward with Paradise,
And to be remembered by Thee
When I am in misfortune,
When the mortals of the world forget me,
And the earth covers,
And I am parted from my loved ones,
And all is severed.
O Most Glorious! O Bestower!
O Most Merciful of those who show mercy!

O God, truly Thou seest my place,
And hearest my words,
And knowest my secrets
As well as what I reveal,
And none of my affairs is concealed from Thee.

I am miserable and poverty-stricken,
A supplicant imploring succor,
Apprehensive and fearful,
Lamenting and confessing and knowing my sins,
Seeking from Thee as the humble seek.
And I implore of Thee with the supplication of an abject sinner,

And I pray to Thee the prayer of a blind and frightened man,
The prayer of him who submits his neck to Thee,
And weeps to Thee,
And is prostrate before Thee.

Do not make me to be wretched, O my Lord;
And be merciful and compassionate toward me,
O Best of those who hear supplications,
And Best of those who bestow.

Lord, guide us with a true guidance,
And adorn us with piety,
And forgive us in the Hereafter—
And the present.

Our Lord, create in my heart light,
In my ears light,
In my eyes light,
In my tongue light,
At my right light,
Above me light,
And create light in my soul—
And for me glorify light!

O God, open my heart
And make my affairs easy!
O God, truly I ask Thee guidance,
And piety, and chastity, and plenty!
O God, for Thee is Praise as Thou sayest,
And the best of what Thou sayest!
O God, truly I seek of Thee Thy pleasure,
And Paradise,
And I take refuge in Thee,
From Thy Wrath, and the Fire,
And from whatever draweth me nearer to it,
Whether by word, or deed, or action!

Our Lord, make this Pilgrimage to be accepted,
And my sins forgiven,
And my deeds righteous and approved.

Our Lord, give us good in this world,
And good in the Hereafter,
And save us from the torments of the Fire.

My God, I have no strength against Thy Wrath,
And no endurance to withstand Thy punishment,
And I cannot be without Thy favor,
Without which I have no power against misfortune,
And no force in me for the struggle!

I seek refuge in Thy pleasure,
From Thy Wrath,
And from the terrible overthrow
Heralding Thy punishment,
O my Hope and my only Hope!
O Best of those who are called upon!
O Most Excellent Giver!
O Thou Whose Mercy exceedeth His Anger!
O my Lord and my King!
O my Confidence! And my Hope! And my Trust!

O God who in hearing one is not prevented from hearing another,
And Whom countless voices have no power to distract,
And for Whom many appeals bring no confusion,
And for Whom languages make no difference,
Who art never vexed by the importuning of those who importune,
And Who art ever able to answer the supplications of those who
     supplicate,
Allow us to know the coolness of Thy pardon,
And the sweetness of Thy forgiveness,
O Most Merciful of those who show mercy!

O God, I come to Thee and halt before Thee,
At this holy place,
Hoping for that which is with Thee—
So make it not that I be disappointed in this visit to Thee,
On this day;
Honor me with Paradise,
And favor me with Thy forgiveness,

And security.
And save me from the Fire,
And part me from any evil of Thy creatures,
And make it to be that I place my hopes in none excepting Thee,
For all doors are closed excepting Thine!
And make me never to depend on other than Thee,
In religion as well as worldly matters,
Even for the twinkling of an eye . . .

And raise me from the baseness of disobedience to the glory of
      submission,
And illuminate my heart, and my grave,
And protect me from all evil,
And gather for me all that is good,
O Most Generous of those who are petitioned,
And Most Excellent of those who bestow!

O God, by Thy light we wish to be guided,
And by Thy favor to be sufficed,
In Thy guardianship, and Thy grace,
And Thy kindness, and Thy beneficence,
In the morning and in the evening.
Thou art the First—
And there are none before Thee!
Thou art the Last—
And there are none after Thee!
Thou art the Visible—
And there is nothing above Thee!
Thou art the Hidden—
And nothing exists below Thee!

We take refuge in Thee,
From indigence,
And slothfulness,
And the torments of the grave,
And the temptation of riches.

I ask Thee the causes of Thy favor,
And certain forgiveness,
And abounding good fortune for my pious deeds,

And salvation from all sin,
And to be granted Paradise,
And escape from the Fire.

O God, O Knower of secrets—
O Hearer of all voices—
O Raiser of the dead—
O Answerer of prayers—
O Fulfiller of the necessities—
O Creator of the earth and the heavens—
Thou art God!
There is no deity except Thee,
The One, the Only, the Solitary,
To Whom all resort;
The Bestower, the Unstinting,
The Clement, Who doth not hesitate;
There is no withstanding Thy decree,
And no arguing Thy Judgement!

Lord of all,
And King of all,
And Predestinator of all—
I pray to Thee to grant me:
Wholesome knowledge,
And virtuous deeds,
And real Faith!
And grant that we may experience:
The repentance of the Faithful,
The submission of the submissive,
And the deeds of the virtuous,
And the conviction of those who are convinced,
The felicity of the God-fearing,
And the High Degree of the successful!

O Most Excellent of those to whom we appeal,
And Most Generous of those we entreat,
And Most Patient of those who give,
How patient Thou art to those who disobey Thee!
And how near Thou art to those who seek Thee!
And how compassionate Thou art toward those who ask of Thee!

None are guided except those guided by Thee,
And none err except those who are made to err by Thee,
And none can be rich except those made rich by Thee,
And none can be poor except those made poor by Thee,
And none can be blameless except those made blameless by Thee,
And none are concealed except those concealed by Thee.

I pray Thee to grant us much favor,
And the joy of meeting with Thee,
And Thy increased blessings,
And benefits from Thee,
And that Thou createst for us:
Light in our life,
And light at our assembly after death,
And light in our graves,
And light with which we may seek mediation with Thee—
And light with which to achieve Thy approval . . .

O God, make the end of my life the best of my life!
And the best of my deeds, their conclusion!
And the best of my days, the day on which I shall meet Thee!

O God, let me hold fast to Thy commands,
And support me with Thine aid,
And provide for me from Thy bounty,
And liberate me from Thy punishment—
On the day when Thou shalt resurrect Thy slaves.

I have come to Thee, hoping for Thy compassion,
And I am far from my land,
And I am performing my devotions,
And fulfilling Thy precepts,
And reading Thy Book,
And praying to Thee,
And lamenting the obstinacy of my heart,
And fearing my sins—
And the wrong I have committed against my soul,
And knowing my guilt.

This is the prayer of one whose shortcomings are multitude,
And whose sins are many,
And from whom hope is severed,
And whose faults remain,
And whose tears fall,
And whose time is terminated:
And this is the prayer of one unable to discover any forgiver,
    except Thee;
And for whose hopes for good there is no bestower, except Thee;
And for whose broken bones there is no joiner, except Thee,
O Most Merciful of those who show mercy!

There is no strength and no power, except from God,
The Most Exalted, and the Supreme!

Our God, deliver me not into Thy punishment,
And keep me not where I will encounter temptation.
My King, I am here, praying to Thee,
And turning my face to Thee in supplication;
And I place my cheek [to the ground] in humility and trepidation,
So accept my prayer and make right the wrong I have committed,
And sever from me my worldly desires and needs,
And make me to desire that which is Thine,
And turn me toward the place of turning of those who mention
    Thy Name,
Whose prayers are accepted,
Whose arguments are upstanding,
Whose sins are forgiven,
Whose Pilgrimage is accepted,
Whose faults are remitted,
Whose mistakes are erased,
Whose affairs are guided;
The place of turning of those who in no thing disobey Thee,
And who do not sin again,
And never again bear any burden of sin;
The place of turning of those whose tongues are honored,
By the utterance of Thy Name,
And whose bodies are cleansed of any uncleanness,
And whose hearts are directed, ·

And whose very being is opened to Islam;
And whose eyes are soothed by Thy pleasure,
And forgiveness before death,
And whose vision Thou tearest from evil,
And whose souls Thou employest in Thy Sacred Way!

And I ask Thee not to make me
The most miserable and sinful of Thy creatures,
And that I not be the most disappointed of those who hope
     before Thee,
And not the most empty-handed of those who seek Thy favor,
And not the most lost—
Of all those who return from this great place of standing,
My King, Lord of the Universe!

O God, I have prayed to Thee with the prayer Thou hast taught
     me,
So do not cut short what hope Thou hast given me,
O Thou to Whom our obedience is not gain,
And for Whom our disobedience inflicts no loss.

And whatsoever Thou bestoweth upon me—
That I desire!
Make it to aid me in the way Thou willest,
And make it best for me.

Make me love submission to Thee,
And the practice of it,
As Thou hast led Thy Favorites to love it,
Until they saw its rewards.
And as Thou hast led me to Islam,
So take it not from me—
Until Thou takest me to Thee,
Still embracing it.

O God, make me love the Faith,
And adorn it in my heart,
And make me abhor disbelief,
And wickedness, and disobedience,
And make me to be one of those who are guided.

O God, make our lives to have a good conclusion,
And make it come to pass that our desires know Thy favor,
And make our way easy, that we may achieve Thy pleasure,
And in every matter make our deeds to be excellent.

O Rescuer of the Drowned!
O Savior of the Lost!
O Witness of every secret thought!
O End of all lamentation!
O Thou Whose beneficence is without beginning or end!
O Thou Whose goodness is Eternal!
O Thou of Whom all things are in need—
And without Whom none can exist!
O Thou Who hath provision for all—
And to Whom all return!
Thee, to Whom the hands of those who supplicate are lifted,
And toward Whom worshipers yearn!
We ask Thee to place us in Thy protection,
And Thy generosity,
And in Thy guardianship,
And Thy refuge,
And Thy shelter,
And Thy security!

O God, truly we take refuge in Thee from extremity,
And from the depths of despondency,
And the mocking of foes,
And from becoming an evil sight;
And keep us from unhappiness in our dwellings:
In wealth, and as concerns our children.

O God, let it not transpire that in this place any sin go unforgiven
      by Thee,
Or that any anguish go uneased by Thee,
And no obligation continue unsettled by Thee,
And no enemy but that is made impotent against us by Thee,
And no wickedness but that is corrected by Thee,
And none who ail but that they be healed by Thee,

And no void but that is filled by Thee,
And no worldly need—or need in the Hereafter,
In which there is Thy pleasure,
And our benefit,
But That is provided by Thee;
Truly, Thou guidest the way,
And joineth the broken,
And maketh rich the poor!

O God, we cannot escape from appearing before Thee,
So grant that our arguments be accepted,
And our sins forgiven,
And that our knowledge be increased,
And our efforts worthy;
I approach, my mortal lips imploring the protection of Thy
    Immortal countenance,
O Possessor of Glory and Might!

O God, none may keep me from Thee if Thou acceptest me—
And none can aid me if Thou refuseth me,
So reject me not because of my small gratitude,
And abandon me not because of my small patience.

O God, make death the best of those things we choose not,
But which we await;
And the grave the best dwelling in which we shall dwell—
And, than death, make best that which follows death.

My Lord, forgive me, and my parents,
And my children, and my brothers,
And my family, and my descendants,
And the Faithful: male and female,
Those who live with us and those who are dead.

O God, I ask Thee Faith to occupy my heart,
And true conviction,
That I may know that naught can befall me, except what Thou
    hast destined for me;

And make me to be content in Thy judgments,
And aid me on this earth,
That I may abstain from that which is unlawful;
And that I be content,
And in religion submissive;
And cleanse my tongue from falsehoods,
And my heart from hypocrisy,
And my deeds from falseness,
And my sight from perfidy—
For Thou knowest the treachery of the eyes
And what the heart concealeth!

O God, have mercy when I fall in death and am lonely in my
grave,
And when I stand between Thy hands,
For I have been a stranger in this world.

O God, Thou art Peace—
And from Thee peace—
Thou art Blessed and Most High,
O Possessor of Majesty and Glory!
O God, Thou art King,
There is no deity except Thee!
And I am Thy Slave!

I have committed wrongs against my soul,
And I confess my guilt—so forgive my trespasses;
Truly, none forgives sin except Thee;
And guide me to the best conduct,
For none can direct the way except Thee;
And turn from me that which is evil,
For other than Thee none can avert it from me!

What is Thy Command? I am here, O God!
Happiness attend Thee!
And all good is in Thy hands,
And I repent unto Thee!
Amen . . .

THE FAREWELL PILGRIMAGE OF THE
PROPHET MUHAMMAD

In the tenth year of the Hejirah the Prophet Muhammad ﷺ had a presentiment of his approaching death and gathered all his family and companions and followers for what has come to be

known as the Farewell Pilgrimage. Muhammad ﷺ had been poisoned in the seventh year of the Hejirah, when he had led an expedition against the Jews of Khaibar, and had never fully recovered.

Now, followed by more than a hundred thousand Believers, all wearing the robes of Ihram, the Prophet observed the rites at Makkah and then visited 'Arafat. Atop the stone mountain, still on camelback, he gazed down over the waiting multitude—then

he spoke. First Muhammad ﷺ addressed the heavens, praising God; he spoke slowly and a black man with a powerful and melodious voice repeated his words a sentence at a time that all might hear.

Worship completed, the Prophet spoke to the thousands on the boulder-covered slopes and in the arid valley surrounding the mountain, and again the black man's voice carried his words to them. The Muslims were exhorted forever to keep from the practice of usury, never to accept any interest whatsoever on money lent; they were to forgive those who had committed crimes against them before the rise of Islam, abandoning the Arab practice of vendetta; they were cautioned as to the rights of their wives, all being equal in Islam; and the calendar was fixed from that day forth: the Muslim lunar calendar, twelve months coordinated to the phases of the moon according to the laws of the earth and the sky.

Then, when the Prophet had done, there was a silence. Then, still in the saddle, he suddenly exclaimed:

O people, remember what I have said here—for I know not whether I shall be with you in this place again after this day has passed. And, above all else, never forget that each Muslim is the brother of all others: for all Muslims in this world form one race of brothers! . . .

O God— he said, his face turned to the sky, *have I fulfilled my mission?*

A vast cry of affirmation rose from the thousands of pilgrims surrounding the mountain:

Yes, O God, truly!

Shaken by the demonstration, Muhammad ﷺ again addressed himself to the sky, crying:

O God, hearken to their testimony!

Shortly afterward, it is told, still on 'Arafat, the Prophet received his final revelation: the words which, chronologically, form the last verse of the Holy Quran. It is chronicled that the revelation descended from the heights with such unearthly force that the Prophet's camel collapsed to its knees. Then Muhammad ﷺ spoke, repeating God's message for all to hear:

This day have I perfected your religion for you, completed my favor upon you, and have chosen for you Islam as your religion. [*Quran 5:4*]

On receiving this pronouncement, there was great joy in the multitude; but Abu Bakr wept—for he understood that the Prophet's mission on earth had in truth come to its close and that Muhammad's ﷺ death was soon to follow.

MUZDALIFAH

No pilgrim may depart from 'Arafat for Muzdalifah until the sun is down. Then, breaking from their camping places, all depart from the sacred mountain at once, hurrying out of the darkling valley like an immense army in defeat. This precipitous rush is called nafrah or ifadhah.

Reading talbyah, the pilgrim horde hastens through the gathering darkness to Muzdalifah, eight kilometers distant, where the parched hills have a sparse growth of thorn bushes and where all must observe the *maghrib* and *'isha* prayers, then search in the wilderness night for forty-nine pebbles to carry on to Mina for *jamrat*—the ritual stoning of the three pillars which symbolize Satan and temptation.

While at Muzdalifah it is best for the pilgrim to pause for Praise
at the roofless mosque called The Sacred Grove, Al Mash'ar
al-Haram.

God is Most Great!
God is Most Great!
God is Most Great!
There is no deity except God—
And unto God, Praise!
God is Most Great!

Du'a Read at the
Mosque of the
Sacred Grove,
Al Mash'ar
al-Haram

O God, as Thou hast made us to halt in this place,
And shown it to us,
So grant that we may repeat Thy Name.
As Thou hast guided us,
So forgive us,
And have mercy on us,
As Thou hast promised us—
And Thy Word is Truth!

Then when ye flow down from 'Arafat
Celebrate the praises of God
At the Sacred Monument,
And celebrate His praises
As He has directed you,
Even though, before this,
Ye were of those who strayed.
Then flow down from the place where men so do,
And ask forgiveness from God,
For God is Oft-Forgiving,
Most Merciful. [*Quran* 2:197–198]

O God, truly we ask Thee,
O Most Forgiving and Most Merciful,
To open for our prayers the doors of acceptance,
O Thou Who respondeth to the petition of the afflicted,
O Thou who sayest to a thing "Be!" and it is!

O God, truly we come in our multitude to Thee,
To appeal for Thy forgiveness for our sins,
And that we not be made to return in despair.

And bestow upon us the best of that
Which Thou hast bestowed upon Thy virtuous slaves,
And make us not to turn from this great and sacred place,
Except with success and happiness, without regrets,
And without further need to be penitent,
And not as those who are astray,
Or who have been led into temptation,
O Most Merciful of those who show mercy!

O God, make us to be guided—
And protect us from the causes of ignorance and destruction,
And save us from the misfortunes of the sicknesses of the soul,
For these are the worst of foes.

And make us to be of those to whom Thou turneth,
And who look not toward other than Thee,
And take our hands and lead us toward Thee,
And have compassion on our supplications before Thee,
O Thou Who art Omnipotent!
When we are crooked, straighten us . . .
Be with us, but never against us.

And make us to live in this world in faithfulness and obedience,
And make us to die as Muslims, and repenting;
And make us to be of those who take the Book with their right
hands,
And make us to be of those who are secure on the Day of Great
Fears!
And Bless us, O God, with the sight of Thy Exalted Countenance,
By Thy Mercy, O Most Merciful of those who show mercy!

MINA: THE PLACE OF SACRIFICE

Mina, already passed once during the outward march from
Makkah to 'Arafat, was a gathering place for desert tribes long
before the time of the Prophet Muhammad ﷺ. Here are the

86   THE SACRED JOURNEY

stone-and-mortar monuments marking the places where Satan
appeared to Isma'il, son of the Prophet Ibrahim, warning that his
father was about to sacrifice him and tempting him to take flight.

The Tale of Ibra-   We are told that the Prophet Ibrahim had
him's Vision and   a dream vision wherein he was commanded to
the Tempting of   sacrifice his son to God. Ibrahim, the tale goes,
Isma'il by Satan   told his son that they would go out together
to find firewood; but then, under the sky, the heartbroken father
confessed to his son what he intended. Isma'il accepted his fate
and obediently prepared to suffer the Divine command as they
mounted toward the site of the sacrifice, as seen in Ibrahim's vision:
the barren place now overlooking the third Jamrat at Mina.

Satan three times appeared to Isma'il—who was lagging behind
his father. The first manifestation took place where the Jamrat
al-Ula now stands, a short, thick phallus-like pillar with rounded
top, at its base closely surrounded by a low, circling wall. Satan
again appeared at the site of the Jamrat al-Wusta, an identical
monument; both in the village street. The Evil One's third manifestation took place on the spot now occupied by the Jamrat
al-'Aqabah, beneath the bluff on which Isma'il believed he was to
die a blood sacrifice. At each of his appearances Satan warned
Isma'il of his father's intentions—and was stoned by the son.

When Isma'il had been bound and lain face downward in preparation for the sacrifice, the Prophet Ibrahim put the knife to his
son's throat; but the blade turned in his hand, refusing to enter the
flesh. Three times Ibrahim bent forward to complete the sacrifice
and three times the knife turned. Then, suddenly, the Angel
Jibra'il appeared, bringing a ram. And Jibra'il told Ibrahim that
God had received the sacrifice without requiring the soul of Isma'il;
the ram was to be offered in his stead.

The crumbling village of Mina lies in a rising valley so narrow
as to be almost a gorge, dwarfed on either hand by ugly boulder-
strewn crags of naked rock riddled with black caves and crevices.
Here, during the Pilgrimage ceremonies which take place at Mina,
camp tens of thousands of the Bedawi pilgrims—creeping into
holes and caves and cracks in the shimmering, burning rock, their
bodies and the soles of their feet almost insensible to pain, but still

seeking on the burning heights some relief from the furnace valley.

Mina is a place of death for many. In the summer the heat is terrible; a midday temperature of Centigrade 50° (125° Fahrenheit) is not exceptional. There are four parallel streets in the village, the widest of which rises toward the summit of the valley. Here, on this street, are the strange pillars or monuments marking each spot where Satan appeared to the son of the Prophet Ibrahim.

Below Mina is the Masjid al-Khayf, where Muhammad ﷺ prayed and where all pilgrims may pray after him. There is a story that in this place seventy of God's prophets have worshiped, among them Moses.

Entering the village, read:

Praise unto God Who hath delivered me here safe and in health—	*Du'a Read on Approaching Mina*

O God, this is Mina!
I have reached it as Thy Slave,
And the son (or daughter) of Thy Slave!
I pray that Thou bestoweth upon me—
That which Thou hast bestowed upon Thy favorites!

O God, I seek refuge,
From deprivation and calamity,
In my Faith and in my worldly life;
O Most Merciful of those who show mercy!
And Peace and Blessings upon our Prince, Muhammad,
And upon his family and companions.

THE JAMRAT AL-'AQABAH AND THE OFFERING OF A BLOOD SACRIFICE

Arriving from Muzdalifah on the tenth day of the month Dhu-al-Hijjah, the day called the Feast of the Sacrifice, 'Id al-Adha, or 'Id al-Qurban, the pilgrim army floods into the stony valley between the naked mountains. Engulfing the settlement, the struggling horde surges toward the "Satans"—for, on arrival, provided the sun is rising or has risen, all must hurry to the Jamrat al-'Aqabah, a masonry monument about three meters high, built against a low cliff-side at the summit of the valley.

Pilgrims suffering from heat exhaustion or other weakness may delay until the pressure has lessened, but it will be better if they can visit the Jamrat al-'Aqabah before the sun reaches its meridian. We are approaching the close of the Hajj, and every effort should be made to fulfill the acts of Pilgrimage in their proper sequence. But remember: we are not required to do that which exceeds our powers.

At the place of Jamrat al-'Aqabah, coming within throwing range of the monument, each pilgrim must cast seven of the forty-nine pebbles gathered at Muzdalifah. The stones should be flung one at a time. At each casting, say:

> *In the Name of God!*
> *God is Most Great!*

From this moment forth the pilgrim no longer is to read talbyah; the time for talbyah has passed.

On each of the next two days in Mina the pilgrim will visit all three "Satans," casting seven pebbles at each of the pillars, but on the first day in Mina only the Jamrat al-'Aqabah is to be stoned.

Then, returning from the site of the Jamrat al-'Aqabah, all pilgrims who can afford the expense should offer up a blood sacrifice. The flesh of the sacrificed animal is to be disposed of in a sensible manner: by putting it aside for subsequent meals to be taken in Mina or distributing it to those in need—but not by leaving it to rot and poison the atmosphere. God does not require an offering for blood's sake, and sacrifice must not become wanton destruction.

> *It is not their meat that reaches God, neither their blood; it is your piety that reaches Him. He has made them subject to you that ye might glorify God for His guidance: and proclaim the good tidings to all who do right.* [Quran 22:37]

The Close of Ihram for Those Who Fulfill the Hajj After the stoning and the sacrifice the pilgrim should cut the hair. This may be merely a token gesture, and we may clip but a few hairs of the head, or a lock of hair—and, again, this is all that is required of female pilgrims—but for men it is better to shave the head.

When this rite has been completed, the pilgrim no longer is in Ihram and the robes can be put off. The period of Ihram has passed —and the Hajj is approaching its closing ceremonies.

The external trappings of Ihram no longer are of significance; the pilgrim who has brought a change of clothing from Makkah will change to his or her more accustomed garb; others will continue to wear the two-piece Ihram garments, but Ihram has closed.

Tawaf Ifadhah: The Second Tawaf of the Pilgrimage However, the prohibitions of Ihram—the abstinence from sexual intercourse, from the use of perfume or scent, from the wearing of jewelry and personal adornment—are not lifted until after the Tawaf Ifadhah, the second tawaf of the Pilgrimage, to be performed as quickly as possible after the stoning of the Jamrat al-'Aqabah, the offering up of a blood sacrifice, and the closing of Ihram with the cutting of the hair.

During those years when the Pilgrimage must be observed during the hottest months of the year, pilgrims should complete the stoning of the first Jamrat, make the sacrifice, and close their Ihram as early in the morning as is possible; then they may hasten to Makkah before the full heat of the day for the performance of the Tawaf Ifadhah.

Tawaf Ifadhah is the foremost of the obligatory rituals which remain to be discharged. The preparation and observances are the same as before. The prayers and Praise may be read unchanged or may be altered by the individual pilgrim.

During this tawaf the pilgrim will know greater satisfaction than before. The exaltation will be much greater—and the humility more profound. And yet there will be a certain quietude, a certain calm—deeper feeling and better understanding.

Remember, mention and offer up prayer for your loved ones, the living and the dead, and for Muslims who are forbidden by godless governments to perform the Hajj and who dwell in despair and slavery and die as martyrs. As you stand in the presence of the Holy Ka'bah, pray that God's mercy may descend upon all Muslims. Ask God to show His compassion, that Muslims of all races and colors may be freed of foreign chains and that evil nations may fall and all roads to Makkah be opened again. And pray for the souls of the heroic races never to be seen in Makkah again—among them the peoples of the Crimea, obliterated by the Soviets—who perished rather than surrender any part of their identity, rather than relinquish any part of their Religion.

Fighting is decreed for you and ye dislike it. But it is possible that ye dislike a thing which is good for you, and that ye love a thing which is bad for you; but God knoweth and ye know not!

They ask thee concerning fighting in the Sacred Month. Say: "Fighting therein is grave, but it is graver in the sight of God to prevent access to the path of God! To deny Him, to prevent access to the Sacred Mosque, and drive out its members!" Tumult and oppression are worse than slaughter. Nor will they cease fighting you until they turn you back from your Faith, if they are able . . .

[Quran 2:215–216]

It is not requisite but instead is a convenience that the Tawaf Ifadhah be made the day of arrival at Mina; its completion releases the pilgrim from all the prohibitions accepted on taking Ihram. Too, in a measure it marks the completion of the Hajj.

Tawaf Ifadhah may be postponed until after the rites in Mina have been fulfilled, as was the Prophet's custom.

However, those pilgrims who hasten to Makkah to perform their Tawaf Ifadhah the same morning they stone the Jamrat al-'Aqabah are warned to remain in Makkah during the hot hours of the day, remaining in the shade of the Sacred Mosque if they wish; but all must return to Mina before sundown.

The Second and Third Days in Mina   We remain in the Valley of Mina for two or three days after the tenth of Dhu-al-Hijjah, for prayer and Praise and for the stoning of the Jamrat. Some pilgrims may prefer to pass most of the daylight hours in Makkah, returning only to sleep at Mina and observe the rite of stoning the pillars, but all must remain in the valley for at least two nights following the night of the tenth. These days are called the Days of Drying Meat, Ayyam al-Tashriq, after the ancient custom of curing the flesh of the sacrificed animals by drying it in the sun.

Celebrate the Praises of God during the numbered days, but if anyone hastens to leave in two days, there is no blame on him; and if anyone stays on, there is no blame on him, if his aim is to do right. Then fear God—and know that ye will surely be gathered unto Him. [Quran 2:202]

During the second day of the stay in Mina pilgrims must stone all three Jamrat, casting seven pebbles at each: a total of twenty-one pebbles. Unlike the first day, on the following days the pelting of the "Satans" is not to begin before the sun passes its meridian.

The observations of the third day are identical with those of the second, exhausting each pilgrim's store of forty-nine pebbles brought from Muzdalifah.

If for any reason whatever a pilgrim intending to return to Makkah on the twelfth day of Dhu-al-Hijjah is delayed past sundown, the return must be postponed until the following day. Then, on the thirteenth day of Dhu-al-Hijjah, the pilgrim must perform an additional stoning of the three Jamrat, gathering the required twenty-one stones in Mina itself. On this occasion the stoning may take place at any time after dawn.

The Close of   All pilgrims must be gone from Mina and
the Pilgrimage   return to Makkah before sundown of the thirteenth day of Dhu-al-Hijjah.

When Mina is behind and the Tawaf Ifadhah has been performed, the Pilgrimage is ended.

The Hajj has been fulfilled.

'UMRAH AFTER HAJJ

Pilgrims who originally came to Makkah with the Ihram of 'Umrah with Tamattu', or 'Umrah with Hajj, need not perform 'Umrah after the close of the Pilgrimage rituals. But all who entered Makkah with the Ihram of Hajj only, preferring to make a separate 'Umrah later, should do so directly after the close of the Pilgrimage.

These pilgrims, or any person dwelling in Makkah who desires to make 'Umrah out of the Pilgrimage season, should go to Tan'im, about five kilometers from Makkah on the camel route to Madinah, and there put on the robes of Ihram. Formally announcing the

Intention, the worshiper must then return to Makkah and make tawaf and sa'y as set forth earlier in this volume, concluding with the rite of cutting the hair.

HAJJ BADAL: THE PILGRIMAGE OF SUBSTITUTION

We are permitted to send others to Makkah in our place if because of an incurable illness or advanced age we cannot personally make the journey. Too, in the *Hadis* we are told of a man who asked if it was lawful to make Pilgrimage in the name of a sister who had vowed to perform Hajj but had died without accomplishing the sacred journey. The Prophet is said to have replied: "If she had left debts, would you have paid them? Then pay also debts due unto God."

We may make Hajj in the name of any person dear to us who dies without making the sacred journey. In this instance it is better if the cost of the Hajj is met with money from the estate of the deceased.

TAWAF AL-WADA'—THE FAREWELL TAWAF

The Farewell Tawaf, the last of the ritual circlings of the Holy Ka'bah, is made only just prior to the pilgrim's departure from Makkah for his or her homeland. Also, it is performed by anyone, in any season, who is leaving Makkah for an undetermined period. The robes of Ihram are not worn; also, we do not increase the gait during part of each of the first three circuits as on former occasions.

Completing the ritual circling of the Ka'bah, the worshiper should go to the place called Al-Multazam, between the Ka'bah's elevated gold and silver doors and the Black Stone, and there read Praise, as was done during the Tawaf al-Qudum and Tawaf Ifadhah. This done, two *rak'ah* should be read at the Place of Ibrahim, Maqam Ibrahim. Then, rising from the prayers, the pilgrim may go to the Black Stone and kiss it in farewell.

Returning again to the place called Al-Multazam, the worshiper should press the upraised hands and the face to the wall of the Ka'bah and read Praise.

After this is done, go to the well Zamzam and drink of its waters; then depart from the Sacred Mosque, going out through the Farewell Gate, Bab al-Wada'—and from Makkah.

Passing out through the gates of Makkah, read:

We are those who have returned to the Lord,
And those who have repented,
And those who have worshiped,
And those who Praise our God.
And God hath fulfilled His promise,
And hath succored His Slave,
And, alone, He hath defeated His foes!

Du'a Read by the Pilgrim Departing from Makkah to Return to His or Her Homeland

PART 2

THE SACRED JOURNEYS TO MADINAH AND JERUSALEM

CHAPTER 9

AL-MADINAH: THE SECOND HOLIEST
OF THE CITIES OF ISLAM

IN THE *HADIS*, the Traditions, we read that as well as making the sacred journey to Makkah, Muslims should visit Madinah and the Masjid al-Aqsa in Jerusalem. Pilgrimage to these latter is most desirable, but is not obligatory. Al-Madinah, the second city of Islam, lies approximately three hundred and seventy-five kilometers north of Makkah. Here, among many of his companions, sleeps the Prophet.

There are several routes leading northward from Jeddah and Makkah to Madinah. The direct Makkah-Madinah road is but a camel track and lightly traveled, but the coastal route, via Jeddah and Rabigh, carries motor traffic: lorries bearing pilgrims to Madinah make the desert journey in from sixteen to twenty-two hours. The landscape is savage and desolate. Between water holes, where occasionally a few date palms are found, there is nothing except sand, a hawk or vulture soaring in the otherwise empty sky, sand-hued antelope vanishing over the heat-shaken horizon, and scorpions hiding in the shade of the desert rocks. During the hot months the trespasser is shriveled and stunned by the awful heat and in the winter the dry cold slashes like a blade. A few Bedawin dwell by each of the wells, selling water and coffee and occasionally supplying dates and food to passers-by.

Traveling northward from Jeddah, the first halt is at Dhahban, the second at Tuwal, and the third at Rabigh. Dhahban and Tuwal are tiny villages, humid and unhealthy like Jeddah; Rabigh, where pilgrims approaching Makkah from the north change to Ihram, is a small harbor.

At Rabigh the road divides, one fork continuing northwesterly along the coast to Masturah, then turning inland to Abiar bin Hasani, Ashshufayyah, Al-Mesejid, Al-Fresh, Abiar 'Ali, and Madinah.

The other fork leading out of Rabigh turns inland immediately, to Bir al-Meberik, Al-Bustan, Um al-Birak, Al-Hafa, and Al-Mafrag, currently reuniting with the other road at Al-Mesejid.

Pilgrims coming from the south and unaccompanied by their Shaykh al-Hajj generally are met at the gates of Al-Madinah by the Shaykh's Agent, called Muzawwir, already informed by letter or wireless. Should the Muzawwir not be present, the town and Hajj officials, members of whom meet all traffic at Madinah's gates, summon the Muzawwir, who then escorts the pilgrims to prepared quarters.

Madinah, the ancient Yathrib, is an oasis of many gardens and is second only to Makkah in sanctity. Muhammad ﷺ sought sanctuary there after his Hejirah or Flight from Makkah. Here it was that he received many of the divine revelations which are incorporated in the Quran. Just outside Madinah is the Jebel Uhud, the mountain where the Prophet and his companions fought the Quraysh in the third year of the Hejirah; and here, in the foothills, are the graves of seventy-three of the companions, one of whom is Hamzah bin Abd-al-Mutallib, the Prophet's uncle.

Nearer Madinah is the battlefield called The Trench, Al Khandaq, where the Quraysh attacked Madinah with ten thousand allies, but were frustrated by a trench the Prophet had caused to be dug in anticipation of the assault, during the fifth year of the Hejirah. In this place are seven mosques and tombs of companions of the Prophet.

Just outside Madinah's walls are the graves of Al-Abbas, another uncle of Muhammad ﷺ and Al Hasan bin 'Ali, the grandson of the Prophet by his daughter Fatimah; and here lies 'Uthman bin 'Affan, son-in-law of Muhammad ﷺ and the third Khalif of Islam. Close at hand are the graves of a number of Muhammad's ﷺ wives. This is the burial ground of Madinah and is called Al Baqi'.

The Sanctuary, the
Tomb, and the
Mosque of the
Prophet

After arriving at Madinah and bathing and changing to fresh clothing, the first place to be visited is the mosque called The Sanctuary of the Prophet, Al Haram al-Nabawi. This was the second mosque built by Muhammad ﷺ, and his faithful followers after the flight from Makkah; the first mosque was erected at Quba', a few kilometers from Madinah on the camel route from Makkah.

The Prophet personally labored on the construction of both mosques, but here in Al Haram al-Nabawi he lies in his tomb. And here, beside him, sleep Abu Bakr and 'Umar.

The original mosque was built of sun-dried brick, the floor was of earth, and the ceiling was constructed of palm fronds covered with mud and supported by pillars of palm wood. Today the floors and pillars are of polished marble—for the Sanctuary of the Prophet has been rebuilt and added to and made splendid by many kings, the last of whom was the Sultan 'Abd-al-Majid; only the Faith is unchanged.

Accompanied by their Shaykh or Muzawwir, pilgrims will enter the mosque through the Bab al-Salam, saying:

In the Name of God—
And by the Religion of the Messenger of God,
On whom be Peace and blessings.

Follow the above with the same words uttered by those entering the Sacred Mosque in Makkah, then read:

O God, Blessings upon our Prince,
Muhammad, and the family of our Prince,
Muhammad; and forgive me my sins,
And open for me the doors of Thy Mercy,
And allow me to enter,
O Most Merciful of those who show mercy!

Du'a Read at   Inside the present mosque are the precincts
the Tomb of   of the Prophet's mosque, its limits marked by
the Prophet   a railing of wrought brass. This place is called
Raudhah and is on the right hand of the domed tomb of the

Prophet Muhammad ﷺ . In the *Hadis* we are told that this is
a fragment of Paradise.

Enter the place called Raudhah and pray two *rak'ah,* then read
the following Praise:

O God, this is a garden of the gardens of Paradise!
Thou hast made it bright and excellent,
And illuminated it with the light of Thy Prophet,
And Thy Beloved, Muhammad,
On whom be Peace and Blessings.
And allow us to congregate with those who shall follow him in
    throngs;
And let us die in his love,
And following his Traditions;
And let us drink from his well,
And from his noble hand,
A pleasant drink which will forever quench our thirst.
O God, Thou hast power to do all things!

Rising now, go in humility to the tomb of the Prophet. The

chamber where lie Muhammad ﷺ and Abu Bakr and 'Umar
is completely enclosed and draped in green silk. In the time of

Muhammad ﷺ this was the site of the house of 'Aisha, his wife.
The length is sixteen meters and the breadth is fifteen meters.
Standing before it, read this greeting:

Peace be with Thee, O Prophet of God,
Peace be with thee, O Chosen of God from all His creatures,
Peace be with thee, O Beloved of God!
I bear witness that there is no deity except God, the One!
And He is without companion!
And thou art truly His Slave and Messenger.

And I bear witness that truly thou didst fulfill thy mission,
And fulfilled thy trust,
Counseled the people,
And fought for the sake of God;
God blessed thee with a blessing
To endure until the Day of Judgement!
O God, grant us good in this world,
And grant us good in the Hereafter,
And save us from the torments of the Fire!
O God, grant him dignity, and favor,
And High Degree;
And resurrect him in the Place of Praise
Thou hast promised for him,
O Most Merciful of those who show mercy!

Du'a Read at the   Concluding the above, the pilgrim may read
Tomb of Abu Bakr   any prayer or Praise which comes to the lips.
This done, go to the tomb of Abu Bakr, and read the following
salutation:

Peace be with thee,
O successor to God's Messenger;
Peace be with thee,
O companion of God's Messenger in the cave;
Peace be with thee,
O thou who wert trusted with confidences;
May God reward thee with the best of the rewards to be granted
    to the people of the Prophet!
Thou didst succeed him as the best successor,
Thou didst walk in his way and on his path,
The best of his followers!
And thou didst support Islam,
Cared for the family of Islam,
And, until death, never departed from the way of the just!
Peace be with Thee,
And God's Mercy,
And Blessings.

Go next to the tomb of 'Umar, and read the salutation:

Peace be with thee, | *Du'a Read at the*
O upholder of Islam; | *Tomb of 'Umar*
Peace be with thee,
O sustainer of Truth against infidelity;
Peace be with Thee,
O ever-truthful;
Thou didst care for the orphans,
And cared for the family of Islam,
And strengthened Islam!
Peace be with thee,
And God's mercy.

Now the pilgrim should read prayers for the good of his, or her, own soul, for loved ones absent from the Hajj and Madinah, and for all Muslims, especially those forcibly prevented from performing the Pilgrimage.

Then, in closing, read Praise.

Departing from the tomb of the Prophet and the Mosque of the Prophet, the pilgrim should visit Al-Baqi', the burial place of Madinah, and there read prayers for the companions of the Prophet and for his wives and relations and followers.

There is no sequence which must be followed, and we may take as much time as we require. Men come to Madinah not that they may return to their homelands and announce that they have been to these places, but that they may worship God in these sites—

where the Prophet Muhammad ﷺ worshiped.

The Mosque of   Visit Quba', a garden village outside Madi-
Piety, Masjid   nah's walls and the location of the first place
al-Taqwa, at Quba'   of worship dedicated by the Prophet and his
companions after they fled Makkah to take refuge in Madinah. This mosque is called the Mosque of Piety, Masjid al-Taqwa.

After Muhammad ﷺ and Abu Bakr had fled Makkah and crossed the desert, they arrived at Quba', where they rested more than ten days. During this pause the Prophet dedicated the Mosque of Piety and here read the first Friday prayers. Then Muhammad ﷺ continued to Madinah.

We are told to read two *rak'ah* here, then to read Praise:

O God, truly this mosque is the mosque of Quba',
And the place where our Prophet prayed,
Our beloved and our Prince, Muhammad,
On whom be Peace, and Blessings.
O God, Thou hast said—
And Thy words are Truth,
In the tongue of Thy Prophet,
Thy Messenger:

This is the mosque founded on piety, from the first day;
It is the most worthy of thy standing forth therein;
In it are men who love purification,
And God loveth those who make themselves pure.

O God, cleanse our hearts of hypocrisy,
And our deeds of false pride,
And our sex from that which is unlawful,
And our tongues of falsehoods and slander,
And our eyes from perfidy—
Truly, Thou knowest the treachery of the eyes,
And what is concealed in the heart!

Our Lord, we have committed wrongs against ourselves,
And unless Thou forgivest us,
And hath mercy on us,
We shall be of those who are lost! . . .

Near the Masjid al-Taqwa is the Well of the Ring, Bir al-Khatam, in early times called Bir 'Aris. At the Prophet's death his seal ring passed into the keeping of Abu Bakr and later to 'Umar, then to 'Uthman. It is told that 'Uthman once came to this well for his ritual ablutions, and as water was being drawn, the ring of

Muhammad ﷺ fell from 'Uthman's hand, dropping into the well. It was searched for but never recovered.

The Mosque of
Two Directions
of Prayer: Masjid
al-Qiblatayn
Next, the pilgrim should visit the Mosque of Two Directions of Prayer, Masjid al-Qiblatayn. When the Prophet first came to Madinah and this place he still directed his prayers toward Jerusalem, but while here he received the divine revelation which established a new direction of prayer, a new qiblah: the Holy Ka'bah, in Makkah.

We see the turning of thy face to the sky [for guidance], so We shall turn thee toward a Qiblah that shall please thee. Turn then thy face in the direction of the Sacred Mosque; wherever ye are, turn your faces in its direction. Truly, the People who have received the Book know well that it is the Truth from their Lord. Nor is God unmindful of what they do. [Quran 2:144]

Read two *rak'ah* at the Mosque of Two Directions of Prayer, and then read the following Praise:

O God, truly this is the Mosque of the Two Directions of Prayer,
And the praying place of our Prophet,
And our beloved, Muhammad,
On whom be Peace, and Blessings.
O God, as Thou hast granted that we reach this place in this
*   world,*
That we may visit it and its noble remains,
So do not, O God, prevent us in the Hereafter,
From knowing his mediation,
Peace and Blessings be with him!

And now the pilgrim should go to the Mosque of Victory, Masjid al-Fath, at Khandaq. Read two *rak'ah* and read Praise. Then visit the Jebel Uhud, the mountain where sleep seventy-three of the Prophet's companions.

Farewell Visit
to the Tomb of
the Prophet
Before leaving Madinah, the pilgrim will make a farewell visit to the tomb of the Prophet and read:

O God, make not this visit to be a last visit
To this noble place;

Grant that I may come here again,
In health and untroubled.
If I live I shall return—
If God wills!

And, should I die,
My trust is in my oath, my bond, my promising, my pact,
From this day of ours until the Day of Resurrection,
That I bear witness:
There is no deity except God,
Alone, without companion!
And that I bear witness:
Muhammad is His Slave,
His Messenger!
Foreign indeed from God, Lord of Glory,
The limits the infidel have placed about His Name!
And Peace be with all His Messengers,
And Praise unto God,
Lord of the Universe! . . .

CHAPTER 10

JERUSALEM: THE THIRD HOLIEST
OF THE CITIES OF ISLAM

JERUSALEM, and more particularly the Sacred Mosque, Al Haram al-Sherif—or the Farther Mosque, Al Masjid al 'Aqsa—is the third holiest place in Islam.

THE MOSQUE OF 'UMAR

The present mosque and surrounding buildings stand on the site of the temple built three thousand years ago by Solomon; five hundred years later razed by Nebuchadnezzar, and rebuilt within the century by Ezra and Nehemiah; converted into a pagan temple by Antiochus Epiphanes, one of Alexander's successors; restored by Herod during the lifetime of the Prophet Jesus; seventy years afterward completely razed to the ground, for the second time in its history, by the Emperor Titus—and finally rebuilt as it stands today by 'Abd-al-Malik, a little more than half a century after the death of Muhammad ﷺ .

We are told that the Prophet paused here after the night journey from Makkah and before ascending to the presence of God to receive the Divine Commands regarding the observance of the periods of prayer.

THE JOURNEY BY NIGHT AND THE NIGHT ASCENT

The Journey by Night, Al Isra', and The Night Ascent, Al Mi'raj, took place on the night of the twenty-seventh of Rajab, the year previous to Muhammad's ﷺ Hejirah from Makkah. Some Muslims contend that the Prophet made the miraculous journey from Makkah to Jerusalem and the ascension from Jerusalem to Paradise, and the return to Makkah, in the flesh. Others are of the opinion that the events as described were seen in a vision while Muhammad ﷺ slept in Makkah. Bodily, or in spirit, the trip was made.

Glory to God Who did take His Slave for a journey by night, from the Sacred Mosque to the Farthest Mosque, whose precincts We did bless—in order that We might show him some of Our Signs: for He is the One Who heareth and seeth [all things].

[*Quran* 17:1]

It is told that the Angel Jibra'il appeared to Muhammad ﷺ while he slept by the Holy Ka'bah. The Prophet was bathed in a golden basin filled with the water of Faith and then mounted a divine steed which bore him to Jerusalem with the speed of light, each bound covering a span measurable only by the distance a man's eye can see.

At Jerusalem, Muhammad ﷺ dismounted at the ancient site of the temple of Solomon and there offered up worship with an assembly of prophets who had preceded him on earth: Ibrahim, Moses, David, Solomon, Jesus . . .

Then, mounting again, Muhammad ﷺ was borne heavenward by his winged steed—halting at last by the Lote Tree, Sidrah al-Muntaha, the heavenly mansion of the Angel Jibra'il, above which is the Throne of God.

Here Muhammad ﷺ received the Divine Command that all Muslims must offer up five prayers each day.

It is no evidence of Piety that ye turn your faces toward East or West; but Piety is: To believe in God, and the Last Day, and the Angels, and the Book, and the Prophets; to spend of your substance out of love for Him, for your kin, for orphans, for the needy, for the wayfarer, for those who ask, and for the ransom of slaves; to be steadfast in prayer, and practice regular charity; to fulfill the contracts which ye have made; and to be firm and patient, in pain, and adversity, and throughout all periods of panic. Such are the people of Truth, the God-Fearing.

[Quran 2:176]

الرّحلة المقدّسة

الى بيت الله الحرام

كتاب يبحث عن احكام الحج وأسراره ووصف المواقف الكريمة
والمشاهد الشريفة ومسجد النبي وقبره الشريف والمسجد الأقصى
وعما يلزم الحجاج في سفرهم واقامتهم

تأليف

الحاج احمد كمال

جمعيّة الاسلام

ترجمة

حسين عولي عطا

١٣٨٠ — ١٩٦٠.

الفهرس

مقدمة

بقلم

صاحب السماحة الامام الاكبر الشيخ محمد بن محمد
مهدي الخالصي رئيس جامعة مدينة العلم ،
الكاظمية ، بغداد ، العراق

●

بسم الله الرحمن الرحيم

الحمد لله الذي وحد كلمة المسلمين على الاعتراف بتوحيده والتصديق بكتابه
والايمان برسوله ، وجمع شملهم في جمعتهم وجـــماعتهم وعيدهم وحجهم والتوجه في
صلواتهم الى قبلة واحدة يعبدون إلـهاً واحداً ، وأشهد أن لا إله إلا الله وحده لا
شريك له ، ظهرت آيات توحيده في جميع مخلوقاته ، في ارضه وسمواته ، وفي الآفاق
والانفس وفي كل شيء ، وأشهد أن محمداً عبده ورسوله ، صدقت رسالته معجزاته
الظاهرة الباهرة الباقية الى الأبد في قرآنه وعلومه ، واحكامه التي تضمن المصالح
للبشر في جميع تطوراتهم ، وتنفي ما يحدث من المفاسد في الجامعة البشرية وافراد
الناس ، وكلما ازدادت العلوم والمكتشفات تقدماً ازداد اعجاز تلك الاحكام وضوحاً
وظهوراً ، فالمعجزة تلو المعجزة تتجدد وتظهر في احكام الرســالة المحمدية بتزايد
العلوم وتقدم المكتشفات ، وكل يوم لنا في رسول الله معجزة ظاهرة . اللهم صلّ على
محمد وآله واصحابه كما صليت على ابراهيم وآل ابراهيم انك حميد مجيد .

وبعد . فاني كنت ولا ازال افكر في امر الاسلام والمسلمين فلا ازداد إلا

عجباً ودهشة من امرين لا ارى بينها وفقاً ولا تقارباً مع انها شيء واحـد
وينبغي ان لا يختلفا . ارى الاسـلام اعلى فلسفة وادق احكاماً واشمل لمصالح
البشر وادعى للعلوم والاتحاد والسعادة والاخوة البشرية وللتربية الصحيحة ولسمو
الاخلاق وللأمر بالمعروف وللنهي عن المنكر ولخفض العيش والغنى والدعة والعافية
والعزة والرفعة والسلامة والعدل والصلاح والسير الى الامام والسلام ، من كل ما
عرفه البشر من انواع العلوم والقوانين والنظم والشرائع . ثم أنظر في حـال
المسلمين فأرام أبعد الأمم عن خيرات الإسلام واحطهم قـدراً واعظمهم وزراً
وأكثرهم جهالة وأضعفهم قوة وافقرهم مالاً وانكدهم عيشاً ، شتاتاً متفرقين لم تقم
لهم جماعة ولم يجمع لهم شمل ، اذلاء صاغرين في بلادهم يخافون ان يتخطفهم الناس
من حولهم ؛ لم يقم فيهم عدل ، ولم يعمل معهم بمعروف ؛ لا مرشد يهديهم ولا قائد
إلى الخير يقودهم ، بعيدين عن كل تقدم . نكدٌ عيشهم مضطربة افكارهم متضاربة
آراؤهم ، مختلفة مذاهبهم ، فما هذا البعد ما بين الاسلام والمسلمين ؟ ومما يزيد
الأسى انهم لم يعرفوا اسرار احكام الاسلام وشرائعه ، وما ترمي اليه من المصالح
الدنيوية والأخروية ، ولا يوجد فيهم من تصدى لذلك من العلماء والكتاب اللهم
إلا القليل النادر في بعض الاحكام .

هذا ما كان يختلج ببالي وكنت اتطلب من ادرك ذلك وشعر به فتصدى له .

وقد شاءت ارادة الله ان تختار السيد احمد كمال ، العامل مع منظمة النجدة
الاسلامية الدولية التابعة لجمعية الاسلام ليملأ هذا الفراغ . واثناء اقامته في بغداد
جرى حديث مفصل بيني وبينه في اسرار شرائع الاسلام ومن جملتها تشريع
الحج وما فيه من الفوائد والمصالح العامـة للبشر وللمسلمين خاصة ، وان احد
الاغراض منه توحيد كلمة المسلمين وجمع شتاتهم ، فلم ترقنا المؤلفات التي كانت بين
ايدينا في الحج ؛ فمنها ما ألفت على مذهب ابي حنيفة ومنها ما كتبت على مذهب
الشافعي أو مالك او ابن حنبل . ثم رأينا كتباً في الحج ألفت على مذهب اهل
البيت الذي دان به الشيعة ولم تتطرق لفتاوى غيرهم . ورأينا من بين تلك الكتب
ما ألف على المذاهب الاربعة . الا كانت جميعها غير وافية بالغرض وناقصة .
وبعد محادثات طويلة افترقنا .

في اواسط شوال من هذه السنة جاءني منه كتاب سماه (الرحلة المقدسة)
ولم ادر ما كتب فيه ، فطلبت من الاستاذ الفاضل (حسين عوني عطا) ان

يُعرّبه فإذا هو مشتمل على كثير مما كنا نطلبه من مؤلفي المسلمين ؛ فشكرت الله على ان قيّض من اخواني البعيدين عني منزلاً من يملك ما املكه من الشعور الديني ويعينني على ما اطلبه للمسلمين من الوصول الى اقصى السعادة برضوان الله والخير في الدنيا والآخرة . واليك وصف هذا الكتاب على الاجمال .

ان فيه حلاوة يستطيبها الذوق السليم ذكرني عند قراءته المثل السائر (ان لله جنوداً منها العسل) واي عسل اشهى واحلى واهنأ وامرأ من الشهـــد الروحي الذي يجلي الروح ويريح البدن ... اقرأ هذا الكتاب تره يصف لك المواقف المقدسة حتى تنسى مكانك وتظن نفسك واقفاً فيهـا . اذا وصف لك الميقات تجد نفسك فيه ، واذا ذكر لك الحرم تحسب نفسك انك داخل فيه ، واذا نعت الكعبة وحددها تجدها نصب عينيك ، واذا ذكر الطواف يخيل لك انك تطوف حول البيت ، واذا مشى بك الى مقام ابراهيم للصلاة او حجر اسماعيل لذكر الله لا تشك في انك قد اتيت المقامين فصليت فيهما وذكرت الله وحده . واذا سعى بك بين الصفا والمروة تخالك ساعياً بينها وانت في مكانك ، وهكذا ينتقل بك من مكة الى عرفات ويصفه لك والطريق المؤدية اليها والافاضة الى المزدلفــة ثم الى منى ، وكأنك بوصفه ترى بعينيك ما وصفه لك ، وتسمع باذنيك الحجــاج محرمين ملبين خاشعين مصلين ساعين واقفين في عرفات ، والمشعر الحرام ، رامين الجمرات سائقين الهدْي راجعين الى مكة ، طائفين ساعين ، عائدين الى منى لرمي الجمرات الباقيات ، خاتمين للحج بطواف الوداع بعد طواف النساء . وبينما انت ترى نفسك تتقلب بقراءتك الكتاب بين تلك المواقف تتلقى أحكام مناسك الحج فتحيط بها علماً ويسهـل امرك وامر مطوّفك ؛ ثم تبصر النصائح التي تلزم لمن يريد الحج من بلده وطريقه ومحط رحله في الحرم وفي المدينة المنورة ، وما يلزم للأكل والشرب واللباس واتقاء الحر والبرد على اختلاف المواسم ، وطريق المعاملة مع اهل مكة والمدينــة والمعاشرة معهم ؛ وتبصر من وصف مسجد النبي صلى الله عليه وآله وسلم وحرمـــه ومحل قبره الشريف ما يمثلها بين عينيك كأنك تراها في وصف الحرم والكعبة ، ولا يقف هذا الكتاب عند هذا الحد ، بل يذكرك بالمائة والثمانين مليوناً من المسلمين المعذبين تحت اثقال الظلـم الأجنبي وكثيرون من هؤلاء محرمون عن اقامة الشعائر الدينية عامة والحج خاصة ، فعلينا ان ندعو الله لإنقاذ هؤلاء المحرومين وان نجاهـد لتحريرهم .

— و —

ومن اهم ما اشتمل عليه كتاب السيد احمد كمال هو الجمع بين مذهبي الشيعة والسنة . ويريك أن الفرق بين الشيعة والسنة أقل من الفرق بين الشافعية والحنفية ، ويدعو المسلمين عامة الى الوحدة الحقيقية الصادقة ونبذ الاختلاف ولا سيما في هذا العصر .

ومع كل ما اشتمل عليه هذا الكتاب لم يهمل ذكر كثير من اسرار أحكام الحج ومصالحها ؛ واذا مر بك على موقف أو مشهد عرفك بذكر شيء من تاريخه وأسباب النسك الذي يجري فيه . وبالجملة ان هذا الكتاب وصف للمناسك والمواقف ، وبيان لأحكام الحج وفوائده وأسراره ، ودعوة للمسلمين الى الاتحاد والتخلص من اسر العبودية والاسترقاق ، وتحذير من الفرقة وسوء ما تجره من البلاء على المسلمين .

وفق الله مؤلفه وشكر سعيه واجزل اجره ومنَّ على مترجمه وناشره بالخير ونفع المسلمين عامة والحجاج خاصة به .

محمد بن محمد مهدي الطالصي الكاظمي

بغداد — ١٣٧٢

كلمة صاحب السماحة المفتي الحاج

محمد امين الحسيني

اجزل الله ثواب المؤلف الكريم ، السيد احمد كمال
ووفقه ووفق جميع الذين يخدمون قضية الاسلام والمسلمين،
والله يكافىء المؤمنين .

بيروت ، لبنان
٢٠ حزيران ــ يونيو ــ ١٩٦٠

كلمة المترجم

لقد اندفعت في سبيل ترجمة هذا السفر النفيس لا سعياً وراء منفعته ، ولا لاني اخذت بسحر بلاغته في لغته الاصلية بل اسرتني تلك الروح التي يفتقدها كل فرد منا في هذه الايام العصيبة التي يجتازها الاسلام في جميع اقطاره وشعوبه ، تلك الروح التي تضع مؤلف هذا الكتاب في صفوف المصلحين المجاهدين الذين يريدون بعث روح السلام ـ السلام الذي لا يخفى خلفه الاعتداء ولا يكمن تحته الاستبداد أو الظلم كالذي نزل على النبي ابراهيم ـ من وراء بعث الاسلام . فقد اسرتني هذه الروح وغمرتني بسحرها عندما استجبت لدعوة سيدي الجليل سماحة العلامة وحجة الاسلام الإمام الخالصي لنقل هذا السفر الى العربية ، فزادتني حماسة على حماسة ولم اشعر الا وانا محاط بجو ارتفع بي الى سعادة ذهنية لا يشعر بها الا من اقتبس هذه الروح في رحلة ذهنية مماثلة .

وانا اذ اتقدم بهـــذه الترجمة الى العالم الاسلامي اتمنى ان تقع في نفوس قراء هذا العالم الواسع موقعاً يحقق الغرض النبيل الذي سعى اليه المؤلف ويسعى اليه سماحة الامـــام الخالصي وامثاله من المصلحين في هذا العصر ، وارجو من الله ان ينزل لها في قلوب المؤمنين المنزلـة التي تستحقها ، ويجعل لهـا في افئدتهم مستقراً ومقاماً . (إنَّ اللهَ اشْترى من المؤمنين أنفُسَهُم وأموالَهم بأنَّ لهُمُ الجَنَّةَ يُقاتِلونَ في سبيل الله فيَقتُلونَ ويُقتَلون وعداً عليه حقاً في التوراة والإنجيل والقرآن ومن أوْفى بعهْده من الله فاستبشروا ببيعِكُمُ الذي بايعتمْ به وذلك هو الفوزُ العظيم). (سورة التوبة الآية ١١٢)

ع . ع . ع

الرحلة المقــــدسة

ذكر انه بعد طرد آدم وحواء من الجنة كسيري القلب توسلا الى الله وهـما بجانب معبد ـ هو على شكل معبد في الجنة تصلي فيه الملائكة ـ ، فترددت بين الجدران الصخرية لصرح المعبد الاصلي أصداء الصلاة الاولى التي نطق بها البشر .

« إِنَّ أَوَّلَ بَيْتٍ وُضِعَ لِلنَّاسِ لَلَّذِي بِبَكَّةَ مُبَارَكاً وَهُدىً لِلْعَالَمِينَ . فِيهِ آيَاتٌ بَيِّنَاتٌ مَقَامُ إِبْرَاهِيمَ وَمَنْ دَخَلَهُ كَانَ آمِناً وَلِلَّهِ عَلَى النَّاسِ حِجُّ البَيْتِ مَنِ اسْتَطَاعَ إِلَيْهِ سَبِيلاً وَمَنْ كَفَرَ فَإِنَّ اللَّهَ غَنِيٌّ عَنِ العَالَمِينَ »

(سورة آل عمران ، الآيتان ٩٦ ـ ٩٧)

تقف الكعبة اليوم ـ وقد زارها ابناء آدم قبل الطوفان وبعد مـا اختفت واحاط الماء بهم ودرسوا . أعاد النبي ابراهيم بناءها مع ابنه اسماعيل ـ في نفس الموقع في جمـال جذاب صرحـاً بسيطاً مكعباً من الصخر والطين تكسوه كسوة سوداء ذات زرقة مزدانة بحروف مذهبة .

ويمكن الدخول الى الكعبة المقدســة ، من اي باب من الابواب الاربعة والعشرين ، وهي تبلغ في الطول اثني عشر متراً وفي العرض عشرة أمتـار وفي الارتفاع خمسة عشر متراً وتسمى (البيت العتيق) .

وفي موسم الحج يفيض على البلاد العربية طوفان من البشر من جميع اقطار الارض من كل فج عميق ، فتنفغر مداخـل مكة المكرمة التي حرمت على غير المسلمين ، وتصبح الكعبة المجللة بالسواد ليلا ونهاراً مركزاً يحيط به سيل متموج من

المؤمنين ، الذين يؤدون فريضة الطواف . ويتبع هؤلاء موج بعد موج من الحجاج المنهوكين الساجدين على الارض أو الراكعين او الجالسين او الواقفين في اوضاع الصلاة والعبادة .

وبعد انتهاء الاعمال الاولى في مكة (وتسمى العمرة ، يبتدىء الحج ، فتسير الجموع منها الى عرفات في الارض الجرداء .

وعرفات (وهي محل المعرفة ، جبل صخري أجرد ، في واد كبير غير ذي زرع . وذكر في وجه تسميتها ان آدم وحواء عندما طردا من الجنة افترقا ، ومرت عليها ، وكل منها يبحث عن الآخر ، مثنا عام دون جدوى ، وحيدين يائسين حتى نزل الملك جبرائيل وأرشد آدم الى حواء .

وهنا على الجبل الصحراوي التقيا مرة اخرى و (عرف) كل منها صاحبه .

وهناك قصة تقول ان في زمن ابراهيم قام الملك جبرائيل بتلقين النبي ابراهيم جميع مناسك الحج ثم سأله هناك (فعرف) ابراهيم ما لقن .

وفي نهاية الوقوف في عرفات يندفع الحجاج - وهم في الاغلب ما يقرب من خمسمائة الف نسمة - في الارض الجرداء الى المزدلفة حيث يقفون ليلا للصلاة فيها وهي مصلى منعزل ، ومن هناك يتحركون الى منى ، ويقال في وجه تسميتها ان ايمان النبي ابراهيم وابنه اسماعيل قد امتحن هناك - اذ أعد الوالد المتحير ابنه قربانا لله ، ولما اراد الشيطان اغراء الشاب ليعصي أباه رماه اسماعيل بحجر .

هذه هي مناظر الحج ، وهاتيك أماكنه المقدسة ، واكثرها قدسية مكة - وفي وسط تلك البلدة المقدسة المحرمة - قلب الاسلام في الارض (القبلة التي أمرنا ان نصلي اليها خمسة اوقات في كل يوم) .

واستحب لنا ان نصلي اليها جماعة ، وذلــك افضل من أن تتعبد على انفراد (غير ان ثلاث صلوات تجب فيها الجماعة ولا تصح فرادى وهي صلاة الجمعة وعيد الفطر وعيد الاضحى) ، فمن مدينة الكاب (رأس الرجاء الصالح) الى سيبريا القطبية ، ومن مندناوا وجزر المحيط الهادي السفلي ، ثم من هناك عــبر القارتين آسيا واوربا الى فنلندة ، ومنها جنوبــاً نحو سواحل افريقيا الاطلسية شرقاً وغرباً ، شمالاً وجنوباً يتوجه في كل يوم سبع البشرية نحو مكة والكعبة متحدين في صلواتهم ، عدا الذين ساقهم سوء الحظ الى الوقوع تحت نير العبودية الشيوعية .

لقد ظلت الاراضي التي تضم مدينة مكة والمواقع المقدسة - وهي محــاطة

من جميع جوانبها بمتاهة من الوديان الصخرية والممرات المفتوحة ، وهي في حـد ذاتها صحراء – منذ اقدم أزمنة التاريخ المعروفة ، نقطة تجـارة وطريق حج يقطع اقسى جزء من الارض الماحلة .

ولم تقم مكة في أرض جرداء قاحلة فحسب ، بل انها في غاية الحر والجفاف ويكاد الحر فيها ان يكون فوق طاقة البشر ، حتى انه قد اودى بحياة الحجاج وسكان مكة بشكل مريع ؛ ونحن نجد في القرآن ابتهالاً الى الله تعالى من النبي ابراهيم في قوله :

« رَبَّنَا إِنِّي أَسْكَنْتُ مِنْ ذُرِّيَّتِي بِوَادٍ غَيْرِ ذِي زَرْعٍ عِنْدَ بَيْتِكَ الْمُحَرَّمِ . رَبَّنَا لِيُقِيمُوا الصَّلَاةَ فَاجْعَلْ أَفْئِدَةً مِنَ النَّاسِ تَهْوِي إِلَيْهِمْ وَارْزُقْهُمْ مِنَ الثَّمَرَاتِ لَعَلَّهُمْ يَشْكُرُونَ » .

(سورة ابراهيم ، الآية ٣٧)

تقع مكة على بعد ثـلاثة وسبعين كيلومتراً من ثغرها الساحلي على البحر الاحمر المشتعل حرارة ، في تجويف غير منتظم بين تلال وجبال بلغ منها أنه في الازمنة القديمة لم يكن من الضروري لحماية المدينة بناء سور لها ، بل كان يكفي سد الوادي من ثلاث نقاط مفتوحة بأبواب محكمة تؤدي الى المدينة . اما اليوم فإن هذه الابواب – التي كان قد اغلقها كفـار قريش في وجه محمد (صلى الله عليه وآله وصحبه وسلم) مرة – لم يبق منها الا آثارها ، وقد تناثرت المساكن ذات الطبقات والخرائب على التـلال الصخرية . ويمتد طريق واسع على طول وادي مكة يقسمها قسمين طولاً ، ويتقاطع هذا الشريان الرئيسي بجانب المسجد الكبير بطريق واسع يقطع الوادي من جانب الى آخر ؛ وبذلك يمر من اشد الاسواق نشاطاً . وهذا الطريق الاخير – وقد سقف ليحمي الحجاج والمكين من حر الصيف الذي لا يوصف – هو الطريق المقدس بين الصفا والمروة (محل السعي) . فهنا ذهبت « هاجر » أم اسماعيل تبحث يائسة عن الماء لولدها الطفل قبل ان توجد مكة .

أما اليوم فان الطريق قد صفت فيه الحوانيت صفاً ، وهي ملأى بأطنان

من المسابح من العنبر والأخشاب النادرة الذكية الرائحة ، ونسخ صغيرة جداً من القرآن الكريم بلغ صغر حجمها ان صفحة كاملة مصورة منها تقل في حجمها عن ظفر المرأة ، ولا تقرأ الا بواسطة مكبرة قوية ، وطعام وشراب ولباس ، والمظلات لاتقاء حرارة الشمس لا للمطر ، والاحجار المموهة التي تشبه الاحجار الكريمة والبخور والمسك والزبار والعطر القوي الرائحة وماء الورد والكوكاكولا ، وعنب الطائف وبطيخه الناضج ، تلك النماذج البسيطة لمكة والمنظر المقدس ـ أمتعة مقدسة وغير مقدسة لإثارة شهية الجم الغفير من الحجاج الغادين والرائحين ، بين الصفا والمروة وهم يؤدون شعائر السعي .

ومع هذا فان مكة ليست موقعاً جغرافياً أو طقساً من طقوس الحج ، بقدر ما هي معتقد جازم ثابت منطبع في القلوب عن ايمان صادق ، فلن يكتشف الحجاج في مكة الا انهم في مكة وحسب ، فنحن لا نأتي الى هنا لنبحث عن الالهام ، بل لأننا ملهمون ، والحج انما هو اعلان عن الايمان لا البحث عنه .

فالاسلام يقوم على خمسة اركان :

الركن الاول هو شهادة أن لا إله إلا الله وأن محمداً رسوله . (وما يتبع ذلك) . والركن الثاني هو الصلاة . فهناك أمور يجب القيام بها لهذا العالم وللعالم الذي يليه .

وايتاء الزكاة هو الركن الثالث ، والصيام هو الركن الرابع اما الركن الخامس فهو الحج .

والحج هو مؤتمر عظيم للمؤمنين من جميع اقطار هذه الارض ، يتعبد فيه المسلمون على اختلاف عناصرهم والوانهم في اتحاد والفة . فيدركون القوة التي تنبعث من الايمان الموحد والعمل المتسق . ان في دعوتنا للتجمع في الاماكن المقدسة فرصة لا مثيل لها لاكتشاف قوتنا المادية والروحية والبدنية . ولا مثيل في العالم لهذا المؤتمر السنوي ، كما ليس هناك شعب يمتاز بمثل هذا المؤتمر لمعرفة وحدة كيانه وغايته .

ان الاسلام اليوم يفتح عينه بعد اغفاءة امتدت الف عام تقريباً . فقد كان معدل ستين الفاً من المؤمنين من غير العرب يحجون في السنوات الواقعة بين الحربين العالميتين الاولى والثانية . وجاء الى مكة في سنة ١٩٤١ مائة وخمسون الفاً وفي سنة ١٩٥٠ اجتمع في مكة وعرفات مئتان وثلاثون الفاً . اما في سنة

١٩٥٢ فقد أدى فريضة الحج خمسمائة ألف حاج . وفي سنة ١٩٦٠ بلغ الحجاج سبعمائة وخمسين ألفاً عدا الحجاج من أهل البلاد .

إن العملاق يتحرك . وعلينا بعد أن استيقظنا واطلعنا على العالم الجديد أن نعمل فوق هذه الأرض لكي نجعل منها محلا تتهيأ فيه الفرص والحبور والحرية للبشرية جمعاء كأننا نعيش أبداً ، وأن نعمل لآخرتنا كأننا نموت غداً .

التهيؤ للحج (الاستطاعة)

إن أول ما يقتضى للحج هو أن يكون الحاج قادراً على أداء الفريضة . فليس علينا أن نحج إذا كان ذلك يؤدي إلى متاعب لأولئك الذين نعولهم .

المنافع في الحج

يجوز للحجاج أن يحملوا معهم أمتعة وبضائع ينفقون من ربحها الحلال على سفرتهم من أوطانهم وإليها وعلى تكاليف الحج نفسه . وفي هذا منفعة لذوي المصالح ولعامة الحجاج الذين ربما بهظتهم ضروريات الحياة لولاه .

الزاد والراحلة

إن في المسلمين أمماً عديدة لكل منها طعامه الخاص ، فمن الحكمة أن يحمل الحجاج ـ الذين ليس لهم من المال ما يكفيهم لتحمل نفقات الحاجات اليومية الكثيرة ـ الطعام الأساسي لهم . وفي ذلك حكمة أخرى من حيث الصحة البدنية ، فإن لوازم الحج على الحاج باهظة ، ومن اللازم التحفظ والاحتياط ضد النكسات الهضمية . وعلى كل حال فإن على الحاج أن يتزود بحيث يستطيع الانفاق بمقدار ضعف ما يتطلبه الانفاق على الرحلة إلى مكة على أوسع تقدير .

أدلاء الحج (الحملدارية) والمطوفون

سواء أكان الحجاج المسافرون إلى مكة منفردين أم مصحوبين برفاق فإن السلطات العربية تتأكد عند وصولهم الحجاز من أنهم جميعاً في عهدة موظفين

منظمين معترف بهم من قبل الحكومة . وهؤلاء الموظفون يسمون (المطوّفين) . وهناك اناس يسمون رؤساء قوافل الحج (الحملدارية) مرتبطون بالمطوفين . ولما كان مما لا مفر منه ان ينضم الحجاج الى مثل هذه القيادة (المطوفين) خلال الحج ، فلعل من الافضل ان يلتحق الحاج منذ البداية بقافلة احد رؤساء قوافل الحج (الحملدارية) في القطر الذي يقطنه الحاج . وهؤلاء الادلاء (الحملدارية) موجودون في جميع الاراضي التي يسكنها المسلمون ما عدا تلك المناطق التي يسيطر عليها الاتحاد السوفياتي او له نفوذ فيها . ان رؤساء قوافل الحج (الحملدارية) هؤلاء يتمهنون رعاية الحجاج الى مكة ، والمطوفون يدلونهم الى مناسك الحج . وان الادلاء (الحملدارية) بشر ، فمنهم الكثيرون من ذوي الكفاءة المخلصين ومنهم من ليسوا كذلك ، والحاج أو الحاجة لهما ان يحسنا الانتقاء منذ بدء الرحلة . ولعل رئيس قافلة الحج (الحملدار) الذي ينبغي له ان يعود مع الحجاج في نهاية موسم الحج ــ والمقيم في البلد الذي يبدأ منه القيام برعاية الحجاج الى الحجاز في السنوات المقبلة ــ حريص أن يصون سمعته . فاسألوا عن اخلاق رؤساء قوافل الحج (الحملدارية) بالاستعانة باولئك الذين ادوا الفريضة في رعايتهم في المواسم السابقة .

وان المطوفين مسؤولون عن رعاية اولئك الحجاج الذين يؤتى بهم من الاراضي الاجنبية ، او الذين يوضعون في عهدته من جانب الموظفين الرسميين العرب في الحجاز ، وهو اجراء تتخذه الحكومة لرعاية قطر الحاج الذي يؤتى منه ، ويخص اولئك الذين يقدمون من دون ان يكون معهم احد من رؤساء القوافل (الحملدارية) لرعايتهم ، وكل مطوف يهيء المسكن من جدة ومكة وخلال الرحلة الى عرفات ومنى . وهو يهيء وسائط النقل ويقود اتباعه لأداء مناسك الحج . ان رئيس قافلة الحج (الحملدار) الذي يكرس نفسه لعمله يساعد الحجاج في معاملاتهم مع السكان في مكة ، ويكون وسيطاً في جميع شؤونهم ، سواء منها الخاصة ، او التجارية ، او الرسمية . وعلى المطوف عند الوصول الى جدة ان يضمن اخراج امتعة كل شخص من دائرة الكمرك . وارساله الى مسكن يهيء له من قبل ؛ وعليه أن يعقب شؤون جوازات السفر ويحصل على « بطاقة مرور ، تبين هوية الحاج بعد أن يسلم أو تسلم مستنداتها ، فان جميع جوازات السفر واوراقه تأخذها السلطات في جدة حتى انتهاء

موسم الحج .

ان رؤساء قوافل الحج (الحملدارية) المخلصين يحمون أتباعهم من جشع أصحاب الحوانيت ويساومون بالنيابة عنهم . ويعملون كمترجمين لهم . ان المطوف أب ، وأخ ، وخادم ، وحارس في آن واحد . ولقد دعي يحمل الحاج . ولن تنتهي مهمته الا بعد أن ينتهي آخر فرد من جماعته من الحج ويركب السفينة او الطائرة او وسيلة النقل الاخرى الى وطنه .

الصـــلاة

ليس هناك من نصح أو نقاش حول مؤهلات الانسان او استعداده للحج ، فذلك شأن بين كل حاج وربه ، غير ان جميع المخلوقات تسبح بحمد الله .

> « أَوَ لَمْ يَرَوْا إِلَى مَا خَلَقَ اللهُ مِنْ شَيْءٍ يَتَفَيَّؤُا ظِلالَهُ عَنِ اليَمِينِ والشَّمَائِلِ سُجَّداً لِلهِ وَهُمْ دَاخِرُون . وَللهِ يَسْجُدُ مَا في السَّمٰوَاتِ وَمَا فِي الأَرْضِ مِنْ دَابَّةٍ والملائكَةُ وَهُمْ لا يَسْتَكْبِرُون» (سورة النحل ، ٤٨ - ٤٩)

> «أَلَمْ تَرَ أَنَّ اللهَ يُسَبِّحُ لَهُ مَنْ في السَّمٰوَاتِ والأَرْضِ والطيرُ صافَّاتٍ كُلٌّ قَدْ عَلِمَ صَلاتَهُ وتَسْبِيحَهُ ، واللهُ عَلِيمٌ بما يفعلون » (سورة النور ، ٤١)

لقد أمرنا بان نولي وجهنا مكة خمس مرات في اليوم ونحن نؤدي الصلاة . ووقت الصلاة الأولى في الفجر وهي صلاة (الصبح) والثانية هي صلاة (الظهر) عندما تكون الشمس في الزوال ، والثالثة صلاة (العصر) في منتصف الوقت بين الظهر والمساء ، والرابعة (المغرب) وهي عند غروب الشمس ، والخامسة صلاة (العشاء) تصلى في الليل .

ولكل صلاة وقت معين وعدد من الركعات ، فبعضها ذات ركعات معينة

وهي (الفرض) والأخرى (السنة) التي اداها النبي محمد (صلى الله عليه وسلم) . ولقد أمرنا عندما نكون في البيت أو على نية البقاء في محل واحد لعدة ايام (الاقامة) ، ان لا نترك أي جزء من هـــذه الصلوات ، الفرض منها والسنة .

وصلاة الصبح ركعتان سنة وركعتان فرض . وصـــلاة (الظهر) أربع ركعات سنة وأربع فرض ، وكذلك صلاة العصر . أما صلاة المغرب فهي ثلاث ركعات فرض وركعتان سنة . وصلاة (العشاء) اربع ركعات سنة وأربع فرض ، ثم ركعتان سنة تلوها عند كثير من المسلمين ركعات اضافية هي (الوتر) تتلى قبل النوم .

ولكننا اذا سافرنا الى أماكن بعيدة ، كالسفر الى مكة فانتـا معفون من اداء صلوات السنة ، ونستطيع تقليل الصلوات الى ركعتين بدلا من اربع ، وذلك بالنسبة الى الركعات الاربع الفرض فقط ، لان ما كان عدد ركعاته ثلاثاً او اثنين لا يقصر .

وعلى ذلك فان في خلال السفر الى مكة وطيلة موسم الحج (الا اذا وصل الحاج الى المدينة مبكراً جداً ، او اذا كان قـــد نوى ان يبقى في محل واحد عدة ايام) تكون صلاة الصبح ركعتين وتكون صـــلاة الظهر والعصر ركعتين وتصليان معاً ، أما صلاة المغرب فتكون ثلاث ركعـــات وركعتان لصلاة العشاء وتصليان معاً .

« وفي فقه أهل البيت وهو مذهب الشيعة جعلت صلاة السنة أربعاً وثلاثين ركعة ضعف صلاة الفرض ؛ للظهر ثمان ركعات قبلها وكذلـــك العصر ، وللمغرب أربع ركعات بعدها ، وللعشاء ركعتان من جلوس بعدها وتعدان بركعة ، واحدى عشرة ركعة قبل الفجر ، وهي صلاة الليل وركعتان نافلة الصبح . وتسمى صلاة السنة النوافل المرتبة أو الرواتب . وحددت الاقامة في السفر التي لا يجوز معها القصر وتقليل الفرائض بنية المكث في محل معين مدة عشرة أيام فأكثر ، وتسقط في السفر نوافل النهار دون نوافل الليل . ويجوز الجمع بين الظهر والعصر والمغرب والعشاء من غير علة ولا سفر) » .

اذا وجدت من الضروري ان تصلي منفرداً فافعل ، ولكن اعلم ان الانسان في هذا العالم ينبغي ان لا يكون منفرداً . فالانسان الوحيد سواء أكان عاملا

أو مصلياً انا هو شيء ضعيف . والامـة المنفردة تنتظر الفنـاء أو العبودية .
اما الاعداد الكبيرة من الرجال المتحدين في الصلاة أو الكفـاح في سبيل الحق
فانها تظهر الهيبة والاحترام . وذلك يرى خلال الحج . لقد انقسم الاسلام بسبب
التوافه والخصومات السياسية القديمة البالغة في القدم ، والتي سمح لها اسلافنا في
جهالتهم ان تصبح مادة للايمان . ولقد تصرفوا وتصرفنا معهم كالمجانين –
ونلنا العقوبة .

ان أغلب شعوب الاسلام تحت الحكم والسيطرة الاجنبية ، ففي المنـاطق
السوفياتية وحدها اكثر من (٣٤) مليون من المسلمين الاتراك و (٤٠) مليون
من المسلمين الصينيين الذين يخافون ان يعبدوا ربهم جهرة ، وهذه الأرقام لا تشمل
الامم الصغيرة الاخرى تحت تلك السيطرة . فان كان واحد منا عبداً ، فليس
احد منا حراً . وما دمنا لا نتسامح مع بعضنا البعض ، وما دمنا لا نعترف
بأن الحنفي والمالكي والشافعي والحنبلي والشيعي والسني ، ليسوا شيئاً وان الاسلام
هو كل شيء ، فان احداً منا لا يستطيع ان يكون حراً .

لقد أمرنا أن نؤدي الصلاة المقدسة مجتمعين والخلافات البسيطة لا أهمية لها .
فيجب ان نتقرب الى الله كل عن الطريق الذي يعرفه خير معرفة ، ولكن يجب
علينا أن لا نحرم اخواننا حق المرور من الطرق المماثلة الاخرى .

فاعبدوا الله جنباً الى جنب . ان ديننا كله في القرآن ، وعقيدتنا هي الاسلام،
وربنا هو رب آدم .

> « ولِكُلٍّ وِجْهَةٌ هُوَ مُوَلِّيها فَاسْتَبِقُوا الخَيْرَاتِ . أَيْنَ ما تَكُونُوا
> يَأْتِ بِكُمُ اللهُ جَمِيعاً إِنَّ اللهَ عَلَى كُلِّ شَيْءٍ قَدِيرٌ . ومِنْ حَيْثُ
> خَرَجْتَ فَوَلِّ وَجْهَكَ شَطْرَ المسجِدِ الحرامِ وإِنَّهُ لَلْحَقُّ مِنْ رَبِّكَ ،
> وما اللهُ بِغَافِلٍ عَمَّا تَعْمَلُونَ » .
>
> (سورة البقرة ، ١٤٨ – ١٤٩)

السفر

لقد كتب انه عندما دنا الطوفان وفاضت عيون الأرض ، توجه نوح الى أولئك

الذين ينبغي انقاذهم :

> « وَقَالَ ارْكَبُوا فِيها بِسْمِ اللهِ مَجْرِيها وَمُرْسَاها إِنَّ رَبِّي لَغَفُورٌ رَحِيمٌ » .
>
> (سورة هود ، ٤١)

وهكذا اليوم ، عندما نسافر من أوطاننا ونذهب الى جدة يقرأ الحجاج بين كل آونة وأخرى خلال السفرة :

> « بِسْمِ اللهِ مَجْرِيها وَمُرْسَاها » . أو « (سُبْحَانَ الَّذِي سَخَّرَ لَنَا هَذَا وَمَا كُنَّا لَهُ مُقْرِنِينَ وَإِنَّا إِلَى رَبِّنَا لَمُنْقَلِبُونَ) » ،
>
> (سورة الزخرف ، ١٣ - ١٤)

الاحرام وثياب الحج المقدسة

ان أول مناسك الحج هو ترك الثياب المعتادة وارتداء ثياب الإحرام ، وهي العادة التي يتميز بها الحجاج عن غيرهم ولكن لا تميز فيها بينهم . فكلهم سواء أكانوا من الطبقة العليا أو من الطبقة الدنيا ، يرتدون أثواباً معينة فيتذكرون بذلك أنهم أمام الله رجال خلقوا متساوين ــ وانهم يوم القيامة سيحاسبون كذلك ــ . والإحرام حالة امتناع مقدس عن عدة أشياء ، فعندما يرتدي الحاج ثياب الاحرام يدخل فترة سلام وانكار للذات . فالعنف بأي شكل من الاشكال ممنوع . وعلى الحاج ان يمتنع عن ملذات الحواس مها كانت مشروعة في غير الحج إلى ان تنقضي مناسك الحج وينتهي الاحرام . فالحلى والزينة الشخصية ممنوعة كما ان العطر والروائح ممنوعة كذلك ، وليس للحاج المحرم ان يقتطع شجرة او ثمراً في حرم مكة . (وفي فقه اهل البيت يجوز للمالك ان يقطع الشجر في ملكه ، وجني الثمار لكل احد جائز) . ويجب ان ينقطع الاتصال الجنسي وترتفع النوازع الجنسية بتاتاً حتى عن التفكير فيها . وفي خلال ايام الحج ينبغي ان لا يكون هناك خصام او جدال ، ولا غلظة او نقاش ولا صيد . فعلى الحاج ان يكرس نفسه بدنياً الى مناسك الحج ، وذهنياً عليه ــ او عليها ــ الانصراف الى الصلاة والتسبيح وترويض النفس .

« الْحَجُّ أَشْهُرٌ مَعْلُومَاتٌ فَمَنْ فَرَضَ فِيهِنَّ الْحَجَّ فَلَا رَفَثَ وَلَا فُسُوقَ وَلَا جِدَالَ فِي الْحَجِّ وَمَا تَفْعَلُوا مِنْ خَيْرٍ يَعْلَمْهُ اللهُ وَتَزَوَّدُوا فَإِنَّ خَيْرَ الزَّادِ التَّقْوَى وَاتَّقُونِ يَا أُولِي الْأَلْبَابِ » .

(سورة البقرة ، ١٩٦)

« يَا أَيُّهَا الَّذِينَ آمَنُوا لَيَبْلُوَنَّكُمُ اللهُ بِشَيْءٍ مِنَ الصَّيْدِ تَنَالُهُ أَيْدِيكُمْ وَرِمَاحُكُمْ لِيَعْلَمَ اللهُ مَنْ يَخَافُهُ بِالْغَيْبِ فَمَنِ اعْتَدَى بَعْدَ ذَلِكَ فَلَهُ عَذَابٌ أَلِيمٌ . يَا أَيُّهَا الَّذِينَ آمَنُوا لَا تَقْتُلُوا الصَّيْدَ وَأَنْتُمْ حُرُمٌ وَمَنْ قَتَلَهُ مِنْكُمْ مُتَعَمِّداً فَجَزَاءٌ مِثْلُ مَا قَتَلَ مِنَ النَّعَمِ يَحْكُمُ بِهِ ذَوَا عَدْلٍ مِنْكُمْ هَدْياً بَالِغَ الْكَعْبَةِ أَوْ كَفَّارَةٌ طَعَامُ مَسَاكِينَ أَوْ عَدْلُ ذَلِكَ صِيَاماً لِيَذُوقَ وَبَالَ أَمْرِهِ عَفَا اللهُ عَمَّا سَلَفَ وَمَنْ عَادَ فَيَنْتَقِمُ اللهُ مِنْهُ وَاللهُ عَزِيزٌ ذُو انْتِقَامٍ . أُحِلَّ لَكُمْ صَيْدُ الْبَحْرِ وَطَعَامُهُ مَتَاعاً لَكُمْ وَلِلسَّيَّارَةِ وَحُرِّمَ عَلَيْكُمْ صَيْدُ الْبَرِّ مَا دُمْتُمْ حُرُماً وَاتَّقُوا اللهَ الَّذِي إِلَيْهِ تُحْشَرُونَ . جَعَلَ اللهُ الْكَعْبَةَ الْبَيْتَ الْحَرَامَ قِيَاماً لِلنَّاسِ وَالشَّهْرَ الْحَرَامَ وَالْهَدْيَ وَالْقَلَائِدَ ذَلِكَ لِتَعْلَمُوا أَنَّ اللهَ يَعْلَمُ مَا فِي السَّمَوَاتِ وَمَا فِي الْأَرْضِ وَأَنَّ اللهَ بِكُلِّ شَيْءٍ عَلِيمٌ » .

سورة المائدة ، (٩٧ ـ ١٠٠)

مــدة الاحرام

ترتدى ثياب الاحرام خلال :

ـ ١١ ـ

١ ـ وصول الحجاج الى مكة للطواف الاول والسعي ، وهو الدوران حول الكعبة والسعي بين الصفا والمروة ذهاباً واياباً سبع مرات .

٢ ـ الوقوف امام جبل عرفات في اليوم التاسع من شهر الحج ، ثم في تلك الليلة عند رمي الحجارة ، والوقفة في الظلام للصلاة في المزدلفة وهي موقع مقدس في الصحراء بين عرفات ووادي منى .

٣ ـ ثم في اليوم العاشر عند رمي الحجــارة في جمرات العقبة ، وهي اكبر ثلاث نصب من الصخر والطين تعين محلات في منى حيث ظهر الشيطان لإسماعيل ابن النبي ابراهيم .

٤ ـ خلال تقديم الهدي في منى .

الاحرام للذكور

تتألف ثياب الإحرام للرجال من قطعتـــين كبيرتين من القماش الابيض لا نقوش فيها ولا زينة ولا خياطة ، ويفضل الكثيرون من الحجاج المناشف القطنية البيضاء فهي افضل من القماش الخفيف للوقاية من حر الصيف المهلك ومن الرياح الفجائية التي تشبه السكاكين عندما يكون الحج خلال الشتاء .

لقد كانت مناسك الحج تقع قبل زمن النبي محمد عليـه الصلاة والسلام في وقت معين من الخريف . ففي سني الجاهليــة كانت الاشهر القمرية تحفظ في أبراجها بإضافة ايام زائدة ، وهو تعامل تركه النبي ، فالسنة الآن قمرية وزمن الحج يتغير فيما من جميع المواسم . وعلى الحجاج ان يتذكروا ذلك ويهيئوا انفسهم بمقتضاه .

وفي الزمن القديم (في عصر الجاهلية) كان الحجاج عندما يقتربون من الكعبة المقدسة يخلعون جميع ملابسهم كعلامة من علامـــات الخضوع ، ويطوفون عراة ويقبلون الحجر الاسود كما نفعل نحن الآن الا التعري . فقد جرت العادة ـ حتى زمن النبي محمد (صلى الله عليه وسلم) ـ ان يذهبوا عراة في الظلام الى الكعبة لأداء المناسك . فلم يرض النبي عن هـــذا التعري ولا عن الضوضاء التي كانت العبادة تجري بها . فجاء بثيــاب الاحرام التي نرتديها اليوم والطريقة الخافتة التي نصلي بها . اما الطقس فانه قديم .

يوضع احد قسمي قماش الاحرام على الكتفين يغطي القسم الاعلى من الجسم ،
ويلف القسم الثاني منه على الخصر ويشد بحزام ، ويجب ان يصل الركبتين ،
ويجب ان تكون كل قطعة من القماش مترين ونصف المتر طولاً ومتراً ونصف
المتر عرضاً ، (وهذا التحديد ليس بواجب عند فقهاء أهل البيت بل المدار
في الثوب الاول ان يرتدى به ويصدق عليه اسم الرداء ، وفي الثاني ان
يؤتزر به ويصدق عليه اسم الازار كيف شاء وان كان الافضل في الثاني ان
يغطي السرة والركبة ، ويصح الاحرام بكل ماتصح الصلاة به) ،، وينبغي ان
لا يرتدي المرء ثوباً فوق هذا الثوب او تحته . غير ان من المتعارف عليه حمل
كيس دراهم على طرف المنكب او حزام للدراهم . فأي من هذين لا بد منه
لأن ثياب الاحرام لا جيوب فيها ، (اذ يحرم على الرجل لبس المخيط في
الاحرام) ، وعلى الرجال ان لا يغطوا رؤوسهم اثناء الحج . كما ان اقدامهم
ينبغي ان لا تكسوها سوى الاخفاف التي لا تغطي اعقاب الارجل . ، (وفي
فقه اهل البيت لا يجوز تغطية تمام ظهر القدم فيباح لبس النعلين المتعارفة دون
الاخفاف) ، .

الاحرام للاناث

يمكن ان لا ترتدي النساء لباس الاحرام التي يرتديها الرجال فلهن ان يبقين
في البستهن الاعتيادية فيكتسين كسوة جديدة بسيطة في وقت الدخول في الاحرام ،
وبالرغم من ان النساء المحرمات لا يتحجبن خلال الحج فان من اللازم تغطية
شعورهن ، وينبغي ان تصل ثياب النساء الى كعوبهن واردانهن الى الرسغ ، ويجب
ان تكون اطراف ما يكتنف الرقبة عالية بحيث تغطي صدورهن .

والنساء الحاجات اللواتي يأتيهن الحيض في وقت الاحرام او خلال ايام
الاحرام . يحرم عليهن ان يؤدين الصلوات اليومية الى ان يتطهرن .

ولكن لهن ان يتلون جميع انواع الذكر اذا لم يكن صلاة (والطواف كالصلاة
يحرم على الحائض) ، ويجب ان تؤخره حتى تطهر ، واذا حضرت ايام الحج احرمت له
واخرت طواف العمرة الى بعد طهرها ، واعتمرت بعد انتهاء افعال الحج فينقلب
حجها افراداً بعد ان كان تمتعاً) .

وليس للمرأة ان تذهب الى الحج الا بصحبة زوجها او – اذا كانت غـير متزوجة – بصحبة اثنين من افراد عائلتها الذكور الادنين الذين ينبغي ان يكون كلاهما من القرب منها بحيث لا يكون هناك احتمال للزواج بهـا .. د (وفي فقه أهل البيت لا يشترط شيء من ذلك ، والمدار ان تأمن المرأة على نفسها وعرضها وان لم يكن لهـا محرم) ، وعلى الرجل ان لا يقرب زوجته جنسياً ، وعلى المرأة ان لا تشجع زوجها على مجامعتها خـلال الاحرام . والادعية والذكر لا يجهر بها الا الحجـاج الذكور . وعلى النساء الحاجات ان لا يرفعن اصواتهن او يلفتن الانظار اليهن ، فعليهن ان ينصرفن عن الرجال انصرافاً تاماً .

الاستعدادات البدنية للاحرام

على من يريد الاحرام رجالاً ونساء ان يقلموا اظفارهم ويزيلوا الشعر من آباطهم وعوراتهم قبل الاحرام . وعلى النساء ان يغسلن شعورهن ، وعلى الرجال ان يغسلوا أو يحلقوا شعورهم « (الا شعر الرأس فانه يستحب للرجال توفيره للحج اتقاء من الحر او البرد والشمس) » ، وذلك لأن تقليم الأظفار أو تقصير شعر اللحية أو حلقها غير مسموح به مدة الاحرام .

> وأتِمُّوا الحَجَّ والعُمرَةَ لِلَّهِ فإنْ أُحصِرتُمْ فَما استَيسَرَ مِنَ الهَدْي ولاَ تَحلِقُوا رُؤوسَكُمْ حتى يَبلُغَ الهَدْيُ مَحِلَّهُ ، فَمَنْ كانَ منكُمْ مَريضاً أوْ بِه أذَىً مِنْ رأسِه فَفِدْيَةٌ مِنْ صِيامٍ أوْ صَدَقةٍ أوْ نُسُكٍ فإذا أَمِنتُمْ فَمَنْ تَمَتَّعَ بالعُمرَةِ إلى الحَجِّ فَما استَيسَرَ مِنَ الهَدْي فَمَنْ لَمْ يَجِدْ فَصِيامُ ثَلاثةِ أيَّامٍ في الحَجِّ وسَبعةٍ إذا رَجَعتُمْ تِلكَ عَشَرةٌ كامِلةٌ ذَلكَ لِمَنْ لَمْ يَكُنْ أهلُهُ حاضِري المسجِدِ الحَرامِ واتقُوا اللهَ وَاعلَمُوا أنَّ اللهَ شديدُ العِقابِ . »

(سورة البقرة ، ١٩٥)

انواع الحـج

للحج انواع ثلاثة يختار منها المرء ما يريد .

١ ـ العمرة او الحج الأصغر .

على اي فرد يزور مكة للمرة الأولى في أي موسم من المواسم ، أو يعود الى
مكة بعد غياب طويل ، أو يرغب في العمل المستحب ، ان يرتدي ثياب الاحرام
ويقوم بزيارة الاماكن المقدسة في مكة لكي يسبح بحمد الله . وهذا هو (العمرة
المفردة) ، والاحرام لاجل العمرة يكون لزيارة الكعبة والطواف والصلاة والسعي
بين الصفا والمروة .

ان العمرة كاملة بنفسها ، وهي الحج الاصغر ـ ولكنها ليست حجاً ـ والذين
يؤدونها لا يستحقون أن يدعوا أنفسهم حجاجاً الا اذا اكملوا مناسك الحج التي
لا يمكن ان تتم الا في وقتها المعين .

ان أشهر شوال وذي القعدة وذي الحجة قـد خصصت للحج الاكبر . فيمكن
اجراء مناسك الحج منذ أوائل شهر شوال في وقت معين للتقرب من مكة ، بينا
لا تجري الفرائض الرئيسية الا في الثامن والتاسع والعاشر من ذي الحجة وهو آخر
الاشهر العربية من السنة حين تبلغ التجمعات اقصاها لغرض تأدية مناسك الحج .

٢ ـ التمتع ـ العمرة والحج معاً .

ان احرام التمتع ـ ويقال له التمتع مع العمرة ـ يمكن ان يقوم به الحجاج
القادمون مبكرين للحج . وبعد الدخول الى مكـــة واكمال الطواف الابتدائي
والسعي تترك ثياب هذا الاحرام مع امتناعات العمرة للمدة المؤقتة ويمكن العودة
الى ارتداء الملابس والملذات الاعتيادية . لقد امر الحجاج الذين منحوا هـــذه
التسهيلات بتقديم الهدي ، وعلى الذين لا يستطيعون تقديمه صيام ثلاثة ايام خـلال
الحج وسبعة ايام بعد الانتهاء منه « (اي رجوع الحاج الى اهله) » . ان هذه
المناسك (بعكس احرام العمرة الذي ينتهي بزيارة الكعبة المقدسة والصفا والمروة
من جانب اولئك الحجاج الذين يرتدون ثياب احرام التمتع) انما هي بداية منظر
عظيم يزلزل الارض ، هو منظر الحج المقبل . وحج التمتع هو العمرة مع الحج .

وينبغي العودة الى ارتداء ثياب الاحرام التي تركت بعـد تأدية الفروض في مكة
قبل حلول الايام المهمة لشهر الحج وهو شهر ذي الحجة . والواجبات التي اتبعت

عند ارتداء ثياب الاحرام لأول مرة هي نفس الواجبات التي يجب اتباعها عنـد العودة اليه .

٣ – الحج الاكبر .

من المتعارف عليه اليوم لدى الحجاج ضم العمرة عند الاحرام الى الحج ، وذلك يمكن بلوغه بشمول (النية) له بكل بساطة عند الاحرام للحج .

ولا يختلف احرام الحج بشيء عن الاحرام الآخر ، الا ان احرام الحج لا يمكن تركه الا اذا تمت مناسك الحج الاكبر كلها . ففي هـذه الناحية يختلف احرام الحج عن احرام التمتع . وبعد ان يدخل الحاج في الاحرام عليـه ان يراعي محظورات وممنوعات الاحرام . وعند القيام بالحج ينبغي على الحجـاج ان يسعوا لتأدية الفرائض المعينة عليهم لاكمال المناسك . فاذا حال المرض او الصد دون ان يقوم الحاج بذلك ، فله عند الوقوف في منى – لانه لا حج من غير عرفات – ان يكمل حجه بصورة رمزية بارسال الهدي الى وادي منى . والهدي يقدم اذا كان المصدود او المريض حاضرين في المسجـد الحرام ، وعلى ذلك فان اولئك المتغيبين مهما كان سبب تغيبهم ينبغي عليهم تقديم الهـدي بالنيابة ، وربما كان ذلك بارسال الحيوانات المقصود اهداؤها الى موقـع الذبح . واذا ما عرف انها وصلت (منى) فيمكن آنذاك انهـاء الاحرام والعودة الى الالبسة الاعتيادية . ويمكن الاستعاضة بالصوم واعطاء الصدقـات عن تقديم الهدي .

« وفي فقه اهل البيت ذكر ان انواع الحج ثلاثة قران وافراد وهما فرض اهل مكة وما جاورها الى اثني عشر ميـلا ويقدم الحج فيها على العمرة ، وفي القران يسوق الحاج هديه معه دون الافراد ، والحج في كلا هذين النوعين مقدم على العمرة ، والنوع الثالث حج التمتع وهو فرض من نأى عن مكة اثني عشر ميلا فأكثر ، وفيه تقدم العمرة على الحج ، فاذا تمت العمرة حل من احرامها وله التمتع بجميع محظورات الاحرام الى ان يحرم الى الحج فيمتنع عـن محظورات الاحرام الى تمام الحج ، ولا تكون هذه الثلاثة الا في اشهر الحج شوال وذي القعدة وذي الحجة ، وهناك عمل آخر هو فرض على كل من يريد ان يدخل مكة في جميع اوقات السنة وهو ان يحرم القادم الى مكة من الميقات ويطوف ويسعى ويحل ولا يرتبط هذا العمل بالحج وتكون الأعمال في مكة مـع العمرة

المفردة اربعة انواع ، وتفصيل احكامها مذكورة في كتب الحج)) .

الاحرام هو وقت التحمل والصبر . والاحرام تجربة في الاخــوة وعظــة للفرقة ووعد اظهار لما يمكن ان يصبح عليه الاسلام اذا مــا اتحدنا . والاحرام تحذير من الذل والهوان المقبل علينا وعلى الاسلام نفسه ، اذا لم يعرف المسلمون كيف يفكرون ويعملون ويتفانون سوية في صبر وانكار للذات – وإذا ما دعا الأمر الى تضحية النفس في سبيل الله وتحسين حال البشر عامة .

مواقيت الاحرام

على الحجاج القادمين من الشمال عن طريق البحر ان يغيروا ملابسهم ويرتدوا ثياب الاحرام عندما تكون سفينتهم امام ثغر (رابغ) الصغير . اما اولئك الذين يأتون من الشمال عن طريق المدينة فعليهم ان يحرموا في « آبار علي » ، وكان اسمها في زمن النبي (ذا الحليفة او مسجد الشجرة) .

وعلى الحجــــاج الذين يأتون من الجنوب بطريق البحر او البر ان يحرموا في (يلمل) . اما الذين يأتون براً من الشرق من نجد والاحساء او الطائف فان عليهم ان يحرموا في (قرن) – وكان اسمها في زمن النبي (ﷺ) (قرن المنازل) او (وادي محرم) .

والحجاج الآتون براً من العراق يجب ان يحرموا في ذات عرق (وهي آخر وادي العقيق) وسكان مكة يحرمون في مكة نفسها . وليس فرضاً الاحرام في هذه الاماكن ، ولكنه مستحب ((وفي فقه اهل البيت هو فرض)) . ولقد تغير العالم الآن وقد يصل الكثيرون من الحجاج اليوم جوا ، فلا يكون ميسوراً عليهم تغيير ملابسهم وهم في الجو طائرون ، فمن الافضل ان يرتدوا ثياب الاحرام في آخر محل ينزلون فيه قبل جدة او بعد وصولهم الى جدة . . (ويمكن ان ينذروا الاحرام قربة الى الله في منازلهم فيرتدوها ويركبوا طــائراتهم محرمين ويجزى عن الاحرام في الميقات)) .

الغسل ــ والوضوء

تبدأ شعائر الاحرام بالغسل . فيستحب عند تغيير الثياب الاعتيادية للاحرام الاغتسال تماماً ، فاذا لم يكن ممكناً فعلى الحاج ان يتوضأ كما يتوضأ للصلاة .

وقد اعتاد كثير من المسلمين القيام بالوضوء في صمت ، تاركين جميع الادعية والاذكار التي يستحب أن تصحب أو تعقب العمل ، ولكن اذا أراد الحاج ان يؤدي الوضوء بالكيفية التي كان النبي محمد (صلى الله عليه وسلم) يؤديها ، فعليه ان يقول في صوت غير جهِر : «أنوي الوضوء للصلاة » .

ثم يغسل يديه ثلاث مرات وهو يقول بنفس الصوت كالسابق : « بِسْم اللهِ الرَّحْمَن الرَّحِيم . الحمدُ للهِ الذي جَعَل المـاءَ طَهُوراً والإسلامَ نُوراً » ثم يتمضمض ثلاث مرات ويقول : (اللَّهُمَّ نَوِّرْ قَلْبي بالقرْآن واجْعَلْني مِنَ المُصَلِّين) ثم يستنشق ثلاث مرات ويقول : «اللهم اجْعَلني مِنَ الذين يَشَمُّونَ رَوَائحَ الجَنَّة » ثم يغسل وجهه ثلاث مرات ويقول : « اللهم بَيِّضْ وَجْهِي يَوْمَ تَبْيَضُّ وُجوهٌ وَتَسْوَدُّ وُجوه » .

ثم بعد ذلك يغسل ذراعه الأيمن ثلاث مرات ويقول : «اللهم أعْطِني كِتَابي في يَمِيني وحاسِبْني حِساباً يَسِيراً » ، ثم الذراع الأيسر قائلاً : (اللَّهُمّ لا تُعْطِني كِتابي في شِمَالي أوْ وَرَاءَ ظَهْري ، ولا تُحاسِبْني حِساباً عَسِيراً) .

ثم يرفع يده اليمنى فوق رأسه ويمسحه من الامام الى الخلف وهو يقول : «اللهم أظِلَّني بِظِلٍّ عَرْشك يومَ لا ظِلَّ إلا ظِلّك » ، ثم يغسل اذنيه وهو يقول : (اللهم اجعَلْني مِنَ الذين يَسْمَعُونَ القولَ فَيَتَّبِعُونَ أحْسَنَه) ويغسل رقبته قائلاً (اللهم نَجِّني مِنَ النار) واخيراً يغسل قدميه مقدماً القدم اليمنى وهو يقول (اللهم ثَبِّتْني على الصِّراط يومَ تَزِلُّ فِيه الأقدام) (اللهمّ تَقَبَّلْ حَسناتي واغْفِرْ لي سَيِّئاتي وخَطِيئاتي) .

وعند الانتهاء من الوضوء يقول (أشْهَدُ أنْ لا إلَهَ إلا اللهُ وَحْـدَهُ لا شَريكَ له وأسْتغفِرُهُ وأنُوبُ إليه وأشْهَدُ أنَّ مُحَمداً عَبْدُهُ ورَسُولُهُ) « (وفي فقه اهل البيت وردت أدعية كثيرة ولم يوجبوا غسل الاذن والرقبة واوجبوا في الرجلين المسح ولم يجوزوا الغسل وقالوا هكذا كان وضوء النبي وكذلك نزل القرآن) » .

التيمم

واذا لم يتيسر الحصول على الماء فان على المسلم ان يؤدي الوضوء بالتراب او الرمل وهو التطهر الرمزي (التيمم) فاضرب راحتيك على أي مـكـان يابس نظيف من الارض فيه تراب .

والأرض مفضلة ، ولكن اذا كان هنـاك ما يدعو الى الشك في طهرها فان للحاج ان يستعمل جداراً او غطاء فيه تراب ، ثم امسح وجهك بكلتي يديك ، واضرب الأرض مرة ثانية وامسح اليد اليمنى حتى المرفق ثم اضرب ثالثاً باليد اليسرى كما فعلت باليمنى وبذلك تكمل الفريضة .

« يا أَيُّها الَّذِينَ آمَنُوا لا تَقْرَبُوا الصَّلاةَ وأَنْتُمْ سُكَارَى حَتَّى تَعْلَمُوا ما تَقُولُونَ ولا جُنُباً إلَّا عابِري سَبِيلٍ حَتَّى تَغْتَسِلُوا وإِنْ كُنْتُمْ مَرْضى أَوْ عَلَى سَفَرٍ أَوْ جاءَ أَحَدٌ مِنْكُمْ مِنَ الغائِطِ أَوْ لامَسْتُمُ النِّساءَ ولَمْ تَجِدوا ماءً فَتَيَمَّموا صَعِيداً طَيِّباً وأَمْسَحُوا بِوُجُوهِكُمْ وأَيْدِيكُمْ إنَّ اللهَ كانَ عَفُوّاً غَفُوراً » .

(سورة النساء ، ٤٢)

ولا يجب ان نتوضأ قبل كل صلاة اذا كنا نعلم واثقين بأننا تجنبنا أي نوع من انواع الحدث منذ آخر فريضة وضوء . وكذلك الامر في لبس ثياب الاحرام – اذا لم يوجد الماء – .

« (وفي فقه أهل البيت لا يجب في التيمم مسح اكثر من الجبهة الى طرف الانف الاعلى والكفين) » .

الصلاة عند الاحرام

على كل حاج بعد الاغتسال ولبس ثياب الاحرام ان يصلي ركعتـين قصيرتين يقرأ فيها :

« بِسْمِ ٱللهِ ٱلرَّحْمٰنِ ٱلرَّحِيمِ . ٱلْحَمْدُ لِلّٰهِ رَبِّ ٱلْعَالَمِينَ . الرَّحْمٰنِ الرَّحِيمِ . مَالِكِ يَوْمِ ٱلدِّينِ . إِيَّاكَ نَعْبُدُ وَإِيَّاكَ نَسْتَعِينُ . اهْدِنَا الصِّرَاطَ ٱلْمُسْتَقِيمَ . صِرَاطَ ٱلَّذِينَ أَنْعَمْتَ عَلَيْهِمْ . غَيْرِ ٱلْمَغْضُوبِ عَلَيْهِمْ . وَلَا الضَّالِّينَ ، آمين.

« سورة الفاتحة »

ثم يتبع ذلك بالآيات التالية :

« بِسْمِ اللهِ ٱلرَّحْمٰنِ الرَّحِيمِ . إِذَا جَاءَ نَصْرُ اللهِ وَٱلْفَتْحُ . وَرَأَيْتَ النَّاسَ يَدْخُلُونَ فِي دِينِ اللهِ أَفْوَاجاً . فَسَبِّحْ بِحَمْدِ رَبِّكَ وَٱسْتَغْفِرْهُ . إِنَّهُ كَانَ تَوَّاباً » .

« سورة النصر »

« بِسْمِ ٱللهِ ٱلرَّحْمٰنِ الرَّحِيمِ . قُلْ أَعُوذُ بِرَبِّ ٱلْفَلَقِ . مِنْ شَرِّ مَا خَلَقَ . وَمِنْ شَرِّ غَاسِقٍ إِذَا وَقَبَ . وَمِنْ شَرِّ النَّفَّاثَاتِ فِي ٱلْعُقَدِ . وَمِنْ شَرِّ حَاسِدٍ إِذَا حَسَدَ » .

« سورة الفلق »

الدعاء خلال الاحرام

ثم يأتي بعد الانتهاء من الصلاة وقت التضرع والحمد . ويستحب تلاوة الدعاء التالي بعد وقت كل صلاة : (اللهُمَّ أنتَ السَّلام . وَمِنْكَ السَّلام . وَاليكَ السَّلام . أحيِنَا يا ربُّ في السَّلام . واقبَلنا في جَنَّتِكَ دار السلام . لك العَظَمَةُ وَالمَجْد . سَمِعنا وأطَعْنا غُفرانَكَ رَبَّنا واليكَ المَصير) .

نيـة الاحرام

على الحجاج الذين يحرمون ان يعلنوا عن نيتهم لفظاً ، فيتوجهوا الى الخالق وهم لا يزالون في وضع الصلاة قائلين : « اللهم إني أنوي العُمرة ، واني أحرم لها فيسِّرها عليَّ وتقبلها مني » . ويستعمل الحجاج الذين يحرمون للحج نفس الالفاظ ولكن باضافة الكلمات اللازمة ((التي تنص على الحج بدل العمرة)) ، ((وفي فقه اهل البيت لا يجب التلفظ للنية بل يكفي عقد القلب)) . ولا يغيب عن بالنا ان الاحرام للحج لا يمكن ان يترك الا اذا نوى الحاج منذ البداية ان يقوم بحج التمتع — حتى اكمال مناسك الحج — . وليس معنى ذلك ان على الحاج ان يلبس ثياب الاحرام الوسخة . ففي وسعنا تبديل ثياب الاحرام ونغتسل ما شئنا مرتدين اثوابا جديدة ولكن ينبغي ان لا نستأنف لبس ثيابنا الاعتيادية . ((وفي فقه اهل البيت لا يجوز للمتمتع ان يجمع العمرة والحج بنية واحدة واحرام واحد بل يجب عليه ان يحل من العمرة وينوي للحج نية مستقلة ويحرم له احراماً مستقلاً)) .

التلبيــة

ان التلبية هي اكثر الالفاظ ترددا في الحج فعلى الحاج ان يقول بعد النية مباشرة « لَبَّيْكَ اللهمَّ لَبَّيْكَ » للحج او « لَبيك اللهم لَبَيك » للعمرة والحج . وان يشفع ذلك بالتلبية التالية :

« لَبيك اللهم لَبَيك ، لَبَيك اللهم لَبَيك ، لَبَيك اللهم لبيك ، لبيك لا شريك لك لبيك ، ان الحمد والنعمة لك ، والمُلكَ لا شريكَ لك لبيك » . وعلينا ان نكرر هذه التلبية مرات لا عداد لها في خلال الحج .

فعلينا ان نكررها اذا انتقلنا واذا صعدنا او نزلنا وعندما نسمع غيرنا ينطق بها . وعند الخوف وقبل النوم وقبـــل أن نخاطب اي انسان . واذا وجدنا اناساً يتخاصمون فعلينا ان نقولهـــا لهم ، ونضيف عليها في بعض الاحايين ، « اللهم صلِّ على محمد . وآل محمد . كما صليتَ على ابراهيمَ . وآلِ ابراهيمَ . إنك حميد مجيد ، اللهم سلم على محمدٍ وآل محمد . كما سلمت على ابراهيمَ وآلِ ابراهيم . إنك حميد مجيد » .

التقرب من مكة

(أَيْنَمَا تُوَلُّوا فَثَمَّ وَجْهُ اللهِ)

جدة ــ والتقرب من مكة

على الحجاج الذين يأتون برّاً او جوّاً عند تقربهم من جدة ان يتلوا : رب
أدخِلني مدخلَ صِدقٍ وأخرجني مخرجَ صدقٍ واجعل لي من لدُنك سلطاناً نصيرا .
وجدة هي الموقع الرئيسي لنزول الحجاج في الحجاز . وهي مبنيــــة على الساحل
المرجاني المفتت المنحدر على البحر الاحمر . وحقّ البحر تصيبه حرارة الجو التي
لا يمكن تحملها وستار ضاغط من الرطوبة فوق المدينة .

وبعد النزول الى البر والخروج من دائرة الجرك يأخـــذ المطوفون الحجاج
الذين اتوا من بلادهم الى منازل مؤقتة في البلدة الساحلية ، وذلك ينطبق ايضاً على
الحجاج الذين تتكون منهم جماعة مصحوبة برئيس من رؤساء قوافل الحج ، سبقهم
الى جدة ومكة بموعد سابق بباخرة مبكرة لكي يعد لكل شيء عدته لاستقبالهم ،
لأنه ملزم باستقبالهم هو أو وكيله في جدة .

والوكيل هو مساعد المطوف المقيم في جدة في غيابه ، ويعمل نيابة عنه في
استقبال الحجاج وإيوائهم والإشراف على احتياجاتهم ، والحصول على مستنــدات
النقل وغير ذلك من الخدمات .

ان الحجاج الذين يصلون منفردين (ويسمون في مكة فلت) ، وليسوا
جزءاً من جماعة خاصة او تحت رعاية رئيس من رؤساء قوافل الحج (حملدار)
معروف تأخدمه سلطات الحجاز الى مركز معين ، ومن هناك يسلمون بعهدة مطوف
يقع في منطقته افراد الحجاج ؛ فان جميع المطوفين منضمون الى جمعيـــات مكية
مقفلة نظمت كل جمعية منها لتضطلع بحاجات امم بعينها وتنطق بلسان ولهجات
تلك الامم وتعرف حاجاتها ــ هذه المعرفة تشبه نصلا ذا حدين فهي تجرح بمقدار
ما تقي .

ان سكان مكة أناس من لحم ودم لا يختلفون عن الحجاج الذين يغمرون
البلاد العربية الا من حيث ان تجار البلدة وكثيراً من سكانها ، ليسوا هنـــاك
لغرض اداء فريضة الحج دائماً بل للاستفادة منه . ولم يجعل توطنهم بالقرب من

الكعبة المكرمة منهم ملائكة . ولقـــد كانت مكة موضع حج دائم منـــذ
آلاف السنين وتعرض اهلها الى اغراء قوي ، حتى ان تفكيرهم قد تأثر بذلك .
وفيهم الطيب والشرير ، والغني والفقير ، ولكنهم جميعاً يعتبرون الحجاج غنيمتهم
الشرعية ، يأخذون منهم مبالغ كبيرة لأغلب الحاجات اليومية الاساسية . وفضلا
عن الدخل الذي يرد الى الحجاز من النفط ، وهو انحصار حكومي ، فان جميع
الموارد التي تدفع للمصاريف الحكومية والاقتصاد القومي ، قائم على اساس الفوائد
التي تجنى من موسم الحج السنوي . وعلى الحجاج الذين يأتون معهم بأموال تجارية
للبيع والانفاق على الحج ان يمارسوا تجارتهم بشيء من التعقل

« لَيْسَ عَلَيْكُمْ جُنَاحٌ أَنْ تَبْتَغُوا فَضْلاً مِنْ رَبِّكُمْ الخ .. » .

(سورة البقرة)

تاجر انت باستقامة وخذ ربحاً معقولاً لبضاعتك – وتحفظ من ان تكون
ضحية لغيرك . وليس في جدة اي امتياز ديني للمسلمين وبلدتها في موقعها الحالي
ليس فيها اي ميزة تاريخية معينة . وتنحصر أهميتها في الواقع في كونهـــا الممر
البحري الى مكة . (« هكذا يقولون تبعاً لما كانوا عليه قبل ولكن الحقيقة غير
ذلك لأنه لا ينكر ان الحكومة العربية السعودية قامت بأعمال كبرى في اجراء
الاحكام الشرعية وحفظ الامن والحرص على راحة الحجاج ، وهي تشكر عـــلى
ذلك . واذا جرى حيف من احد المواطنين في الحجاز فانما يكون من حيث يخفى
على الحكومة ويكفي في رفعه ان يخبر من اصابه حيف او جور اقرب موظف
للحكومة اليه فيرى العدل والأمن محسوساً تقر به عينه ويطمئن له باله) » .

ينقل الحجاج من جدة الى مكـة بالسيارات بمختلف انواعهـــا من اللوريات
والباصات والصالونات وغيرها وبواسطة الجمال والحمير . ويفضل بعض المسلمين
التنقل على الجمال لأن تلك هي الواسطة التي كانت في زمن النبي . وكيفما كانت
واسطة النقل فان اصوات الجموع المحتشدة من الحجـــاج الذين يلبون في رحلتهم
المقدسة تجعل من الطريق الصحراوي نوعاً من السحر .

وذلك هو النوع الوحيد من السحر الحلال في الاسلام . لقد امرنا ان نلبي
على الدوام اثناء المراحل الاخيرة من تقربنا الى مكة . ويمكن قطع المسافة بين
جدة ومكة بأقل من ساعتين بالسيارة ، ولكن هناك من بين الجموع الحاجة من يمكن

رؤيتهم سائرين على الأقدام ــ كما قطعوا القارة الأفريقية من (سيراليوني) و (ساحل الذهب) و (الكونغو) . وقبل بضع سنوات ، اي قبل ان تقع الصين وآسيا الوسطى تحت الحكم الشيوعي ويمنع الحج ، كان الحجاج يأتون مشاة من «كانسو في الصين» ويقتضي لهم قضاء سنتين أو ثلاث سنوات لإنهاء هذه الرحلة التي تكاد لاتصدق .

ليس علينا إن نهلك انفسنا باسم الدين ، كما ان الفقر ليس حجة . فالحج واجب على الناس لله ولكن على اولئك الذين يطيقون تكاليفه ، وكل مَن يستنفد جميع موارده لكي يقوم بالحج ويحرم عائلته من احتياجاتها ويترك اطفاله مغرقين في الديون لكي يصل مكة ، انما يقترف اثماً .

ان الطريق الى مكة كله صحراء فيها بعض الواحات المنعزلة بجانب الطريق الملتهب . وير الطريق المبلط من تحت التلول الصخرية التي تزينها بقايا الاستحكامات والابراج التي بنيت في زمن الاتراك لصد هجمات البدو على قوافل الحجاج . واول موقف يفتشون فيه من جانب الشرطة العربية هو في « ام السلام » وهي ثكنة ومركز حراسة تشبه الخيمة في الصحراء . والموقف الثاني للتفتيش ايضاً من قبل الشرطة هو في « سجرا » حيث يوجد مقهى « كالح » بجانب نقطة الحراسة . اما الموقف الثالث فهو في « الشميسي » الذي كان يسمى من قبل « الحديبية » وهو الحاجز الذي لا يتخطاه غير المسلمين ، ليدخلوا الأرض المقدسة . فعليك ان تلبي في هذا الموقع ففيه وقعت معاهدة الحديبية ، فقد ذكر لنا ان النبي محمداً (صلى الله عليه وسلم) عندما كان في المدينة في السنة السادسة من هجرته من مكة التي كانت لا تزال حصن الكفار من قريش المعادين له رأى في نومه انه عاد فدخل مكة مسقط رأسه من دون أن يعارضه احد . فلما استيقظ عزم على محاولة الحج حتى في مقاومة اعدائه ، وكانت قريش الكافرة في حالة حرب مع النبي ، حتى لقد هاجمت (المدينة) غير ان العادة العربية كانت تقضي بتحريم جميع اعمال العنف اثناء شهور الحج المقدسة .

فسار محمد صلى الله عليه وسلم في حوالي الف واربعمائة او الف وخمسمائة من اصحابه واتباعه إلى مكة . وكانوا جميعاً غير مسلحين . فكان لا بد من ان لا يجعل لقريش عذراً ، صحيحاً كان او غير صحيح ، لاستعمال وسائل العنف في المنطقة المقدسة . ولكن المسلمين لم يكونوا يعرفون شدة قريش . ففي السنوات الست

منذ ان هاجر محمد صلى الله عليه وسلم مضطراً ـ وهو نفسه من قريش ـ من مكة لـكي يحمي نفسه ويحمي اتباعه ، رأى المكيون ان قوتهم اخذت تهدد . فقد ظهرت قوة الاسلام المعنوية والروحية في تنظيمه ومقاومته . وقد رد النبي والمسلمون عدة مرات هجمات متفوقة شنها المكيون عليهم . فعندما وصل الحجاج الذين يقودم محمد (صلى الله عليه وسلم) الى الوادي انذرهم احد الموالين بأن قريشاً قد اعدت سلاحها وارتدت جلود النمور ـ وهي علامة الشجاعة عندهم ـ واقسمت ان تحول دون ان يضع النبي قدمه على ارض مكة ، مخالفة بذلك جميع التقاليد العربية ، وركب الفرسان الكافرون ليردوا الحجاج القادمين من (المدينة) ويضطروهم الى اليأس من اداء مناسك الحج .

فقام النبي محمد (صلى الله عليه وسلم) بحركة سوقية ، فزحف عن طريق صحراوي وصل منه رتل الحجاج منهوكين الى « الحديبية » فضربت الخيام على الحدود الحالية للحرم وأحاط بها الرجال وجمالهم والبدن والتي جاءوا بهـا من (المدينة) ، وحاول النبي الدخول في مفاوضـة مع قريش التي اغلقت أبواب مكة بوجه .

فأرسل النبي محمد صلى الله عليه وسلم رسولاً يخبر المكيين بأنه ورفاقه لم يأتوا الا للحج ، ولكن رسول النبي عندما حاول ان ينفذ رسالته ، عقر المكيون ناقته بسيوفهم وأساءوا معاملته ، فعاد الى مخيم المسلمين في الحديبية مرفقاً بمبعوث من قريش هدد النبي ومسلمي (المدينة) وكانوا جميعاً محرمين .

وجاء مبعوث آخر من مكة جعل الحجاج يذكرونه غاضبين بأن يقدم الاحترام اللازم لزعيمهم . فلما عاد المبعوث الى قريش التي تنتظره قال لهم : « لقد رأيت قيصر وكسرى في مواكبهم ، ولكن لم أجد رجلا يحترم رفاقه كمحمد » . حاولت فئة من مشاة مكة ان تغزو مخيم المسلمين فقبض عليهم وجيء بهم الى محمد (صلى الله عليه وسلم) فعفا عنهم عندما وعدوا بالكف عن العدوان . ثم في الاخير اتى مبعوثون منظمون من قريش بعد مفاوضات وانتهى الخلاف الى هدنة سميت صلح الحديبية او بيعة الرضوان . وقد نصت هذه البيعة على ان يكون هناك صلح بين الموقعين عليها مدة عشر سنوات . ويجب اعادة المهاجرين من كفار قريش الى المسلمين خلال هذه السنوات العشر ، ولا يعاد المسلمون المهاجرون الى قريش . والقبائـل التي ترغب في الاشتراك في هذه المعاهدة كاحلاف لأي من الطرفين يمكن قبولها . واخيراً فإن

على محمد (صلى الله عليه وسلم) واتباعه ان يولوا ظهورهم مكة ولا يزوروها او يزوروا الكعبة — ولكنهم يستطيعون العودة ودخول مكة في السنة التالية — بشرط أن يأتوا غير مسلحين . وقد عارض اتباع النبي الفقرة التي تشير الى متاركة المسلمين وقريش بعضهم البعض ، معارضة مريرة وقنطوا .

ولكن هذه المعاهدة مع ذلك اثبتت اخيراً انها اعظم نصر حازه المسلمون حتى ذلك الحين . فان الذين ارسلوا الى مكة ممن دخلوا في الاسلام اصبحوا دعاة الدين في حصن العهد ، وكانت الحرب بين محمد (صلى الله عليه وسلم) وكفار قريش تحول دون انتشار الدين الجديد . وقد اصبح الآن من الممكن للطرفين المتخاصمين ان يتلاقوا في سلام ويتناقشوا في معتقداتهم .

لقد ذهب محمد (صلى الله عليه وسلم) الى الحديبية في اقل من الف وخمسمائة من اتباعه ، وعاد في السنة التي تلتها الى مكة لمدة ثلاثة ايام هو وجماعته في خلالها الحج الاصغر — وهو العمرة — ورحلوا في سلام . وقد حافظ المسلمون على تطبيق فقرات المعاهدة — الى ان خرق احـد افراد قبائل مكة المتحالفة الهدنة بقيامه بهجوم . وعند ذلك وبعد سنتين فقط من التوقيع عليها زحف النبي على مكة في جيش قوامه عشرة آلاف ؛ فتم الاستيلاء على البلدة وكسرت الاصنام وعادت الكعبة المقدسة الى دين آدم وابراهيم الحنيف . ومعاهدة بيعة الرضوان التي ظن عند وضعها انها موجبة لاخـتذال المسلمين ، فتحت مكة لهم ، واكدت الى العالم الذي لم يكن يدري ولكنه كان ينتظر ، مجيء الدين الجديد . وهنا في « الشميسي » — الحديبية — حيث جرى كل ذلك يدخل الحجاج الارض المقدسة ، فلا يدخل اي شخص من غير هذا الدين فيها ولا يضع قدمه ، فهي ارض محرمة ، واتل التلبية بصورة مستمرة . ونقطة الحراسة التالية هي « ام الدود » على بعد سبعة كيلو مترات من مكة . وتليها آخر وقفة عند ابواب مكة .

وعلى الحجاج عندما يقتربون اخيراً من مكة ان يقولوا :

« اللهُمَّ اجْعلْ لِي بِهَا قَرَاراً وَأَرْزُقْنِي فِيهَا رِزْقاً حَلالاً » .

ثم يمرون من الابواب الى داخل المدينة ويقولون :

« اللّهُمَّ إنَّ هذا الحَرمَ حَرَمُك والبَلَدَ بَلَدُك ، والأَمْـنَ أَمْنُكَ والعَبْدَ عَبْدُك ، جِئْتُكَ مِنْ بِلادٍ بَعِيدةٍ ، بِذُنُوبٍ كَثِيرةٍ وأعمَالٍ سَيِّئةٍ ، أَسْأَلُكَ مَسْألَةَ الْمُضطَرِّين إلَيْك ، الْمُشفِقِينَ مِنْ عَذَابِكَ ، أنْ تَسْتَقْبِلَني بِمَحْضِ عَفْوِك ، وأنْ تُدْخِلَني في فَسِيحِ جَنَّتِكَ جَنَّةِ النَّعِيم ؛ اللّهُمَّ إنَّ هذا حَرَمُك وحَرَمُ رَسُولِك ، فَحَرِّمْ لَحْمِي ودَمِي وعَظْمِي على النَّار ، اللّهُمَّ آمِنِّي مِنْ عَذَابِـكَ يَوْمَ تَبْعَثُ عِبَادَك . أَسْأَلُك بِأَنَّكَ أَنْتَ اللهُ الذي لا إلَهَ إلّا أنْتَ الرحمنُ الرحيم أنْ تُصَلِّي وتُسَلِّمَ على سَيِّدِنا مُحَمَّدٍ وعَلى آلِهِ وصَحْبِهِ وسَلِّمْ تَسْلِيماً كَثِيراً أبداً . »

او يقرأون الدعاء التالي :

« اللّهُمَّ إنِّي أَسْأَلُكَ في مَقامِي هـذا في أوَّلِ مَنَاسِكِي أنْ تَقْبَلَ تَوْبَتي وأنْ تُجَاوِزَ عَنْ خَطيئَتي وَتَضَعَ عَنِّي وِزري . الحمْدُ لله الذي بَلَّغَني بَيْتَهُ الحَرام . اللّهُمَّ إنِّي أَشْهَدُ أَنَّ هذا بَيْتُكَ الحَرامُ الذي جَعَلْتَهُ مَثَابَةً للنَّاسِ وأمْناً ومُبَارَكاً وهُدىً للعالَمِين . اللّهُمَّ إنِّي عَبْدُكَ والبَلَدَ بَلَدُكَ ، والبَيْتَ بَيْتُكَ ، جِئْتُ أَطلُبُ رَحْمَتَكَ وأوُمُّ طاعَتَكَ مُطيعاً لأَمْرِكَ راضِياً بِقَدَرِكَ . أَسْأَلُكَ مَسْألَـةَ الْمُضطَرِّ إلَيْكَ ، الخَائِفِ لِعُقُوبَتِك ، اللّهُمَّ آفْتَحْ لي أبوابَ رَحْمَتِكَ واسْتَعْمِلْني بِطاعَتِكَ ومَرْضَاتِك . »

مكة

ان الدخول الى مكة تجربة عاطفية عظمى . فالناس لا يعرفون لماذا اجتمعوا
حول هذه الاشياء القديمة بدلاً من الجديدة . ولعل سبب ذلك ان القديم قـد
اثبت جدارته وان الجديد ــ مثلنا ــ لم يثبت . ان اجداد اجدادنا منذ فجر
التاريخ قد تعبدوا حول الكعبة المقدسة ، وما لم يسيطر الكفار فان احفـاد
احفادنا سيتعبدون حولها الى آخر الزمان .

ان مكة ليست مكاناً ، انها ، البداية ، و ، الحاضر ، و ، الابدية ، وكل
من يدخلها يشعر بذلك فيهزه .

ان اغلب الحجـاج يفدون الى مكة لكي يؤدوا الفريضة الى الله . ولكن
الناس منذ البداية كانوا يأتون الى الكعبة ليلتجئوا الى الله ، الالتجاء الجسدي من
أذى العدو ويده ، والالتجاء الروحي حيث يستطيع القلب المضطرب ان يجـد
الطريق ، والروحُ الجريحة ان تلتئم جروحها . واليوم ايضاً يوجد حجاج يجدون
في الكعبة والاماكن المقدسة مأوى يلتجئون اليه بعـد مشاق هائلة واضطهاد لا
هوادة فيه ــ حجاج هربوا من ارض اسلامية تحت الحكم الاجنبي الملحـد ــ .
لقد هلك عدد لا يحصى من المسلمين الذين فرض عليهم ان يكونوا امّا هي الآن
سوفيتية ، والذين منعهم الشيوعيون من عبادة الله واداء الحج ، وم يحاولون اجتياز
الحدود المغلقة ليأتوا الى هنا . وقد جعل بضعة آلاف ممن بقي منهم من جـدة
ومكة موطناً وملجأً لهم وم يتسلون لقربهم من الاماكن المقدسة .

فاذا مررت من البلدة فتخلق بالتعفف ! ان المكيـين سوف يقدمون لك من

ماء زمزم في أوعية للشرب ، فاذا قبلت فأعطهم هبـــة مـن المال لقاء ذلك .
ولا تنس ان مـا هو مقدس لا يمكن شراؤه . وانت هنا لا تعبد الاشياء وانما
تعبد الله . ان هذا الماء من محل مقدس ، ولكنه في حد ذاته ليس إلَـهيّا . بل
هو مجرد ماء .

ان مكة بلدة من هذه التربة والارض يسكنها الناس . والكعبة المقدسة من
صخور جبلية وقد صنعت كسوتها ايد بشرية . فالاله الوحيد في مكة هو الله .

وفي داخل ابواب مكة يستجوب الحجــاج من قبل السلطات وممثلي لجنـة
الحج الذين يسألونه عن اسم المطوف . فاذا لم يكن المطوف في صحبة الحاج ،
او لم يكن لدى الباب في استقباله ، فان الموظفين يأمرون من تكون وسائط النقل
في عهدته ان يأخذه الى حيث يجده .

وبعد ذلك ، اي بعد تعيين موطن السكنى ، والعناية بالامتعة وتهيئة وسائل
الراحة والنظافة الجسمية والروحية ، يتجه كل حاج او حاجة نحو البيت الحرام ،
والمسجد الكبير ، حيث يقبل على الكعبة في الفسحة المفتوحـة وتحت السماء .
في وسط الوادي تحيط الاسواق والحوانيت من جميع الجهــات يجدران
البيت الحرام الخارجية وفي بعض الاقسام بيوت المكيين بيوت المكيين العالية التي تشرف طبقاتها
العليا على الساحة الداخلية وعلى الكعبة . والبيوت القريبة تعلوها بيوت أخرى
أقيمت على أرض عالية من ورائها . وجميع نوافذها شرقية كميون ترد على سؤال
مفاجيء . وترعى على الدوام المسجد الحارس كنزه . لا يوجد وقت في الليل
او النهار ، في أية ساعة كانت ، وفي اي موسم كان او في أي جو من الاجواء ،
تكون الكعبة فيه خاليــة . ففي الظهيرة التي تعمي العيون وتخمــد الانفاس
بحرها وفي ظلمة الليــل ، هناك اناس او اشباح على الدوام تطوف وتسعى بـين
الصفا والمروة خارج جدران المسجد العظيم .

ومن المستحب ان يجدد الحجــاج القادمون حديثـاً وضوءم قبل ان
يقربوا من البيت الحرام . وهناك يجانب المسجد محلات للوضوء ، احدها داخل
(باب السلام) وآخر في (باب العمرة) غير انه عندما يكون الحــج في
أوجه يصبح الزحام شديداً ، فاذا لم يتيسر المــاء في مسكن الحاج في مكة
فيمكن شراؤه من اي مقهى من المقاهي المحيطة بالمسجد او في الشوارع والطرق
التي تؤدي اليها . وعلى الحجــاج ان لا يفترقوا عن جماعتهم لشدة اشتياقهم

الى زيارة الاماكن المقدسة . فإن حوالي نصف المليون من الحجاج أغلبهم ينطقون القليل من العربية او لا ينطقونها بتاتاً ، سيكونون في سيول من البشر الذين تزدحم بهم شوارع مكة الضيقة ، عرضة للحر والغبار . وفي النهار تكون الشمس المحرقة على الرأس ، وتزفر الجدران الصخرية للبيوت العالية في الليل زفيرا كزفير الاتون . وكثير من الحجاج يصيبهم الدوار من التعب وشدة الحر ، ولا يستطيعون مقاومة الا بشعورهم الديني . وهناك الاندنسيون والجاويون والسودانيون والسومطريون والدياقيون وحجاج من برما والملايو وسيام ، ومن مندناوا في المحيط الهادىء ، وايرانيون واتراك واكراد وهنود وافغانيون وباكستانيون وبربر ومغاربة ومراكشيون وطوارق ، وحجاج من السنغال وكينيا الافريقيــة ونيروبي ، ورجال ونساء من امم وشعوب قارة افريقيا طولاً وعرضاً . وهناك التتر النازحون من جماعات هم الآن في المانيا وفنلندا . ولقد كان هناك قبل الآن – وسوف يعود يوماً ما ان شاء الله – حجـاج من البانيا والبوسنة والهرسك ومن بولونيا والقوقاس والقرم ، ومن تركستان وقازان وسيبريا ، ومن الصين ومن جميع ارجاء الاراضي الاخرى التي حرم الدين فيها الآن ، ومنع فيها الحج وجميع انواع السفر .

(وبعض هذه الشعوب كسكان القرم قد ابيدوا ، فـلا يمكن رؤيتهم في مكة مرة اخرى ، والآخرون يعيشون الآن في عبودية ، وسوف تكون هناك اوقات ندعو لهم ونترحم عليهم في خلال الحج) .

سيكون هناك من جميع العنـاصر والالوان من سكان سيبريا البيض الى الافريقيين العاجيين ، ومن جميع الالسنة واللهجات . فاحذر من ان تضيع : واحذر من ان تنفصل عن اصحابك . ومن وسائل الحذر ان تحفظ اسماء الذين يرعونك ويدلونك وتكتبها مع عنوان المسكن على ورقة لـكي تظل في حماية ذلك الشخص على الدوام . وافعل مثل ذلك لأولئك الذين لا يعرفون القراءة والكتابة من رفاقك . فاذا ضللت مع كل هذه التدابير فاستعمل ذكاءك .

ان شمس الحجاز مميتة فاجتنب زحــام الحجــاج وابحث عن محل ظليل يمكن ان تراقب منه الغادين والرائحين ، فاذا وجدت حاجاً يبدو انه من جنسك فتحدث اليه ، فان كان من بلدك فان مطوفه سيكون نفس مطوفك ، وسيكون قادراً على ان يعيدك الى جماعتك . فاذا اعددت نفسك فاذهب الى

البيت الحرام بصحبة رفاقك ، ومن الافضل للحجاج الذين لم يتعودوا على حرارة الحجاز الملتهبة التي تحيط بمكة والحجاز كله عندما تكون الشمس عالية ، ان يؤخروا تقربهم من المسجد الى الليل .

البيت الحرام – المسجد الكبير

في مكة

كانت مساكن زعماء القبائل في ايام الجاهلية تحيط بالكعبة المقدسة والمداخل الاربعة والعشرين للمسجد العظيم وساحته القائمة اليوم ، هي كما قيل محل المرات بين تلك المساكن . وكان الحرم في ذلك الزمن يضم منطقة صغيرة مفتوحة حوالي الكعبة المقدسة من غير جدران أو اروقة ، ولم يكن اي قسم منها مغطى من الشمس المحرقة ، وبتوسع وانتشار الاسلام اشترى الخلفاء الاوائل المساكن المحيطة وافسحوا المجال للمزيد من الحجاج الذين يفدون كالسيل الى الموقع المقدس .

وبعد ذلك وسع حكام مكة المساحة المحيطة بالكعبة واضافوا أروقة وتوسيعات حوالي ساحة المسجد . وهناك كما اسلفنا اربعة وعشرون باباً يمكن الدخول الى البيت الحرام منها ، ولكن الافضل للحاج ان يدخل من باب السلام .

والنساء اللواتي يأتيهن الحيض يجب عليهن الانتظار اذا كان هناك وقت كاف إلى ان يزول الحيض قبل ان يؤدين الفروض الاولى في الكعبة . واذا لم يكن هناك وقت كاف ، واذا كانت مناسك الحج توشك ان تبدأ فلهن ان يشرعن بها دون ان يؤدين الطواف . وتذكر الاحاديث ان اولئك اللواتي هن في سعة من العيش يقدمن الاضاحي بعد ذلك .

واقرأ عند دخولك باب السلام :

اللّٰهُمَّ أَنْتَ السَّلَامُ ، ومِنْكَ السَّلَامُ ، فَحَيِّنَا رَبَّنا بِالسَّلَامِ ، وأَدْخِلْنَا الجَنَّةَ دارَ السَّلَامِ ، تَبَارَكْتَ رَبَّنا وتعَالَيْتَ يا ذا الجَلَالِ والإِكْرَامِ ، اللّٰهُمَّ أَفْتَحْ لي أبوابَ رَحْمَتِك ومَغْفِرَتِك . وأَدْخِلْني فيها . بِسمِ اللهِ والحَمْدُ لله . والصَّلاةُ والسَّلامُ على رسولِ الله صلى الله عليه وسلم) .

والآن تتجه انظار الحجاج الى الكعبة المقدسة ، فسيطر على عواطفك ، ان هذه هي ساعة التقديس وهي تجربة الحياة الكبرى فادع قائلاً :

(لا إِلَهَ إِلَّا الله (ثلاثاً) الله أَكْبَرُ (ثلاثاً) ثم قل : (لا إِلَهَ إِلَّا اللهُ وَحْدَه ، لا شَرِيكَ لَهُ ، لَهُ المُلكُ وَلَهُ الحَمْدُ وَهُوَ عَلَى كُلِّ شَيءٍ قَدِير ، أَعوذُ بِرَبِّ البَيْتِ مِــــنَ الكُفْرِ والفَقْرِ ، ومِنْ عَذابِ القَبْرِ ، وضِيقِ الصَّدْرِ وصَلَّى اللهُ على سَيِّدِنا مُحَمَّدٍ وعلى آلِهِ وصَحْبِهِ وسَلَّم . اللهُمَّ زِدْ بَيْتَكَ هـذا تَشْرِيفاً وتَكْرِيماً وَتَعْظِيماً ، ومَهَابَةً ورِفْعَةً وبِرًّا ، وزِدْ يا رَبِّ مَنْ شَرَّفَهُ وَكَرَّمَهُ وَعَظَّمَهُ مِّمَنْ حَجَّهُ وأَعْتَمَرَهُ تَشْرِيفاً وتَكْرِيماً وتَعْظِيماً ومَهَابَـــةً ورِفْعَةً وبِرًّا) .

الكعبة المقدسة

تقف الكعبة في جلال وسط الساحة العظيمة وهي مغطـاة من القمـة الى القاعدة بكسوة موشاة في القسم الذي يعلو الوسط من الارض بآيات من القرآن الكريم كتبت بالذهب معرضة للهواء والسماء وتضيئها في الليـل المصابيح والبرق الذي كثيراً ما يلمع فوق البلاد العربية ، وقـــد ترطبت من الطـل في الليل وجفت من حرارة الشمس في النهار .

وفي خلال الحج تزدحم الساحة بالآلاف المحتشدة وتصبح الكعبة محور هذا الجريان الذي لا ينقطع من العباد الذين يؤدون فريضة الطواف . وعندما ينتهي الحجاج من الطواف السابع يأتي آخرون وقد تعلق الأطفال بثياب آبائهم المحرمين او ناموا مرهقين بين ايديهم ، وتمتلىء الاماكن بالعشرات الجديـــدة من الآلاف المقبلين من جدة والعالم الخارجي . غير ان هناك فترة هدوء نسبي من منتصف الليل الى قبيل ساعة واحدة من الفجر يُحسن صنعاً اولئك الذين ينتظرون الى

ذلك الوقت لكي يؤدوا الطواف ، خاصة في السنوات التي يقع الحج خلالها في أشد أشهر الحر ويقع خارج نطاقه اولئك الذي يؤدون الطواف بعيدين عن الكعبة ، ولكن ضمن المنطقة المبلطة بالمرمر والحجر التي تحيط بالبيت العتيق ، وتشير الى الحدود الاصلية للعبادة (بئر زمزم) و (مقام ابراهيم) الذي تظلله مقصورة مقببة تحتها المنبر اللولبي الذي تتلى منه خطب الجمعة ، والطريق ذو السقف المقوس المعترف به للتقرب من السياج المقدس .

ان جميع ساحة المسجد مكسوة بالحصى ذي اللون العنبري تقطعه تسع طرق حجرية عريضة ، احدها واسع عظيم ينبثق من الكعبة . ويستحب للحجاج الذين يقطعون السياج المقدس في الطريق الممتد من باب السلام ويمرون تحت الطريق المقوس ان يقرأوا :

(وَقُلْ رَبِّ أَدْخِلْنِي مَدْخَلَ صِدْقٍ وَأَخْرِجْنِي مَخْرَجَ صِدْقٍ وَأَجْعَلْ لِي مِنْ لَدُنْكَ سُلْطَاناً نَصِيراً . وَقُلْ جَاءَ الْحَقُّ وَزَهَقَ الْبَاطِلُ إِنَّ الْبَاطِلَ كَانَ زَهُوقاً) .

(سورة الاسراء)

والى اليسار من الطريق المظلل بسقف مقوس بينه وبين البناء ذي الطابقين الذي يضم بئر زمزم ، يقع السلم الذي يستعمل للصعود الى عتبة الكعبة العالية المكونة من ثلاث عشرة درجة ، لأن عتبة الكعبة تعلو بمقدار مترين عن مستوى الارض ، ولا تنقل السلالم وتبقى في محلها الا عندما تفتح الابواب الذهبية والفضية ، والا فان السلالم تعوق طريق الذين يطوفون . وبواجه الحاج المقبل من الطريق ذي السقف المقوس مقام ابراهيم مباشرة ، وهو الصخرة الموجودة داخل بناء ، والتي يقال ان النبي ابراهيم وقف عليها عندما كان يقوم ببناء الكعبة ويتعبد ، وعلى بعد منه في منطقة الطواف التي يكسو ارضها المرمر تقع الكعبة المكسوة وعليها الستائر النفيسة التي تخفي ابوابها . ويقع الى الركن الجنوبي الشرقي من الكعبة في اطار من الفضة « الحجر الاسود » الذي تلقاه النبي اسماعيل من الملك جبرائيل أثناء اعادة بناء البيت الحرام ، ولا يرى الحجر لأول وهلة . فقد وضع في علو تصل اليه ايدي او أفواه الذين يمرون خلال الطواف ، وتحجبه عن الانظار سيول المؤمنين ، ولن يرى الا من تجمع الحجاج هناك لكي يقبلوه او يلمسوه .

— ٣٣ —

ويقع المنبر المرتفع الى يمين مقام ابراهيم وموازياً له . ويقع الى الخلف ـ بحيث يخفي الجانب الاسفل من وجه الكعبة المتجه الى الشمال داخل المنطقة التي يضمها الطواف ـ جدار شيد بأحجار ضخمة بني على شكل نصف دائرة هو (الحطيم) يعلو بمقدار الكتف ، ويضم الجدار محلاً للصلاة يسمى (الحجر) ـ وقد قيل ان قد دفن هناك تحت الارض المرمرية المسحوقة ، سبعون من الانبياء بينهم اسماعيل . وقيل ان هاجر ام النبي اسماعيل مدفونة هنا ايضاً .

وهنا نام النبي محمد صلى الله عليه وسلم في ليلة السابع والعشرين من رجب قبل سنة واحدة من هجرته من مكة الى المدينة ، عندما نزل الملك جبرائيـل بالجواد السماوي المطهم (البراق) ، ومن هذه البقعة اسرى النبي محمد صلى الله عليه وسلم الى بيت المقدس ، وكان معراجه الى السماوات السبع وعاد قبل الفجر . واذا فات الحاج خلال رحلته الى مكة شيء من الصلوات الخمس اليومية فمن المستحب ان يقضيها هنا قبل بداية طواف الزيارة وهو اول طوافات الحج الثلاثة .

الطواف حول الكعبة

قيل ان الملائكة في الجنة يعبدون الله بالطواف حول كعبة اخرى ويسبحون بحمده . وقد ظل الناس آلاف السنين وهم يطوفون في المنطقة المماثلة نفس الطواف ويؤدون الفريضة نفسها ، حتى انقلبت الاماكن المقدسة في زمن الجاهلية الطويل الظلام الى عبادة الاصنام .

لقد عرفت الكعبة والحجر الاسود بمسير المؤمنين ثم مسير الكفار . ثم طواف المؤمنين الأول للتسبيح والحمد ، ثم طواف الكفار الاعمى وتعزيمهم المحموم . لقد حطم النبي محمد صلى الله عليه وسلم الأصنام العديدة ، واعاد الاماكن المقدسة الى الغرض الاول منها : وهو تمجيد الله الواحد الأحد . ثم تلقى النبي محمد صلى الله عليه وسلم الوحي الالهي الذي منع منذ تلك اللحظة الكفار من دخول المسجد المقدس بقوله :

(يا أيُّهَا الَّذِينَ آمَنُوا إِنَّمَا المُشْرِكُونَ نَجَسٌ فَـلا يَقْرَبُوا المَسْجِدَ الحَرَامَ بعد عَامِهِمْ هـذا) .

(سورة التوبة ، ٢٩)

ومنـــذ ذلك الحين لم يسمح لمشرك (وهو معروف) بالتقرب من الكعبة،
احترم هذا المكان لقدمه ولكل ما ينبثق منه ، ولكن لا تنس ان الكعبة المقدسة ،
وهي بيت الله في ايام النبي ابراهيم ، اصبحت بيتاً للأصنام قبل ان يولد محمد
صلى الله عليه وسلم بكثير . وكان الحجاج العائدون من مكة يحملون معهم في
البداية قطعاً من احجار الكعبة ، وكانت عادة العرب ان تحمل هذه القطع اينا
سار حاملوها فتكون لهم نقطة مقدسة يمكن ان تبـدأ منها العبادة والطواف .
فكانت الخطوة الاولى للاحتفاظ بهذه القطع ان الجهال شرعوا يعطون احجارهم
قوى اعجازية ، ثم كانت الخطوة الثانية انهم شرعوا يعبدونها هي نفسها بدلاً من
ان يعبدوا خالقها ، ثم وضعت هذه الاحجـار في تجاويف اجسام او رؤوس
اشباح منحوتة ، وجعلوا لهذه الاشباح أرواحاً ، ثم تجمع الناس حول هذه الأصنام
فعبدوها . وقد قيل إن النبي محمداً صلى الله عليه وسلم حطم ثلاثمائة وستين إلـهاً
مزيفاً عندما طهر مكة ثانية .

اننا نحترم مكة اليوم ونحترم الكعبة والحجر الأسود وبئر زمزم وماءه ،
ومقام ابراهيم والامكنة المقدسة ، لتاريخها وما يتعلق بها ، ولكن لا لنفسها هي .
فالله ، والله وحده هو غرض ، عبادتنا فلا تنس ذلك .

وعندما يكون الحاج متهيئاً للبدء بالطواف عليه أو عليها ان يذهب الى نقطة
امام الحجر الأسود . وفي هذه الفترة يحصل توقف وقتي في سيل الحجاج الطائفين
وكذلك المندفعون نحو الركن المقدس ، وهناك تلحظ لمعان الحجر الاسود المكسو
بالفضة ، الا قسماً يكفي الحاج ان يدخل رأسه ويقبل الحجر او يلمسه .

نيـــــة الطـــواف

لا تقاطع الآخرين في طوافهم ، ولا تـدافع بالمناكب . وحالما تجد لك مكاناً
اشرع بالقول : (بِسمِ اللهِ الرَّحمَنِ الرَّحِيمِ . اللّهُمَّ إنِّي أُرِيدُ طَوَافَ
بَيتِنكَ الحَرَامَ فَيَسِّرْهُ لي وَتَقَبَّلْهُ مِنِّي سَبعَةَ أشوَاطٍ طَوَافَ الحَجِّ
أُو العُمْرَةِ أو الوَدَاع) . واذا ما انتهيت فانو فيها اذا كان طوافك هـذا
للعمرة (او للحج او للعمرة والحج معاً) كما كانت النية عليـه عند الشروع
بالإحرام . وليكن مشغولاً في طوافه سيا طواف الفريضة بقراءة القرآن والذكر
والدعاء والصلاة على النبي (صلى الله عليه وآله) وآله عليهم السلام . وليقرأ

بعض الأدعية المأثورة فيه منها :

« أَللّٰهُمَّ إِنِّي أَسْأَلُكَ بِاسْمِكَ ٱلَّذِي يُمْشَى بِهِ عَلَى ظُلَلِ ٱلْمَاءِ كَمَا يُمْشَى بِهِ عَلَى جُدَدِ ٱلْأَرْضِ وَأَسْأَلُكَ بِاسْمِكَ ٱلَّذِي يَهْتَزُّ لَهُ إِقْدَامُ مَلَائِكَتِكَ وَأَسْأَلُكَ بِاسْمِكَ ٱلَّذِي دَعَاكَ بِهِ مُوسَى مِنْ جَانِبِ ٱلطُّورِ فَٱسْتَجَبْتَ لَهُ وَأَلْقَيْتَ عَلَيْهِ مَحَبَّةً مِنْكَ وَأَسْأَلُكَ بِاسْمِكَ ٱلَّذِي غَفَرْتَ بِهِ لِمُحَمَّدٍ (صَلَّى ٱللهُ عَلَيْهِ وَآلِهِ وَسَلَّمَ) مَا تَقَدَّمَ مِنْ ذَنْبِهِ وَمَا تَأَخَّرَ وَأَتْمَمْتَ نِعْمَتَكَ عَلَيْهِ أَنْ تَفْعَلَ بِي كَذَا وَكَذَا .. » .

ويذكر كل ما احب من الدعاء المشروع ؛ وكلما ينتهي الى باب الكعبة يصلي على محمد وآله (عليهم الصلاة والسلام) ؛ وليقل في الطواف :

« اللّٰهُمَّ إِنِّي إِلَيْكَ فَقِيرٌ وَإِنِّي خَائِفٌ مُسْتَجِيرٌ فَلَا تُغَيِّرْ جِسْمِي ، وَلَا تُبَدِّلْ ٱسْمِي » .

وينبغي استلام اليماني في كل شوط من اشواطه ويقول :

« اللّٰهُمَّ تُبْ عَلَيَّ حَتَّى أَتُوبَ ، وَأَعْصِمْنِي حَتَّى لَا أَعُودَ » .

ثم يرفع يده الى السماء ويقول :

« يَا ٱللهُ ، يَا وَلِيَّ ٱلْعَافِيَةِ وَخَالِقَ ٱلْعَافِيَةِ وَرَازِقَ ٱلْعَافِيَةِ وَٱلْمُنْعِمَ بِٱلْعَافِيَةِ وَٱلْمَنَّانَ بِٱلْعَافِيَةِ وَٱلْمُتَفَضِّلَ بِٱلْعَافِيَةِ عَلَيَّ وَعَلَى جَمِيعِ خَلْقِكَ ؛ يَا رَحْمٰنَ ٱلدُّنْيَا وَٱلْآخِرَةِ وَرَحِيمَهُمَا ، صَلِّ عَلَى مُحَمَّدٍ وَآلِ مُحَمَّدٍ وَٱرْزُقْنَا ٱلْعَافِيَةَ وَدَوَامَ ٱلْعَافِيَةِ وَتَمَامَ ٱلْعَافِيَةِ وَشُكْرَ ٱلْعَافِيَةِ فِي ٱلدُّنْيَا وَٱلْآخِرَةِ ، يَا أَرْحَمَ ٱلرَّاحِمِينَ » .

وينبغي ايضاً ان يستقبل الميزاب ويقول :

> « اللّهُمَّ أَعْتِقْ رَقَبَتِي مِنَ النَّارِ وأَوْسِعْ عَلَيَّ مِنْ رِزْقِكَ
> الْحَلَالِ وَأَدْرَأْ عَنِّي شَرَّ فَسَقَةِ الْجِنِّ والإِنْسِ وأَدْخِلْنِي الْجَنَّةَ
> بِرَحْمَتِك . »

ويستحب للحجاج الذكور ان يلبسوا النصف الاعلى من ثياب الاحرام على الكتف الايسر وتحت الابط الايمن ، كما فعل النبي محمد صلى الله عليه وسلم ، والعاجز والمقعد من اي من الجنسين يستطيع ان يستأجر من يحملونه في محفة ويطوفون به سبع مرات . فقد روي ان النبي محمداً صلى الله عليه وسلم طاف على ظهر الجمل مرة واحدة على الاقل وهذا غير مسموح به بعد ، ولكن الحمالين يمكن ايجادهم لهذا الغرض . وقد جرت التقاليد على بدء الطواف بلمس او تقبيل الحجر الاسود ، على انه اذا كان ضغط الحجاج مع ذلك شديداً خلال الحج ولم يمكن الوصول الى الحجر الاسود من دون ان يزيد المرء في الاضطراب الموجود فعلاً ، فقم باشارة من بعيد بدل اللمس وامرر يدك على وجهك قائلاً :

> « بِسْمِ اللهِ ، واللّهُ أَكْبَرُ وللّهِ الْحَمْدُ ، اللّهُمَّ إِيمَاناً بِكَ ،
> وتَصْدِيقاً بِكِتَابِكَ ، وَوَفَاءً بِعَهْدِك ، وأَتْبَاعاً لِسُنَّةِ نَبِيِّكَ مُحَمَّدٍ
> صَلَّى اللهُ عَلَيْهِ وَسَلَّمَ . »

أو قل :

> « اللّهُمَّ أَمَانَتِي أَدَّيْتُها ، ومِيثَاقِي تَعَاهَدْتُهُ لِتَشْهَـدَ لِي
> بالموافاة ، اللّهُمَّ تَصْدِيقاً بِكِتَابِكَ وعَلَى سُنَّةِ نَبِيِّكَ أَشْهَدُ أَنْ لا
> إِلَهَ إِلَّا اللهُ وَحْدَهُ لا شَرِيكَ لَهُ وأَنَّ مُحَمَّداً عَبْدُهُ وَرَسُولُهُ ؛
> آمَنْتُ بِاللهِ وَكَفَرْتُ بِالجِبْتِ والطَّاغُوتِ وباللّاتِ والعُزَّى وعِبَادَةِ
> الشَّيَاطِينِ وعِبَادَةِ كُلِّ نَدٍّ مِنْ دُونِ اللهِ . »

« فإن لم يستطع ان يقول ذلك كله فبعضه » ، وليقل :

« اللّٰهُمَّ إِلَيْكَ بَسَطْتُ يَدِي وفِيمَا عِنْدَكَ عَظُمَتْ رَغْبَتِي فَاقْبَلْ مسحتِي (وفي نُسْخَةٍ سُبْحتِي) وأغْفِرْ لِي وأرْحَمْنِي. اللّٰهُمَّ إِنِّي أَعُوذُ بِكَ مِنَ الكُفْرِ والفَقْرِ ومَواقِفِ الخِزْيِ في الدُّنيا والآخِرَة » .

ويستحب ايضاً ان يقول اذا استلم الحجر :

« الحمْدُ للهِ الذي هَدانا لِهٰذا وما كُنّا لِنَهْتَدِيَ لَوْلاَ أنْ هَدَانا اللهُ . سُبحانَ اللهِ والحَمْدُ للهِ ولا إِلٰهَ إلا اللهُ واللهُ أكْبَرُ . أكْبَرُ مِنْ خَلْقِهِ وأكْبَرُ مِّمَّنْ أخشى وأحْذَرُ ، ولا إِلٰهَ إلا اللهُ وَحْدَهُ لا شَرِيكَ لَه . لَهُ المُلْكُ ولَهُ الحَمْدُ يُحْيِي ويُمِيتُ . ويُمِيتُ ويُحْيِي ، بِيَدِهِ الخَيْرُ وَهُوَ عَلَى كُلِّ شَيْءٍ قَدِير » .

ويصلي على النبي وآل النبي ويسلم على المرسلين بقوله :

« السلامُ على انبياءِ اللهِ ورُسُلِه » .

ويقول اني :

« أُوْمِنُ بِوَعْدِكَ وأُوفِي بِعَهْدِكَ » .

ثم يقول :

« أَللّٰهُمَّ أَمَانَتِي أَدَّيْتُها وَمِيثَاقِي تَعَاهَدْتُهُ » .

الى قوله : « في الدنيا والآخرة » . وهي نهاية الدعاءين المذكورين آنفاً ، والأوْلى في فقه اهل البيت أن يضيف الى الشهادة بالرسالة بعدها :

« وأَنَّ الأئمَّةَ مِنْ ذُرِّيَّتِهِ » .

ويسميهم واحداً بعد واحد :

« (حُجَجُهُ في أَرْضِهِ وَشُهَداوُهُ عَلَى عِبَادِهِ) ».

وبهذه الكلمات يبدأ الطواف فيترك الحاج (الكعبة) و (ركن الحجر الأسود) وينضم الى السيل الذي يغدو ويروح حول البيت العتيق ماراً بالعتبة الى جهة الركن العراقي ، ثم من الجدار الواطىء « الحطيم » وموضع العبادة المسيج « الحجر » ، ثم (من الركن الشامي) و (الركن اليماني) لتكمـــل الطواف بالعودة الى الحجر الاسود المقدس .

وفي الركن اليماني حجر آخر تحيط به خيوط من فضة . وكان من عـــادة النبي ان يلمس هذا الركن عند مروره في الطواف ، واليوم عندما يكون الحج في ابانه يشق كثيراً التقرب منه ، ويمكن اغفال لمسه لمساً فعلياً ، غير ان على الحاج عندما يمر من الركن اليماني والحجر الاسود ان يقرأ :

(رَبّنا آتِنا في الدُّنْيا حَسَنَةً وَفِي الآخِرَةِ حَسَنَةً وَقِنَا عَذابَ النّارِ . وَأَدْخِلْنَا الْجَنَّةَ مَعَ الأَبْرارِ . ياعَزِيزُ ياغَفَّارُ يارَبَّ الْعَالَمِين) .

ويقرأ كلما مر من الحجر الاسود اما لامساً او رافعاً يده اليمنى بعلامة اللمس:

(بِسْمِ اللهِ وَاللهُ أَكْبَرُ وَلِلهِ الْحَمْدُ) .

وفي اثناء الاشواط الثلاثة حول الكعبة على جميع الحجاج الذكور ان يسيروا قسماً من المسافة بخطوات سريعة متبعين مطوفهم او شيخهم . وليس على الحاجات ان يسرعن ولكن عليهن ان يكملن طوافهن بخطوات هادئة .

الشوط الاول

يتقدم المطوف جماعته في الدعاء في خلال كل شوط من الاشواط السبعة . وفي الشوط الاول يتلو بصوت عال ويردد اتباعه اقواله من بعده :

(سُبْحَانَ ٱللهِ وَٱلْحَمْدُ لِلهِ وَلَا إِلَهَ إِلَّا ٱللهُ وَٱللهُ أَكْبَرُ
وَلَا حَوْلَ وَلَا قُوَّةَ إِلَّا بِٱللهِ ٱلْعَلِيِّ ٱلْعَظِيمِ ، وَٱلصَّلَاةُ وَٱلسَّلَامُ
عَلَى رَسُولِ ٱللهِ صَلَّى ٱللهُ عَلَيْهِ وَسَلَّمَ ، أَللَّهُمَّ إِيمَاناً بِكَ وَتَصْدِيقاً
بِكِتَابِكَ وَوَفَاءً بِعَهْدِكَ وَٱتِّبَاعاً لِسُنَّةِ نَبِيِّكَ وَحَبِيبِكَ مُحَمَّدٍ صَلَّى
ٱللهُ عَلَيْهِ وَسَلَّمَ . أَللَّهُمَّ إِنِّي أَسْأَلُكَ ٱلْعَفْوَ وَٱلْعَافِيَةَ وَٱلْمُعَافَاةَ ٱلدَّائِمَةَ
فِي ٱلدِّينِ وَٱلدُّنْيَا وَٱلْآخِرَةِ ، وَٱلْفَوْزَ بِٱلْجَنَّةِ وَٱلنَّجَاةَ مِنَ ٱلنَّارِ) .

ويقول بين الركنين في كل شوط :

(رَبَّنَا آتِنَا فِي ٱلدُّنْيَا حَسَنَةً وَفِي ٱلْآخِرَةِ حَسَنَةً وَقِنَا عَذَابَ
ٱلنَّارِ . وَأَدْخِلْنَا ٱلْجَنَّةَ مَعَ ٱلْأَبْرَارِ ، يَا عَزِيزُ يَا غَفَّارُ يَا رَبَّ ٱلْعَالَمِينَ) .

الشوط الثاني

وخلال الشوط الثاني حول الكعبة يتلو المطوف ويردد اتباعه خلفه :

(أَللَّهُمَّ إِنَّ هَذَا ٱلْبَيْتَ بَيْتُكَ وَٱلْحَرَمَ حَرَمُكَ وَٱلْأَمْنَ أَمْنُكَ
وَٱلْعَبْدَ عَبْدُكَ وَأَنَا عَبْدُكَ وَٱبْنُ (أَوْ أَبْنَةُ) عَبْدِكَ ، وَهَذَا
مَقَامُ ٱلْعَائِذِ بِكَ مِنَ ٱلنَّارِ ، فَحَرِّمْ لُحُومَنَا وَبَشَرَتَنَا عَلَى ٱلنَّارِ .
أَللَّهُمَّ حَبِّبْ إِلَيْنَا ٱلْإِيمَانَ وَزَيِّنْهُ فِي قُلُوبِنَا وَكَرِّهْ إِلَيْنَا ٱلْكُفْرَ
وَٱلْفُسُوقَ وَٱلْعِصْيَانَ ، وَٱجْعَلْنَا مِنَ ٱلرَّاشِدِينَ . أَللَّهُمَّ قِنِي عَذَابَكَ
يَوْمَ تَبْعَثُ عِبَادَكَ ، أَللَّهُمَّ ٱرْزُقْنِي ٱلْجَنَّةَ بِغَيْرِ حِسَابٍ) .

الشوط الثالث

وفي خلال الشوط الثالث يتلو المطوف ويردد اتباعه وراءه :

(أَللَّهُمَّ إِنِّي أَعُوذُ بِكَ مِنَ ٱلشَّكِّ وَٱلشِّرْكِ وَٱلشِّقَاقِ وَٱلنِّفَاقِ وَسُوءِ ٱلْأَخْلَاقِ وَسُوءِ ٱلْمُنْظَرِ وَٱلْمُنْقَلَبِ في ٱلْمَالِ وَٱلْأَهْلِ وَٱلْوَلَدِ . أَللَّهُمَّ إِنِّي أَسْأَلُكَ رِضَاكَ وَٱلْجَنَّةَ ، وَأَعُوذُ بِكَ مِنْ سَخَطِكَ وَٱلنَّارِ . أَللَّهُمَّ إِنِّي أَعُوذُ بِكَ مِنْ فِتْنَةِ ٱلْقَبْرِ وَأَعُوذُ بِكَ مِنْ فِتْنَةِ ٱلْمَحْيَا وَٱلْمَمَاتِ) .

الشوط الرابع

وفي خلال الشوط الرابع يتلو المطوف ويردد اتباعه خلفه :

(أَللَّهُمَّ ٱجْعَلْهُ حَجًّا مَبْرُوراً وَسَعْياً مَشْكُوراً وَذَنْباً مَغْفُوراً وَعَمَلاً صَالِحاً مَقْبُولاً وَتِجَارَةً لَنْ تَبُورَ ، يَا عَالِمَ مَا في ٱلصُّدُورِ ، أَخْرِجْنِي يَا أَللَّهُ مِنَ ٱلظُّلُمَاتِ إِلَى ٱلنُّورِ . أَللَّهُمَّ إِنِّي أَسْأَلُكَ مُوجِبَاتِ رَحْمَتِكَ وَعَزَائِمَ مَغْفِرَتِكَ وَٱلسَّلَامَةَ مِنْ كُلِّ إِثْمٍ وَٱلْغَنِيمَةَ مِنْ كُلِّ بِرٍّ وَٱلْفَوْزَ بِٱلْجَنَّةِ وَٱلنَّجَاةَ مِنَ ٱلنَّارِ . رَبِّ قَنِّعْنِي بِمَا رَزَقْتَنِي وَبَارِكْ لِي فِيمَا أَعْطَيْتَنِي وَأَخْلِفْ عَلَيَّ كُلَّ غَائِبَةٍ لِي مِنْكَ بِخَيْرٍ) .

الشوط الخامس

وفي خلال الشوط الخامس يقرأ المطوف ويردد اتباعه وراءه :

(اَللَّهُمَّ أَظِلَّني تَحْتَ ظِلِّ عَرْشِكَ يَوْمَ لا ظِلَّ إِلّا ظِلُّكَ وَلا
باقِيَ إِلّا وَجْهُكَ ، وَاَسْقِني مِنْ حَوْضِ نَبِيِّكَ سَيِّدِنا مُحَمَّدٍ صَلَّى اَللَّهُ
عَلَيْهِ وَسَلَّمَ شُرْبَةً هَنِيئَةً مَرِيئَةً لا نَظْمَأُ بَعْدَها أَبَداً . اَللَّهُمَّ إِنِّي
أَسْأَلُكَ مِنْ خَيْرِ ما سَأَلَكَ مِنْهُ نَبِيُّكَ سَيِّدُنا مُحَمَّدٌ صَلَّى اَللَّهُ عَلَيْهِ
وَسَلَّمَ . وَأَعُوذُ بِكَ مِنْ شَرِّ ما اَسْتَعاذَكَ مِنْهُ نَبِيُّكَ سَيِّدُنا مُحَمَّدٌ
صَلَّى اَللَّهُ عَلَيْهِ وَسَلَّمَ . اَللَّهُمَّ إِنِّي أَسْأَلُكَ اَلْجَنَّةَ وَنَعيمَها وَما
يُقَرِّبُني إِلَيْها مِنْ قَوْلٍ أَوْ فِعْلٍ أَوْ عَمَلٍ ، وَأَعُوذُ بِكَ مِنَ اَلنّارِ
وَما يُقَرِّبُني إِلَيْها مِنْ قَوْلٍ أَوْ فِعْلٍ أَوْ عَمَلٍ) .

الشوط السادس

وفي الشوط السادس يقرأ المطوف ويردد اتباعه :

(اَللَّهُمَّ إِنَّ لَكَ عَلَيَّ حُقوقاً كَثيرَةً فيما بَيْني وَبَيْنَكَ ،
وَحُقوقاً كَثيرَةً فيما بَيْني وَبَيْنَ خَلْقِكَ ، اَللَّهُمَّ ما كانَ لَكَ مِنْها
فَاَغْفِرْهُ ، وَما كانَ لِخَلْقِكَ فَتَحَمَّلْهُ عَنِّي وَأَغْنِني بِحَلالِكَ عَنْ
حَرامِكَ ، وَبِطاعَتِكَ عَنْ مَعْصِيَتِكَ ، وَبِفَضْلِكَ عَمَّنْ سِواكَ ،
يا واسِعَ اَلْمَغْفِرَةِ ؛ اَللَّهُمَّ إِنَّ بَيْتَكَ عَظيمٌ وَوَجْهَكَ كَريمٌ
وَأَنْتَ يا اَللَّهُ حَليمٌ كَريمٌ عَظيمٌ ، تُحِبُّ اَلْعَفْوَ ، فَاَعْفُ عَنِّي).

الشوط السابع

وفي خلال الشوط السابع وهـــو آخر طواف حول الكعبة يقرأ المطوف ويردد اتباعه وراءه :

> (أَللّٰهُمَّ إِنِّي أَسْأَلُكَ إِيمَاناً كَامِلاً وَيَقِيناً صَادِقاً وَرِزْقاً وَاسِعاً
> وَقَلْباً خَاشِعاً وَلِسَاناً ذَاكِراً وَحَلالاً طَيِّباً وَتَوْبَةً نَصُوحاً وَتَوْبَةً
> قَبْلَ أَلْمَوْتِ وَرَاحَةً عِنْدَ أَلْمَوْتِ وَمَغْفِرَةً وَرَحْمَةً بَعْـــدَ أَلْمَوْتِ
> وَالْعَفْوَ عِنْدَ أَلْحِسَابِ وَالْفَوْزَ بِأَلْجَنَّةِ وَالنَّجَاةَ مِنَ أَلنَّارِ بِرَحْمَتِكَ
> يَا عَزِيزُ يَا غَفَّارُ ، رَبِّ زِدْنِي عِلْماً وَأَلْحِقْنِي بِالصَّالِحِين) .

وكل حاج لا يستطيع ان يتابع ألفاظ المطوف او يعجز عـن السماع بسبب الضجيج او البعد عنه من شدة الزحام ، او الذي لا يستطيع ان يستعيد السطور على هذه الصفحات يستطيع بكل اطمئنان ان يستعيض عنها بأي دعاء ، وحمد الله بأي لغة كانت ، فهناك عدة اجناس من البشر وعدة لغات ولكن هناك رب واحد يعرف ما تخفي الصدور ومعاني جميع اللغات .

المستجار (الملتزم)

وعلى الحجاج الذين اكملوا الطواف سبع مرات ان ينفصلوا عن اولئك الذين لا يزالون مشغولين فيه ، لكي يذهبوا الى جدار الكعبة في محل المستجار ، بين ابواب الذهب والفضة العالية وبين الحجر الاسود ، فاذا لم يكن هناك محل للوقوف جنب الجدار فللحاج ان يواجه المستجار عن قرب كأن يقف على حدود الطائفين ، ويكفي ان يقف قرب مقـام ابراهيم ، الذي يقع مقابل عتبة الكعبة المقدسة العالية .

ويرفع الحاج في مواجهة البيت العتيق وهو في ظله او قريب منه ، كلتي

يديه ويبسط راحتيه ويلمس الجدار المقدس او يقبض على الكسوة السندسية ، أو يتعلق بالعتبة المقدسة ، او من مسافة متوسطة ببسط ذراعيه كمن يستلم ويقول :

(أَللَّهُمَّ يَا رَبَّ ٱلْبَيْتِ ٱلْعَتِيقِ أَعْتِقْ رِقَابَنَا وَرِقَابَ آبَائِنَا وَأُمَّهَاتِنَا وَإِخْوَانِنَا وَأَوْلَادِنَا مِنَ ٱلنَّارِ ، يَا ذَا ٱلْجُودِ وَٱلْكَرَمِ وَٱلْفَضْلِ وَٱلْمَنِّ وَٱلْعَطَاءِ وَٱلْإِحْسَانِ . أَللَّهُمَّ أَحْسِنْ عَاقِبَتَنَا فِي ٱلْأُمُورِ كُلِّهَا ، وَأَجِرْنَا مِنْ خِزْيِ ٱلدُّنْيَا وَعَذَابِ ٱلْآخِرَةِ . أَللَّهُمَّ إِنِّي عَبْدُكَ وَٱبْنُ (أَو ٱبْنَةُ) عَبْدِكَ . وَأَقِفُ تَحْتَ بَابِكَ . مُلْتَزِمٌ بِأَعْتَابِكَ . مُتَذَلِّلٌ بَيْنَ يَدَيْكَ أَرْجُو رَحْمَتَكَ . وَأَخْشَى عَذَابَكَ . يَا قَدِيمَ ٱلْإِحْسَانِ. أَللَّهُمَّ إِنِّي أَسْأَلُكَ أَنْ تَرْفَعَ ذِكْرِي . وَتَضَعَ وِزْرِي . وَتُصْلِحَ أَمْرِي . وَتُطَهِّرَ قَلْبِي . وَتُنَوِّرَ لِي فِي قَبْرِي . وَتَغْفِرَ لِي ذَنْبِي . وَأَسْأَلُكَ ٱلدَّرَجَاتِ ٱلْعُلَى مِنَ ٱلْجَنَّةِ). آمِين .

او يقول :

(أَللَّهُمَّ ، ٱلْبَيْتُ بَيْتُكَ ، وَٱلْعَبْدُ عَبْدُكَ ، وَهُنَا مَكَانُ ٱلْعَائِذِ بِكَ مِنَ ٱلنَّارِ ؛ أَللَّهُمَّ مِنْ قِبَلِكَ ٱلرَّوْحُ وَٱلْفَرَجُ وَٱلْعَافِيَةُ ؛ أَللَّهُمَّ إِنَّ عَمَلِي ضَعِيفٌ فَضَاعِفْهُ لِي ، وَٱغْفِرْ لِي مَا ٱطَّلَعْتَ عَلَيْهِ مِنِّي وَخَفِيَ عَلَى خَلْقِكَ).

وبعد الانتهاء من هذا الدعاء ، على الحاج أن يصلي ركعتين ، والأفضل لإدائها ان يذهب الى مقام ابراهيم ، ويحصل على محل في داخله ، وتقع اربعة اعمدة من اعمدة الستة على اركان الحجر الذي قيل ان النبي ابراهيم وقف عليه وصلى . وقد أحيطت الآن بتشبيك مزين ، والمسافة بين العمودين القريبين

الى الطريق المقوس – الذي يمكن الوصول الى السياج المقدس بواسطة واحد منها – مفتوح لكل داخل .

والافضل ان نقرأ في الركعة الاولى بعد الفاتحة سورة الكافرين :

(بِسْمِ ٱللهِ ٱلرَّحْمٰنِ ٱلرَّحِيمِ . قُلْ يا أَيُّها ٱلْكافِرُونَ . لا أَعْبُدُ مَا تَعْبُدُونَ . وَلا أَنْتُمْ عَابِدُونَ ما أَعْبُدُ وَلا أَنا عَابِدٌ ما عَبَدْتُمْ . وَلا أَنْتُمْ عَابِدُونَ ما أَعْبُدُ . لَكُمْ دِينُكُمْ وَلِيَ دِينِ) .

وفي الركعة الثانية أُتل (سورة الاخلاص) :

(بِسْمِ ٱللهِ ٱلرَّحْمٰنِ ٱلرَّحِيمِ . قُلْ هُوَ ٱللهُ أَحَدٌ . ٱللهُ ٱلصَّمَدُ . لَمْ يَلِدْ وَلَمْ يُولَدْ وَلَمْ يَكُنْ لَهُ كُفُواً أَحَدٌ) .

واذا انتصبت قائماً فاقرأ :

(أَللّٰهُمَّ إِنَّكَ تَعْلَمُ سِرّي وَعَلانِيَتِي ، فَٱقْبَلْ مَعْذِرَتِي ، وَتَعْلَمُ حَاجَتِي فَأَعْطِنِي سُؤْلي ، وَتَعْلَمُ ما في نَفْسِي فَٱغْفِرْ لِي ذُنُوبِي . أَللّٰهُمَّ إِنِّي أَسْأَلُكَ إِيماناً يُبَاشِرُ قَلْبِي ، وَيَقِيناً صَادِقاً حَتّى أَعْلَمَ أَنَّهُ لا يُصِيبُنِي إِلّا ما كَتَبْتَ لِي ، رِضاً مِنْكَ بِما قَسَمْتَ لِي ، أَنْتَ وَلِيِّي في ٱلدُّنْيَا وَٱلآخِرَةِ ، تَوَفَّنِي مُسْلِماً وَأَلْحِقْني بِالصَّالِحِينَ . أَللّٰهُمَّ لا تَدَعْ لَنا في مَقَامِنا هذا ذَنْباً إِلّا غَفَرْتَهُ ، وَلا هَمّاً إِلّا فَرَّجْتَهُ ، وَلا حَاجَةً إِلّا قَضَيْتَها وَيَسَّرْتَها ، فَيَسِّرْ أُمُورَنا وَٱشْرَحْ صُدُورَنا وَنَوِّرْ قُلُوبَنا وَٱخْتِمْ بِالصَّالِحاتِ أَعْمَالَنا . أَللّٰهُمَّ تَوَفَّنا مُسْلِمِينَ وَأَحْيِنا مُسْلِمِينَ وَأَلْحِقْنا بِالصَّالِحِينَ ، غَيْرَ خَزَايا وَلا مَفْتُونِينَ) .

الحجر

يزور أولئك الذين يرغبون في اداء الصلاة قرب الكعبة ، ذلك السياج الذي يشبه نصف الدائرة ، والذي يقع بين الركن العراقي والركن الشامي ويسمى الحجر ، وهو قرب جدار الكعبة وقطع الصخر الكبيرة الموضوعة على الارض والتي قيل انها تشير الى قبري هاجر واسماعيل ، ويقال ان النبي محمداً صلى الله عليه وسلم رقد هنا ليلة سفرته (الاعجازية) المعراج . فصلِّ ركعتين واقرأ ما شئت من الأذكار والأدعية كيفما كان نوعها سواء من الادعية المأثورة او ما يختلج ببالك . ان جميع الادعية حسنة ، وما من دعاء لاحسن فيه ، فإن ذكر الله حسن على كل حال . والمهم ما في القلب لا الكلمات ، وما لا يجري على اللسان يعلمه الله .

(واللهُ عَليمٌ بِذاتِ الصُّدُور) .

ادع لأسلافنا وادع لأخلافنـا ، وادع لمن تحبهم ، ادع جهرة لأولئك الذين يتكتمون في صلاتهم ، ادع للمسلمين الذين هم في اسر العبودية . وما هو طواف الزيارة . وهناك طوافان آخران قبل انتهاء الحج والعودة الى الوطن من مكة . والطواف الثاني – وهو طواف الافاضة – بعد العودة ، من عرفات ، والثالث من طواف الوداع . اما الحجاج الذين يعتمرون بعد الحج فعليهم ان يطوفوا طوافاً آخر للعمرة قبل طواف الوداع .

« (وفي فقه أهـل البيت يجب على المتمتع الطواف ثلاثاً ، الاول طواف العمرة سبعة أشواط ، والثاني طواف الافاضة للحج كذلك ، وهذان الطوافان ركنان تفسد العمرة بترك طوافها والحج بترك طوافه ، والطواف الثالث طواف النساء ، وليس بركن بل هو واجب ؛ ومن تركه تحرم عليه النساء حق يقضيه هو او نائبه ، ويستحب له الطواف الرابع وهو طواف الوداع بعد الحج) » .

والآن قبل ان تغادر الكعبة المقدسة ، اذهب الى بـئر زمزم واشرب من مائها واستعد للعناء الذي يتلو ذلك ، فإن ماء هذه البئر ، بالرغم من الاعماق التي تأتي دلاء القائم على البئر منها ، مج وفاتر نوعاً ما . وهو الذي اطفأ عطش هاجر واسماعيل ، وكشف عنه الملك جبرائيل عندما بقوا في هذه الصحراء التي تشبه الأتون قبل أن توجد مكة .

ان الطين الذي جمع بين صخور الكعبة قد خلط من ماء هـــذه البئر .

ومحمد الطفل ، ومحمد الرجل ، ومحمد النبي صلى الله عليه وسلم ، شرب من هذا الماء القديم . فقد كان من عادته ان يشرب من زمزم في ختام طوافه وهو يعد نفسه للسعي . « (ويستحب في السعي بعــد الفراغ من ركعتي الطواف وارادة الخروج الى الصفا « تقبيل الحجر واستلامــه » ، فان لم يتمكن فالاشارة اليه « والاستقاء بنفسه » من زمزم دلواً أو دلوين وليشرب منه وليصب على ظهره وبطنه قائلاً وهو مستقبل الكعبة :

(أَللّٰهُمَّ أَجْعَلْهُ عِلْماً نَافِعاً وَرِزْقاً وَاسِعاً وَشِفَاءً مِنْ كُلِّ دَاءٍ وَسَقَمٍ ، يَا أَرْحَمَ ٱلرَّاحِمِين) .

وليكن ذلك من الدلو الذي بحــذاء الحجر بل الأولى استلام الحجر قبــل الشرب وبعده عند خروجه الى الصفا ، بل يستحب له اتيان زمزم والتطلع فيها والاستقـــاء منها بالدلو المزبور والشرب والصب على بعض جسده وان لم يرد السعي) » .

وقل عندما تفارق البيت الحرام من باب الصفا :

« إِنَّ ٱلصَّفَا وَٱلْمَرْوَةَ مِنْ شَعَائِرِ ٱللّٰهِ فَمَنْ حَجَّ ٱلْبَيْتَ أَوِ ٱعْتَمَرَ فَلَا جُنَاحَ عَلَيْهِ أَنْ يَطَّوَّفَ بِهِما . وَمَنْ تَطَوَّعَ خَيْراً فَإِنَّ ٱللّٰهَ شَاكِرٌ عَلِيم » . (سورة البقرة ، ١٥٨)

وعلى الحجاج ان يسعوا بعد الانتهاء من الطواف – بضمن ذلــك ان يدعوا بما شاؤوا من الأدعية والتسبيحات الآنية التي تصدر من قلوبهم لأن ذلك جزء من سنن الطواف ، وان الوقت المخصص لهذه الأدعية لم يشرع عبثاً وكذلك شرب الماء .

السعي بين الصفا والمروة

لقد قيل في قصة قديمة نسي واضعها ولا يعرف قائلها انه بعد ان ترك ابراهيم بلاد الكلدان وراء ظهره ، وهي ارض آبائه واجداده ، ذهب في رحلة الى مصر ،

واخذ معه زوجته سارة .

وقد قيـل ان سارة كانت من الجمال فوق كل وصف فوصلت انبـاء جمال هذه المرأة الأجنبيـة الى القصر . وكان الفرعون « سلاطيس » جباراً في أرضه يأخذ كل ما يراه ويطمع فيـه ، ولم يجرأ أحد أن يرده عن زوجتـه ، ولا كانت زوجة احد بمنجى منه . بل كانت جميلات مصر معدودات من عبيده ، وهكذا جيء بزوجة ابراهيم امام هـذا الفرعون ، وذلك لأن « سلاطيس » انصت للشائعات فأراد ان يرى المرأة الاجنبية . وقد قيل انه وجد مـا رأى دون ما سمع ، ولما تركت سارة لوحدها مع هذا الجبار ورأت نظرة الاثم في عينيه ، أخذت تتوسل اليه ، وترجو ان تعاد الى زوجها . ولكن « سلاطيس » لم يكن يسمع ما تقول بل كان يحاول ان يغتصب زوجة ابراهيم .

ولما لم تكن المرأة قـادرة على ان تمنع المصري عن جسدها ، ركعت تصلي ورجت منه ان يتركها الى ان تنتهي من صلاتها . فرضي « سلاطيس » وهو بين ساخط ومغتبط من ذلك الاسلوب الذي لجأت اليه في يأسها ، لكي تحول دون أن يستولي عليها أو ان تؤخر ذلك الاستيلاء .

ولكنه بعد ذلك ، وقد ضجر فجأة ، واخذه جمال سارة حتى في صلاتها ، تقرب من زوجة ابراهيم وهو يريد أن يستولي عليها وهي تصلي ــ فأصابه ضعف تشنجي تركه في حالة نزع موقت . وحاول ثلاث مرات أن يمتلكها ــ فخر منهاراً في المرات الثلاث ، وبعد ذلك تراجع المصري مرعوباً وقد أدرك أن هذه المرأة قد اصبحت في رعاية سماوية .

وهناك رواية اخرى لهذه الأسطورة تقول ان ابراهيم كان في غرفة اخرى مجاورة عند محاولة هتك زوجته . فأخذ الجـدار المبني بالآجر الذي يفصل بين الغرفتين يشف قليلا قليلا امام عيني ابراهيم حتى رأى هو ــ ولكن لم يره أحد ــ ما كان يجري هناك .

وعندما اطلق الفرعون سارة لكي تعود الى زوجهـا اعطاها إحدى جواريه كهدية للذكرى .

فسارع ابراهيم بالخروج من مصر وقد اخذ معه زوجته وجاريتها الى كنعان حيث استقروا هناك .

ولم تكن سارة قد حملت باسحاق بعد ، وكانت تتحرق الى ان تحقق ما كان

يصبو ابراهيم اليه ، فأخـذت تظن انها اصبحت عاقرا ، وان زوجها يريد ان يكون له ولد لأنه طالما دعا الله ان يرزقه ولداً فقدمت اليه جاريتها هاجر .

ودعا ابراهيم ربه فاستجاب الله له هذه المرة وحملت هاجر ولداً ذكراً اسموه اسماعيل .

وفي البداية كانت سارة تحب ابن زوجها من جاريتها الجميلة ، ولكنها عندما رأت تعلق ابراهيم به وتدليلـه لذلك الطفل ، ورقته في معاملة هاجر ادركتها الغيرة وظلت غيرتها تتزايد حتى سممت حياتها فأصبحت لا تطاق ـ وأخذت تكره الطفل وامه الجارية .

وبعد ان اصابها هذا التغير طلبت الى ابراهيم أن يأخذ هاجر والطفـل الى الصحراء ويتركها هناك .

وطلب ابراهيم هداية ربه ، وبعد وقت ذهب مع هاجر ـ التي اصبحت هي الاخرى حياتها لا تطاق بسبب سارة ـ ذهب جنوباً من كنعان الى ان وصل الى حيث تقع مكة الآن . وهنا في الموقع الذي سمي بوادي العطش ترك الأم وطفلها ، وترك معها زاداً واستدار يريد اهلـه . وعندما ترك ابراهيم الوادي القاحل والقى آخر نظرة على الاثنين ركضت هاجر وراءه وهي تدعوه . وجاءت اليه دامعة العين تسأله هل سيتركها حقاً مع الطفل في هذه الصحراء المحلة ؟ فهز برأسه ، وقد عرف بحكمته النبوية أن شراً لا يمكن أن يصل الاثنين في هذا الموقع . وهذه هي الارض التي قامت عليها الكعبة في الأصل قبل الطوفان .

(ويقول بعض المؤرخين انه كان هناك في زمن ابراهيم خرائب تـدل على ان الكعبة كانت قبل الطوفان ، وانـه اشار الى هذا عندما دعا بعد ترك (وادي العطش) وهاجر وابنها في دعائه التالي :

« رَبَّنَا إِنِّي أَسْكَنتُ مِنْ ذُرِّيَّتِي بِوَادٍ غَيْرِ ذِي زَرْعٍ عِنْـدَ بَيْتِكَ ٱلْمُحَرَّمِ ، رَبَّنَا لِيُقِيمُوا ٱلصَّلَاةَ فَٱجْعَلْ أَفْئِدَةً مِنَ ٱلنَّاسِ تَهْوِي إِلَيْهِمْ وَٱرْزُقْهُم مِّنَ ٱلثَّمَرَاتِ لَعَلَّهُمْ يَشْكُرُونَ » .

« سورة ابراهيم ، ٣٧ »

وأصاب الرعب هاجر بعد أن ظلت لوحدها خوفاً على حياة ابنها . فتركت

الطفل قرب محل الكعبة المقدسة اليوم وذهبت تفتش عن الماء ، وكانت هنـاك ربوة صغيرة فصعدتها وناشدت الله ان يمنحها عونه . وهذه الربوة هي الصفا .

ونظرت الى الشمال فرأت شيئًا بدا لها كأنه بحـيرة . فنزلت من الصفا راكضة وماشية ، مسرعة نحو البحيرة . ثم صعدت تلًا منخفضًا آخر وهي تبحث عن الماء المختفي ، وكان العلو الذي تقف عليه هو المروة .

ثم أرجعت طرفها الى حيث أتت فرأت بحيرة صغيرة اخرى ، فتركت كرة ثانية وهي تركض تارة وتمشي اخرى ، وعادت الى الصفا . وفعلت ذلك وهي مرعوبة سبع مرات بين التلين في ذلك الحر الذي لا يطاق وفي ذلك السراب .

وفي المرة السابعة نظرت هاجر يائسة نحو البقعة التي تركت فيها ابنها فرأت شخصًا واقفًا بجانب الطفل ، فأسرعت نحو الرجل الغريب ، ثم ابطـأت في سيرها لأنها عندما تقربت منه عرفت فيه الملك جبرائيل ، فضرب جبرائيـل الارض وانبثق الماء ، وكان ذلك بداية بئر زمزم .

وهناك رواية اخرى تقول إن هاجر بعد ان تغلب عليهـا القلق ، نظرت الى حيث وضعت طفلها فرأت الماء ينبثق من الارض ويسيل في كل الاتجاهات . فلما عادت الى جانب اسماعيل الطفل وجدت ان الماء انبثق من حفرة احدثتها قدم الطفل . فلما رأت السائل الثمين يتدفق من الرمال المحيطة صاحت : « زومي يا مباركة »! فتكونت بركة مـاء ، وكان ذلك بداية زمزم . فسكنت هاجر بجانب هذه البركة المقدسة وهي تعني بولدهـا وتثق بالله الذي اثار فيها الخوف والعطش ، وطمأنها من بعد ذلك .

ثم حدث بعد ذلك ان قبيلة من قبائل اليمن مرت فوجدت هاجر والصغير اسماعيل والبئر حيث لم يكن ماء من قبل ، فوقفوا وطلبوا المـاء ، وضربوا الخيام قرب البركة .

ويقول بعض المحدثين ان ابراهيم كان يذهب مرة في العام الى حيث وادي العطش ليرى ان عائلته على ما يرام ، ولكنه لا يترجل قط ، لأنه أقسم لسارة ان لا يترك ظهر جمله خلال زياراته لهاجر وابنها .

ويقول غيرهم ان سنين عديدة مرت ، وان اسمـاعيل كبر وتزوج امرأة من القبيلة التي سكنت قرب بئر زمزم قبل أن يعود النبي ابراهيم الى وادي العطش

على أمل أن يرى أثراً للاثنين اللذين تركها الى رحمة ربه .

وكانت هاجر قد ماتت وذهب اسماعيل للصيد . ولم يكن الوادي قابلا
للزراعة ، وكان سكانه يعيشون على القنص . وبدون ان يكشف الشيخ عـن
شخصيته اخذ يفتش عن زوجة ابنه . فشكت المرأة من حياتها مع زوجهـا
الصياد ، ولم تقدم للغريب قرى . فعاد ابراهيم وقد ترك مع المرأة الشابة خـبراً
مفاده ان عتبتهم لم تكن حسنة .

وعندما عاد اسماعيل من الصيد وسمع قصة الشيخ وكلماته ادرك ان أباه
هو الذي جاء وعـــاد مرة اخرى ، وفهم مغزى رسالته فترك زوجته واخذ
اخرى ، وحدث ذلك مرة اخرى في السنة التالية . ثم قام النبي ابراهيم برحلة
متعبة من ارض كنعان جاء للمرة الثالثة وسأل أيضاً عن ابنه الذي كان غائباً
فاستقبلته زوجته ، ودعته الى دخول الدار ، واعتذرت اليه عن فقرهما ، ولكنها
كانت ملأى بالفخر باسماعيل .

وعندما رفض ابراهيم ان يترجل ، وبقي على ظهر جمله دون ان يدخل دار
ابنه الذي تركه الا بعد ان سمع ترحيب ابنه من فمه ، جاءته الزوجة الشابـة
باللحم والخبز واللبن . وقبل ان يذهب النبي ابراهيم تحدث الى زوجة ابنه وقال
لها أن تخبر زوجها ان عتبته حسنة ، وان عليه ان يحملها ثابتة . وعندمـا سمع
اسماعيل هذه الكلمات أدرك مغزاها وأكرم زوجها .

وبعد ذلك ، في ارض كنعان ، تلقى النبي ابراهيم الأمر الإلهي الذي أرسله
مرة اخرى الى الوادي القاحل حيث يعيش ابنه الصياد ، وحيث عليه أن يبني
محلا للعبادة ، ويعيد بناء الكعبة التي ذهبت منذ زمن نوح والطوفان . وأطاع
ابراهيم الأمر فرحاً . واشتغل الاب والابن جنباً الى جنب ، ابراهيم واسماعيل
في الشمس المحرقة واقاما الكعبة . وعندما انتهيا صعد ابراهيم الى القمة ودعـا
جميع البشر الى العبادة .

والسعي هو الفريضة التي يؤديها الحجاج في الذهاب والغدو بين الصفا والمروة
سبع مرات ، كما فعلت هاجر في تفتيشها عن الماء لطفلها . وقد تلقى النبي ابراهيم
من الله ذلك لكي يأمر به الناس كافة :

« وَإِذْ بَوَّأْنَا لِإِبْرَاهِيمَ مَكَانَ ٱلْبَيْتِ أَنْ لَا تُشْرِكْ بِي شَيْئًا وَطَهِّرْ بَيْتِيَ لِلطَّائِفِينَ وَٱلْقَائِمِينَ وَٱلرُّكَّعِ ٱلسُّجُودِ . وَأَذِّنْ فِي ٱلنَّاسِ بِٱلْحَجِّ يَأْتُوكَ رِجَالًا وَعَلَى كُلِّ ضَامِرٍ يَأْتِينَ مِنْ كُلِّ فَجٍّ عَمِيقٍ لِيَشْهَدُوا مَنَافِعَ لَهُمْ وَيَذْكُرُوا ٱسْمَ ٱللَّهِ فِي أَيَّامٍ مَعْلُومَاتٍ عَلَى مَا رَزَقَهُمْ مِنْ بَهِيمَةِ ٱلْأَنْعَامِ . فَكُلُوا مِنْهَا وَأَطْعِمُوا ٱلْبَائِسَ ٱلْفَقِيرَ ، ثُمَّ لْيَقْضُوا تَفَثَهُمْ وَلْيُوفُوا نُذُورَهُمْ وَلْيَطَّوَّفُوا بِٱلْبَيْتِ ٱلْعَتِيقِ . » (سورة الحج ، ٢٦ - ٢٩)

ألبيت العتيق

وفي ايام الجاهلية ، بعد النبي ابراهيم بزمن طويل ، وضعت الأصنام في كل من الصفا والمروة ، فكان على الاول صنم ذكر وعلى الثاني صنم انثى قيل انها قد مسخا حجرين يجرم الزنا . وكان الحجاج عند تأديتهم السعي يلمسون الصنم الذكر في بداية الفريضة ، ثم يذهبون الى المروة ويلمسون الصنم المؤنث ويكررون ذلك سبع مرات .

وبعد ان سقطت مكة في يد قوات النبي محمد ﷺ المسلمة أزيلت الأصنام من المدينة وبعثرت ، غير انه قام بعد ذلك جدال بين اتباع محمد ، فقد قالت فئة انه ما دام السعي من طقوس الجاهلية فيجب الكف عنه . اما المعارضون فإنهم كانوا يرون أن السعي قد أخذه الكفار عن الأوائل من المؤمنين بابراهيم وآدم . وقد زال بعد ان نزلت الآية :

« إِنَّ ٱلصَّفَا وَٱلْمَرْوَةَ مِنْ شَعَائِرِ ٱللَّهِ فَمَنْ حَجَّ ٱلْبَيْتَ أَوِ ٱعْتَمَرَ فَلَا جُنَاحَ عَلَيْهِ أَنْ يَطَّوَّفَ بِهِمَا ، وَمَنْ تَطَوَّعَ خَيْرًا فَإِنَّ ٱللَّهَ شَاكِرٌ عَلِيمٌ . » (سورة البقرة ، ١٥٨)

التي تتلى من قِبَل كل حـاج عندمـا يخرج من البيت الحرام في طريقه الى الصفا .

السعي بين الصفا والمروة

على الحجاج الذكور الذين ينتهون من الطواف في المسجد المقدس ان يذهبوا الى قمة الصفا . وليس على النساء الحاجات أن يصعدن الى القمة اذا مـا اشتد الازدحام على الدرجات ، بل يبدأن سعيهن من الأسفل .

وكما هو الحـال في الطواف ، فان اولئك الذين لا يستطيعون السعي على اقدامهم ان يستأجروا محفـة . وبخلاف الطواف ، فان اية واسطة نقل يمكن استخدامها . ولكن يجب ان لا يغيب عنك ان الذين يستطيعون بدنياً من كلا الجنسين أن يقوموا بالسعي ويستخدمون واسطة نقل بين الصفا والمروة للتهرب من الفروض ومناسك الحج انما يجعلون من هذه الفريضة المقدسة مسخرة .

ان الدين ليس رسماً من الرسوم ، ولا الإيمان مجرد كلمات تلفظ . والعقيدة لا يمكن ان تقاس بعدد الركعات يصليها المسلم ، ولا بالوسم في الجبهـة . ولا يكفي التظاهر في التقديس ، والحج ليس دليلا . ان الشعائر تصبح بلا معنى اذا لم يكن هناك ادراك لها ، والصلاة لا تكون صحيحة الا عندمـا تنبثق من القلب الى الفم ، ولا قيمة للسجود اذا لم يكن هناك خشوع حقيقي . والحج لا يبلغ مرحلته الاخيرة '. الغاية منه الا اذا كانت هناك اخوة ومحبة بين المسلمين .

نية السعي

يستحب للحاج ان يتوجه الى الكعبة المقدسة ويقول :

« أَللّهُمَّ إِنِّي أُرِيدُ أَنْ أَسْعَى بَيْنَ ٱلصَّفَا وَٱلْمَرْوَةِ سَبْعَةَ أَشْوَاطٍ سَعْيَ ٱلْحَجِّ (أَوِ ٱلْعُمْرَةِ) لِلّهِ تَعَالَى عَزَّ وَجَلَّ » .

او يقول : (أَسْعَى بَيْنَ الصَّفا وَالمَروَةِ سَبْعَةَ أَشْوَاطٍ لِعُمْرَةِ التَّمَتُّعِ إِلَى حَجِّ الإِسْلَامِ لِوُجُوبِهِ قُرْبَةً إِلَى اللهِ تعالى)» . فاذا كان نائباً عن

احد قال لوجوبه نيابة عن (فلان) الخ ؛ فإن كان سعيه للحج قال : لحج التمتع؛ بدل قوله : لعمرة التمتع ؛ ويستحب التلفظ بالنية) .

وعليه ان يصرح عما اذا كان هذا السعي للعمرة او للحج ، او للعمرة والحج معاً كما نوى عند الاحرام وقبل طواف القدوم (طواف الزيارة) . ويفعل كما يفعل الحجاج حوله ، او يتبع مطوفه ، فيرفع كلتا يديه عالياً كأنه يريـد ان يصل الى الكعبة وهو يقول :

« أَللّهُ أَكْبَرُ اللّهُ أَكْبَرُ اللّهُ أَكْبَرُ وَلِلّهِ أَلْحَمْدُ » .

وعندما ينزل من الصفا يذهب نحو المروة ، وهي على بعـد حوالي (٤٠٥) أمتار ، ويتبع الطريق المقدس (المسعى) خلال مكة والبيت الحرام . والاعمدة الخضراء تشير الى حدود المنطقة ؛ حيث ينبغي على اولئك الذين يؤدون فريضـة السعي ان يهرولوا ، مسافة حوالي اربعين متراً .

ومن المحتمل ان يكون الحر بالغاً اقصاه . وفي أغلب اوقات الحج يكون هناك غبار على جميع انحاء مكة ، واشده فوق (المسعى) ؛ فتكون هناك جماهير عظيمة تتدافع في اتجاهات مختلفة بلا هوادة ، يريد كل منهم ان يشق طريقه في صفوف الآخرين بالقوة . ويزحف بعض الاعراب في جماعات مشتبكي الاذرع يكتسحون من يكون امامهم من الآخرين ؛ وهناك الآلاف المؤلفة من غير نظام او ترتيب ، الى ان يبلغوا احد التلين المقدسين ، حتى يبلغ (السعي) في الليل والنهـار شكل موقعة حربية من مواقع ما قبل حروب قرطاجنة ، في عدد لا يحصى من المقاتلين المرتدين ثياباً بيضاء يتماوجون في معركة شديـدة الغبـار والحر ، ويصبح السعي اشبه الى الخصام منه الى عبادة دينية .

وفي هذا ايضاً اشارة وانذار للمسلمين لكي يبتعدوا عن الماضي ويتركوا الفردية البدائية التي اخذت في نهاية العصور الوسطى تضعف الامم الاسلامية وأدت في الاخير الى سقوطها .

سيكون سلوك الحجاج في السعي في المستقبل قياساً متيناً على تقدم شعبنا نحو احترام النظام الاجتماعي ، وتكريس الجهود للصالح العام دون صالح الفرد ، او العائلة ، او القبيلة ، أو أية أمة بفردها .

وعندما يصبح السعي منظماً مرة اخرى بالرقابة الحكيمة ــ ويمكن ان يتم ذلك في ساعة واحدة ، أو يصبح كذلك من تلقاء ذاته خلال ربع قرن ، فإما اذا

تلقى جميع المصلين الفرصة الثقافية الكافية — سيكون ذلك علامة على ان الاسلام اصبح على وشك النهوض لكي يكون نوراً للعالم . وسوف ترجف الارض تحت اقدام الكفّار والظالمين .

ابتعد عن الزحام وسيل البشر المتد ، وكن على الطرف الخارجي من الطريق المقدس . وسبّح باسم الله او تابع صلوات المطوّف ؛ واذا تعذر عليك ذلك ، اتل اسماء الله أو اي دعاء وتسبيح بأية لغة كانت .

واذا ما وصلت درجات المروة وصعدتها ، فاتجه نحو الكعبة واجعل ذراعك مرة اخرى على شكل الوصل والمس واقرأ مرة أخرى .

دعاء السعي الاول

الله أكبرُ الله أكبرُ الله أكبرُ .

« اللهُ أكبرُ كبيراً وَالحمدُ للهِ كثيراً وَسُبحانَ اللهِ العظيمِ وَبحَمدِهِ الكَريمِ بُكرَةً وَأصيلاً ، وَمِنَ اللّيلِ فَأسجُدْ لَهُ وَسبّحْهُ لَيْلاً طويلاً ، لَا إلهَ إلّا اللهُ وَحدَه ، أنجَزَ وَعدَه ، وَنَصَرَ عَبدَه ، وَهزَمَ الأحزابَ وَحدَه ، لَا شيءَ قَبلَهُ وَلَا بَعدَه ، يُحي ويُميتُ وَهوَ حيٌّ دائمٌ لَا يَموتُ وَلَا يَفوتُ أبداً ؛ بِيَدِهِ الخَيْرُ وَإلَيْهِ المصيرُ وَهوَ عَلَى كُلِّ شَيءٍ قَديرٍ .

(رَبِّ اغفِرْ وَارحَم وَاعفُ وَتَكرَّمْ وَتَجاوَزْ عَمّا تَعْلَمُ ؛ إنّكَ تَعلَمُ ما لا نَعلَمُ ، إنّكَ أنتَ اللهُ الأعزُّ الأكرَم) .

رَبّنا نَجّنا مِنَ النّارِ سالِمينَ غانِمينَ فَرِحينَ مُستَبشِرينَ مَعَ عِبادِكَ الصّالِحينَ ، وَحَسُنَ أولئكَ رَفيقاً ، ذلكَ الفَضلُ مِنَ اللهِ ، وَكَفى بِاللهِ عَليماً ؛ لَا إلهَ إلّا اللهُ حَقّاً حَقّاً ، لَا إلهَ إلّا اللهُ

تَعَبُّداً وَرِقًّا ، لَا إِلهَ إِلَّا اللهُ وَلَا نَعْبُدُ إِلَّا إِيَّاهُ ، مُخْلِصِينَ لَهُ الدِّينَ وَلَوْ كَرِهَ الْكَافِرُونَ .

(إِنَّ الصَّفَا وَالْمَرْوَةَ مِنْ شَعَائِرِ اللهِ ، فَمَنْ حَجَّ الْبَيْتَ أَوِ اعْتَمَرَ فَلَا جُنَاحَ عَلَيْهِ أَنْ يَطَّوَّفَ بِهِمَا وَمَنْ تَطَوَّعَ خَيْراً فَإِنَّ اللهَ شَاكِرٌ عَلِيمٌ) .

دعاء السعي الثاني

اللهُ أَكْبَرُ اللهُ أَكْبَرُ اللهُ أَكْبَرُ وَلِلهِ الْحَمْدُ ؛ لَا إِلهَ إِلَّا اللهُ الْوَاحِدُ الْفَرْدُ الصَّمَدُ الَّذِي لَمْ يَتَّخِذْ صَاحِبَةً وَلَا وَلَداً ، وَلَمْ يَكُنْ لَهُ شَرِيكٌ فِي الْمُلْكِ وَلَمْ يَكُنْ لَهُ وَلِيٌّ مِنَ الذُّلِّ وَكَبِّرْهُ تَكْبِيراً . اللَّهُمَّ إِنَّكَ قُلْتَ فِي كِتَابِكَ الْمُنْزَلِ ادْعُونِي أَسْتَجِبْ لَكُمْ ، دَعَوْنَاكَ رَبَّنَا فَاغْفِرْ لَنَا كَمَا أَمَرْتَنَا ، إِنَّكَ لَا تُخْلِفُ الْمِيعَادَ . رَبَّنَا إِنَّنَا سَمِعْنَا مُنَادِياً يُنَادِي لِلْإِيمَانِ أَنْ آمِنُوا بِرَبِّكُمْ فَآمَنَّا ؛ رَبَّنَا فَاغْفِرْ لَنَا ذُنُوبَنَا وَكَفِّرْ عَنَّا سَيِّئَاتِنَا وَتَوَفَّنَا مَعَ الْأَبْرَارِ . رَبَّنَا وَآتِنَا مَا وَعَدْتَنَا عَلَى رُسُلِكَ وَلَا تُخْزِنَا يَوْمَ الْقِيَامَةِ ، إِنَّكَ لَا تُخْلِفُ الْمِيعَادَ ، رَبَّنَا عَلَيْكَ تَوَكَّلْنَا وَإِلَيْكَ أَنَبْنَا وَإِلَيْكَ الْمَصِيرُ ، رَبَّنَا اغْفِرْ لَنَا وَلِإِخْوَانِنَا الَّذِينَ سَبَقُونَا بِالْإِيمَانِ ، وَلَا تَجْعَلْ فِي قُلُوبِنَا غِلًّا لِلَّذِينَ آمَنُوا ، رَبَّنَا إِنَّكَ رَؤُوفٌ رَحِيمٌ .

(رَبِّ اغْفِرْ وَارْحَمْ وَاعْفُ وَتَكَرَّمْ وَتَجَاوَزْ عَمَّا تَعْلَمُ ، إِنَّكَ تَعْلَمُ مَا لَا نَعْلَمُ ، إِنَّكَ أَنْتَ اللهُ الْأَعَزُّ الْأَكْرَمُ) .

(إِنَّ ٱلصَّفَا وَٱلْمَرْوَةَ مِنْ شَعَائِرِ ٱللَّهِ فَمَنْ حَجَّ ٱلْبَيْتَ أَوِ اعْتَمَرَ فَلَا جُنَاحَ عَلَيْهِ أَنْ يَطَّوَّفَ بِهِمَا ، وَمَنْ تَطَوَّعَ خَيْرًا فَإِنَّ ٱللَّهَ شَاكِرٌ عَلِيمٌ) .

دعاء السعي الثالث

ٱللَّهُ أَكْبَرُ ٱللَّهُ أَكْبَرُ ٱللَّهُ أَكْبَرُ وَلِلَّهِ ٱلْحَمْدُ ، رَبَّنَا أَتْمِمْ لَنَا نُورَنَا ، وَٱغْفِرْ لَنَا ، إِنَّكَ عَلَى كُلِّ شَيْءٍ قَدِيرٌ . ٱللَّهُمَّ إِنِّي أَسْأَلُكَ ٱلْخَيْرَ كُلَّهُ ، عَاجِلَهُ وَآجِلَهُ ، وَأَسْتَغْفِرُكَ لِذَنْبِي ، وَأَسْأَلُكَ رَحْمَتَكَ يَا أَرْحَمَ ٱلرَّاحِمِينَ . (رَبِّ ٱغْفِرْ وَٱرْحَمْ وَٱعْفُ وَتَكَرَّمْ وَتَجَاوَزْ عَمَّا تَعْلَمُ ، إِنَّكَ تَعْلَمُ مَا لَا نَعْلَمُ ، إِنَّكَ أَنْتَ ٱللَّهُ ٱلْأَعَزُّ ٱلْأَكْرَمُ) رَبِّ زِدْنِي عِلْمًا وَلَا تُزِغْ قَلْبِي بَعْدَ إِذْ هَدَيْتَنِي وَهَبْ لِي مِنْ لَدُنْكَ رَحْمَةً ، إِنَّكَ أَنْتَ ٱلْوَهَّابُ . ٱللَّهُمَّ عَافِنِي فِي سَمْعِي وَبَصَرِي ، لَا إِلَهَ إِلَّا أَنْتَ . ٱللَّهُمَّ إِنِّي أَعُوذُ بِكَ مِنْ عَذَابِ ٱلْقَبْرِ . لَا إِلَهَ إِلَّا أَنْتَ سُبْحَانَكَ إِنِّي كُنْتُ مِنَ ٱلظَّالِمِينَ ؛ ٱللَّهُمَّ إِنِّي أَعُوذُ بِكَ مِنَ ٱلْكُفْرِ وَٱلْفَقْرِ . ٱللَّهُمَّ إِنِّي أَعُوذُ بِرِضَاكَ مِنْ سَخَطِكَ وَبِمُعَافَاتِكَ مِنْ عُقُوبَتِكَ ، وَأَعُوذُ بِكَ مِنْكَ ، لَا أُحْصِي ثَنَاءً عَلَيْكَ أَنْتَ كَمَا أَثْنَيْتَ عَلَى نَفْسِكَ ، فَلَكَ ٱلْحَمْدُ حَتَّى تَرْضَى (إِنَّ ٱلصَّفَا وَٱلْمَرْوَةَ مِنْ شَعَائِرِ ٱللَّهِ ، فَمَنْ حَجَّ ٱلْبَيْتَ أَوِ ٱعْتَمَرَ فَلَا جُنَاحَ عَلَيْهِ أَنْ يَطَّوَّفَ بِهِمَا وَمَنْ تَطَوَّعَ خَيْرًا فَإِنَّ ٱللَّهَ شَاكِرٌ عَلِيمٌ) .

دعاء السعي الرابع

أَللهُ أَكْبَرُ اللهُ أَكْبَرُ اللهُ أَكْبَرُ اللهُ وَللهِ ٱلْحمْد .

أَللّهُمَّ إِنِّي أَسْأَلُكَ مِنْ خَيْرِ مَا تَعْلَمُ ، وَأَعُوذُ بِكَ مِنْ شَرِّ مَا تَعْلَمُ ، وَأَسْتَغْفِرُكَ مِنْ كُلِّ مَا تَعْلَمُ، إِنَّكَ أَنْتَ عَلَّامُ ٱلْغُيُوبِ ؛ لَا إِلَهَ إِلَّا اللهُ ٱلْمَلِكُ ٱلْحَقُّ ٱلْمُبِينُ ، مُحَمَّدٌ رَسُولُ اللهِ ٱلصَّادِقُ ٱلْوَعْدِ ٱلْأَمِين . أَللّهُمَّ إِنِّي أَسْأَلُكَ كَمَا هَدَيْتَني لِلْإِسْلامِ أَنْ لَا تَنْزِعَهُ مِنِّي حَتَّى تَتَوَفَّاني وَأَنَا مُسْلِم ؛ أَللّهُمَّ ٱجْعَلْ فِي قَلْبِي نُوراً ، وَفِي سَمْعِي نُوراً ، وَفِي بَصَرِي نُوراً ، أَللّهُمَّ ٱشْرَحْ لِي صَدْرِي وَيَسِّرْ لِي أَمْرِي ، وَأَعُوذُ بِكَ مِنْ شَرِّ وَسْوَاسِ ٱلصَّدْرِ ، وشَتَاتِ ٱلْأَمْرِ ، وَفِتْنَةِ ٱلْقَبْرِ ؛ أَللّهُمَّ إِنِّي أَعُوذُ بِكَ مِنْ شَرِّ مَا يَلِجُ فِي ٱللَّيْلِ ، وَشَرِّ مَا يَلِجُ فِي ٱلنَّهَارِ ، وَمِنْ شَرِّ مَا تَهُبُّ بِهِ ٱلرِّيَاحُ ، يَا أَرْحَمَ ٱلرَّاحِمِين . سُبْحَانَكَ ، مَا عَبَدْنَاكَ حَقَّ عِبَادَتِكَ يَا الله ، سُبْحَانَكَ مَا ذَكَرْنَاكَ حَقَّ ذِكْرِكَ يَا الله .

(رَبِّ ٱغْفِرْ وَٱرْحَمْ وَٱعْفُ وَتَكَرَّمْ وَتَجَاوَزْ عَمَّا تَعْلَمُ ، إِنَّكَ تَعْلَمُ مَالَا نَعْلَمُ ، إِنَّكَ أَنْتَ اللهُ ٱلْأَعَزُّ ٱلْأَكْرَم) .

(إِنَّ ٱلصَّفَا وَٱلْمَرْوَةَ مِنْ شَعَائِرِ اللهِ فَمَنْ حَجَّ ٱلْبَيْتَ أَوِ ٱعْتَمَرَ فَلَا جُنَاحَ عَلَيْهِ أَنْ يَطَّوَّفَ بِهِمَا وَمَنْ تَطَوَّعَ خَيْراً فَإِنَّ اللهَ شَاكِرٌ عَلِيم) .

دعاء السعي الخامس

(أَللهُ أَكْبَرُ اللهُ أَكْبَرُ اللهُ أَكْبَرُ وَللهِ ٱلْحَمْد ، سُبْحَانَكَ
ما شَكَرْنَاكَ حَقَّ شُكْرِكَ يا أَلله ، سُبْحَانَكَ ما أَعْلَى شَأْنَكَ يا أَلله ،
أَللَّهُمَّ حَبِّبْ إِلَيْنا ٱلْإِيمانَ وَزَيِّنْهُ في قُلُوبِنا ، وَكَرِّهْ إِلَيْنا ٱلْكُفْرَ
وَٱلْفُسُوقَ وَٱلْعِصْيانَ ، وَٱجْعَلْنا مِنَ ٱلرّاشِدين (رَبِّ ٱغْفِرْ وَٱرْحَمْ
وَٱعْفُ وَتَكَرَّمْ وَتَجاوَزْ عَمّا تَعْلَمُ ، إِنَّكَ تَعْلَمُ ما لا نَعْلَمُ ،
إِنَّكَ أَنْتَ اللهُ ٱلْأَعَزُّ ٱلْأَكْرَم) . أَللَّهُمَّ قِني عَذابَكَ يَوْمَ تَبْعَثُ
عِبادَك ، أَللَّهُمَّ ٱهْدِني بِالْهُدَى ، وَنَقِّني بِالتَّقْوَى ، وَٱغْفِرْ لي في
ٱلْآخِرَةِ وَٱلْأُولَى ، أَللَّهُمَّ ٱبْسِطْ عَلَيْنا مِنْ بَرَكاتِكَ وَرَحْمَتِكَ
وَفَضْلِكَ وَرِزْقِكَ ، أَللَّهُمَّ إِنِّي أَسْأَلُكَ ٱلنَّعِيمَ ٱلْمُقِيمَ ٱلَّذي لا يَحُولُ
وَلا يَزُولُ أَبَداً ، أَللَّهُمَّ ٱجْعَلْ في قَلْبي نُوراً ، وَفي سَمْعي نُوراً ،
وَفي بَصَري نُوراً ، وَفي لِساني نُوراً ، وَعَنْ يَمِيني نُوراً ، وَمِنْ
فَوْقي نُوراً ، وَٱجْعَلْ في نَفْسي نُوراً ، وَعَظِّمْ لي نُوراً ؛ رَبِّ
ٱشْرَحْ لي صَدْري ، وَيَسِّرْ لي أَمْري (إِنَّ ٱلصَّفا وَٱلْمَرْوَةَ مِنْ
شَعائِرِ ٱلله ، فَمَنْ حَجَّ ٱلْبَيْتَ أَوِ ٱعْتَمَرَ فَلا جُناحَ عَلَيْهِ أَنْ
يَطَّوَّفَ بِهِما ، وَمَنْ تَطَوَّعَ خَيْراً فَإِنَّ ٱلله شاكِرٌ عَلِيم) .

دعاء السعي السادس

(ٱللهُ أَكْبَرُ ٱللهُ أَكْبَرُ ٱللهُ أَكْبَرُ وَلِلهِ ٱلْحَمْدُ ، لا إِلهَ إِلَّا
ٱللهُ وَحْدَهُ ، صَدَقَ وَعْدَهُ ، وَنَصَرَ عَبْدَهُ ، وَهَزَمَ ٱلْأَحْزَابَ
وَحْدَهُ ، لا إِلهَ إِلَّا ٱللهُ ، وَلا نَعْبُدُ إِلَّا إِيَّاهُ ، مُخْلِصِينَ لَهُ ٱلدِّينَ
وَلَوْ كَرِهَ ٱلْكَافِرُونَ ، ٱللّهُمَّ إِنِّي أَسْأَلُكَ ٱلْهُدَى وَٱلتُّقَى وَٱلْعَفَافَ
وَٱلْغِنَى ، ٱللّهُمَّ لَكَ ٱلْحَمْدُ كَٱلَّذِي نَقُولُ وَخَيْراً مِمَّا نَقُولُ .
ٱللّهُمَّ إِنِّي أَسْأَلُكَ رِضَاكَ وَٱلْجَنَّةَ ، وَأَعُوذُ بِكَ مِنْ سَخَطِكَ وَٱلنَّارِ
وَمَا يُقَرِّبُنِي اِلَيْهَا مِنْ قَوْلٍ أَوْ فِعْلٍ أَوْ عَمَـلٍ . ٱللّهُمَّ بِنُورِكَ
اهْتَدَيْنَا ، وَبِفَضْلِكَ ٱسْتَغْنَيْنَا ، وَفِي كَنَفِكَ وَإِنْعَامِكَ وَعَطَائِكَ
وَإِحْسَانِكَ أَصْبَحْنَا وَأَمْسَيْنَا ، أَنْتَ ٱلْأَوَّلُ فَلا قَبْلَكَ شَيْءٌ ،
وَٱلْآخِرُ فَلا بَعْدَكَ شَيْءٌ ، وَٱلظَّاهِرُ فَلا شَيْءَ فَوْقَكَ ، وَٱلْبَاطِنُ
فَلا شَيْءَ دُونَكَ ، نَعُوذُ بِكَ مِنَ ٱلْفَلَسِ أَوِ ٱلْكَسَلِ وَعَذَابِ
ٱلْقَبْرِ وَفِتْنَةِ ٱلْغِنَى ، وَنَسْأَلُكَ ٱلْفَوْزَ بِٱلْجَنَّةِ .

(رَبِّ ٱغْفِرْ وَٱرْحَمْ وَٱعْفُ وَتَكَرَّمْ وَتَجَاوَزْ عَمَّا تَعْلَمُ ،
إِنَّكَ تَعْلَمُ مَا لا نَعْلَمُ ، إِنَّكَ أَنْتَ ٱللهُ ٱلْأَعَزُّ ٱلْأَكْرَمُ) .

(إِنَّ ٱلصَّفَا وَٱلْمَرْوَةَ مِنْ شَعَائِرِ ٱللهِ ، فَمَنْ حَجَّ ٱلْبَيْتَ أَوِ ٱعْتَمَرَ
فَلا جُنَاحَ عَلَيْهِ أَنْ يَطَّوَّفَ بِهِمَا ، وَمَنْ تَطَوَّعَ خَيْراً فَإِنَّ ٱللهَ
شَاكِرٌ عَلِيمٌ) .

وعند اقترابك من الصفا والمروة في السعي السابع اقرأ الدعاء التالي :

دعاء السعي السابع

(أَللّٰهُ أَكْبَرُ اللّٰهُ أَكْبَرُ اللّٰهُ أَكْبَرُ كَبِيراً وَٱلْحَمْدُ لِلّٰهِ كَثِيرا ، أَللّٰهُمَّ حَبِّبْ إِلَيَّ ٱلإِيمَانَ ، وَزَيِّنْهُ فِي قَلْبِي ، وَ كَرِّهْ إِلَيَّ ٱلْكُفْرَ وَٱلْفُسُوقَ وَٱلْعِصْيَانَ ، وَٱجْعَلْنِي مِنَ ٱلرَّاشِدِينَ «رَبِّ ٱغْفِرْ وَٱرْحَمْ وَٱعْفُ وَتَكَرَّمْ وَتَجَاوَزْ عَمَّا تَعْلَمُ ، إِنَّكَ تَعْلَمُ مَا لَا نَعْلَمُ ، إِنَّكَ أَنْتَ ٱللّٰهُ ٱلأَعَزُّ ٱلأَكْرَمُ » .

أَللّٰهُمَّ ٱخْتِمْ بِٱلْخَيْرَاتِ آجَالَنَا ، وَحَقِّقْ بِفَضْلِكَ آمَالَنَا ، وَسَهِّلْ لِبُلُوغِ رِضَاكَ سُبُلَنَا ، وَحَسِّنْ فِي جَمِيعِ ٱلأَحْوَالِ أَعْمَالَنَا ، يَا مُنْقِذَ ٱلْغَرْقَى ، يَا مُنْجِيَ ٱلْهَلْكَى ، يَا شَاهِدَ كُلِّ نَجْوَى ، يَا مُنْتَهَى كُلِّ شَكْوَى ، يَا قَدِيمَ ٱلإِحْسَانِ يَا دَائِمَ ٱلْمَعْرُوفِ يَا مَنْ لَا غِنَى بِشَيْءٍ عَنْهُ ، وَلَا بُدَّ لِكُلِّ شَيْءٍ مِنْهُ . يَا مَنْ رَزَقَ كُلَّ شَيْءٍ عَلَيْهِ ، وَمَصِيرُ كُلِّ شَيْءٍ إِلَيْهِ . أَللّٰهُمَّ إِنِّي عَائِذٌ بِكَ مِنْ شَرِّ مَا أَعْطَيْتَنَا وَمِنْ شَرِّ مَا مَنَعْتَنَا ، أَللّٰهُمَّ تَوَفَّنَا مُسْلِمِينَ وَأَلْحِقْنَا بِالصَّالِحِينَ ، غَيْرَ خَزَايَا وَلَا مَفْتُونِينَ ، رَبِّ يَسِّرْ وَلَا تُعَسِّرْ رَبِّ أَتْمِمْ بِالْخَيْرِ . « إِنَّ ٱلصَّفَا وَٱلْمَرْوَةَ مِنْ شَعَائِرِ ٱللّٰهِ ، فَمَنْ حَجَّ ٱلْبَيْتَ أَوِ ٱعْتَمَرَ فَلَا جُنَاحَ عَلَيْهِ أَنْ يَطَّوَّفَ بِهِمَا ، وَمَنْ تَطَوَّعَ خَيْراً فَإِنَّ ٱللّٰهَ شَاكِرٌ عَلِيمٌ » .)

٭ (وفي فقه اهل البيت يستحب في السعي الخروج من الباب الذي يقابل الحجر الاسود بسكينة ووقار حتى يقطع الوادي ، والصعود الى الصفا بحيث ينظر الى البيت ان لم يكن حاجب ؛ وليستقبل الركن الذي فيه الحجر ويحمد الله عز وجل ويثني عليه ثم يذكر من آلائه وبلائه وحسن ما صنع اليه مايقدر على ذكره ، ثم يكبر الله تعالى (سبعاً) ويهلله (سبعاً) ويقول :

(لا إِلٰهَ إِلَّا اللهُ وَحْدَهُ لَا شَرِيكَ لَهُ ، لَهُ اَلْمُلْكُ وَلَهُ اَلْحَمْدُ يُحِيي وَيُمِيتُ ، وَهُوَ حَيٌّ لَا يَمُوتُ ، بِيَدِهِ اَلْخَيْرُ وَهُوَ عَلَى كُلِّ شَيْءٍ قَدِيرٌ) ثلاثَ مَرَّاتٍ ثُمَّ يُصَلِّي عَلَى اَلنِّبِيِّ « صَلَّى اللهُ عَلَيْهِ وَآلِهِ وَسَلَّمَ » وَيَقُولُ : (أَللهُ أَكْبَرُ ، اَلْحَمْدُ لِلّهِ عَلَى ماهَدَانا وَاَلْحَمْدُ لِلّهِ عَلَى ما أَوْلانا وَاَلْحَمْدُ لِلّهِ اَلْحَيِّ اَلْقَيُّومِ وَاَلْحَمْدُ لِلّهِ اَلْحَيِّ اَلدَّائِمِ) ثلاثَ مَرَّاتٍ وَيَقُولُ : (أَشْهَدُ أَنْ لَا إِلٰهَ إِلَّا اللهُ ، وَأَشْهَدُ أَنَّ مُحَمَّداً عَبْدُهُ وَرَسُولُهُ ، لَا نَعْبُدُ الَّا اِيَّاهُ ، مُخْلِصِينَ لَهُ اَلدِّينَ وَلَوْ كَرِهَ اَلْمُشْرِكُونَ) ثلاثَ مَرَّاتٍ (أَللّٰهُمَّ إِنِّي أَسْأَلُكَ اَلْعَفْوَ وَاَلْعَافِيَةَ وَاَلْيَقِينَ في اَلدُّنْيا وَاَلْآخِرَةِ) ثلاث مرات (أَللّٰهُمَّ آتِنا في اَلدُّنْيا حَسَنَةً وَفي اَلْآخِرَةِ حَسَنَةً وَقِنا عَذابَ اَلنّارِ) ثلاث مرات ثُمَّ يُكَبِّرُ الله (مِائَةَ مَرَّةٍ) وَيُهَلِّلُ (مائة مرة) وَيَحْمَدُهُ (مِائَة مَرَّة) وَيُسَبِّحُهُ (مائة مرة) وَيَقُولُ : (لَا إِلٰهَ الَّا اَللهُ وَحْدَهُ أَنْجَزَ وَعْدَه ، وَنَصَرَ عَبْدَه ، وَغَلَبَ اَلْأَحْزابَ وَحْدَه ، فَلَهُ اَلْمُلْكُ وَلَهُ اَلْحَمْدُ وَحْدَه ، وَحْدَه ، أَللّٰهُمَّ بَارِكْ لي في اَلْمَوْتِ وَفِيما بَعْدَ اَلْمَوْتِ ، اللَّهُمَّ اِنِّي أَعُوذُ بِكَ مِنْ ظُلْمَةِ اَلْقَبْرِ وَوَحْشَتِهِ ، أَللّٰهُمَّ أَظِلَّني في ظِلِّ عَرْشِكَ يَوْمَ لَا ظِلَّ إِلَّا ظِلُّكَ) .

وليكثر من استيداع الله دينه ونفسه واهله ويقول :

(أَسْتَوْدِعُ اللهَ الرَّحْمَنَ الرَّحِيمَ ، الَّذِي لا تَضِيعُ وَدَائِعُهُ ، دِينِي وَنَفْسِي وَأَهْلِي ؛ أَللَّهُمَّ اسْتَعْمِلْنِي عَلَى كِتَابِكَ وَسُنَّةِ نَبِيِّكَ ، وَتَوَفَّنِي عَلَى مِلَّتِهِ وَأَعِذْنِي مِنَ الْفِتْنَةِ) .

ثم يكبر ثلاثاً :   ثم يعيدها مرتين :   ثم يكبر واحدة :

ثم يعيدها ، وليطل وقوفه على الصفا فإن النبي (صلى الله عليه وآله وسلم) كان يقف على الصفا بقدر ما يقرأ سورة البقرة مترسلاً ، وان طول الوقوف عليه يكثر المال ، وليستقبل الكعبة ثم يرفع يديه ثم يقول :

(أَللَّهُمَّ اغْفِرْ لِي كُلَّ ذَنْبٍ أَذْنَبْتُهُ قَطُّ ، فَإِنْ عُدْتُ فَعُدْ عَلَيَّ بِالْمَغْفِرَةِ ، فَإِنَّكَ أَنْتَ الْغَفُورُ الرَّحِيمُ ؛ أَللَّهُمَّ افْعَلْ بِي مَا أَنْتَ أَهْلُهُ ، فَإِنَّكَ إِنْ تَفْعَلْ بِي مَا أَنْتَ أَهْلُهُ تَرْحَمْنِي ، وَإِنْ تُعَذِّبْنِي فَأَنْتَ غَنِيٌّ عَنْ عَذَابِي وَأَنَا مُحْتَاجٌ إِلَى رَحْمَتِكَ ، فَيَا مَنْ أَنَا مُحْتَاجٌ إِلَى رَحْمَتِهِ ارْحَمْنِي . أَللَّهُمَّ وَلا تَفْعَلْ بِي مَا أَنَا أَهْلُهُ ، فَإِنَّكَ إِنْ تَفْعَلْ بِي مَا أَنَا أَهْلُهُ تُعَذِّبْنِي ، وَلَنْ تَظْلِمَنِي ؛ أَصْبَحْتُ أَتَّقِي عَدْلَكَ وَلا أَخَافُ جَوْرَكَ فَيَا مَنْ هُوَ عَدْلٌ لا يَجُورُ ارْحَمْنِي) .

وليقل ايضاً :

(أَللَّهُمَّ إِنِّي أَسْأَلُكَ حُسْنَ الظَّنِّ بِكَ عَلَى كُلِّ حَالٍ وَصِدْقَ النِّيَّةِ فِي التَّوَكُّلِ عَلَيْكَ) .

وليصعد المروة ايضاً على نحو ما سمعته في الصفا وليصنع كما صنع فيه ، وان كان لا يتأكد فيها ذلك . ويستحب المشي حال السعي ، وان جاز الركوب على الدابة وفي المحمل ، وينبغي ان يكون على سكينة ووقار حتى يأتي المنارة وهي طرف السعي فليسع حينئذ ملء فروجه وليقل :

(بِسْمِ اللهِ وَاللهُ أَكْبَرُ وَصَلَّى اللهُ عَلَى مُحَمَّدٍ وَعَلَى أَهْلِ بَيْتِهِ . أَللَّهُمَّ اغْفِرْ وَأَرْحَمْ وَتَجَاوَزْ عَمَّا تَعْلَمُ وَأَنْتَ الْأَعَزُّ الْأَكْرَمُ) .

حتى يبلغ المنارة الاخرى فاذا جاوزها قال :

(يَا ذَا الْمَنِّ وَالْفَضْلِ وَالْكَرَمِ وَالنَّعْمَاءِ وَالْجُودِ اغْفِرْ لِي ذُنُوبِي ، إِنَّهُ لا يَغْفِرُ الذُّنُوبَ إِلَّا أَنْتَ) (وَهَكَذَا يَفْعَلُ فِي كُلِّ شَوْطٍ) .

ان الدعاء السابع يختم السعي . واذا كان السعي للعمرة او للتمتع مع العمرة فيبقى هناك تقصير الشعر وترك ثياب الاحرام فقط « (وفي فقه اهل البيت لا بد من النية للتقصير) » . وتتم العمرة من جانب اولئك الذين يأتون لزيارة الاماكن المقدسة وللذين نذروا العمرة .

وقص الشعر ما هو الا علامة ذكرى ففي وسعنا ان نقص خصلة من الشعر ، وذلك كل ما يقتضي للنساء ، ولكن من الافضل للرجال ان يحلقوا رؤوسهم وبعد الحلق يمسك الحاج بيده ناصيته ويقول :

(أَللهُ أَكْبَرُ اللهُ أَكْبَرُ اللهُ أَكْبَرُ ، أَللَّهُمَّ هَذِهِ نَاصِيَتِي بِيَدِكَ فَاجْعَلْ لِي بِكُلِّ شَعْرَةٍ نُوراً يَوْمَ الْقِيَامَةِ ، وَاغْفِرْ لِي ذَنْبِي يَاوَاسِعَ الْمَغْفِرَةِ ... آمين) وَيَقُولُ أَيْضاً : « الْحَمْدُ لِلّهِ عَلَى مَا هَدَانَا ، وَالْحَمْدُ لِلّهِ عَلَى مَا أَنْعَمَ بِهِ عَلَيْنَا » .

وَبَعْدَ الْفَرَاغِ مِنْهُ يُكَبِّرُ ثَلاثاً نُسْكاً وَيَقُولُ :

(اَلْحَمْدُ لِلّٰهِ الَّذِي قَضَى عَنِّي نُسْكِي ، اَللّٰهُمَّ آتِنِي بِكُلِّ
شَعْرَةٍ حَسَنَةً ، وَاَمْحُ عَنِّي بِهَا سَيِّئَةً ، وَارْفَعْ لِي بِهَا دَرَجَةً ،
وَاَغْفِرْ لِي وَلِلْمُحَلِّقِينَ وَاَلْمُقَصِّرِينَ وَلِجَمِيعِ اَلْمُسْلِمِينَ. اَللّٰهُمَّ
زِدْنَا إِيمَاناً وَيَقِيناً ، وَتَوْفِيقاً وَعَوْناً ، وَاَغْفِرْ لَنَا وَلِآبَائِنَا وَأُمَّهَاتِنَا.
وَصَلَّى اَللّٰهُ عَلَى سَيِّدِنَا مُحَمَّدٍ وَعَلَى آلِهِ وَصَحْبِهِ وَسَلَّمْ . آمِين) .

وأولئك الذين جاؤا مبكرين الى مكة ، لينتظروا مناسك الحج المقدسة ،
قبل بضعة اسابيع من موسم الحج ، والذين يحرمون للتمتع مع العمرة ، عندما
يخلعون ثيابهم تباح لهم محظورات الإحرام ، ولكنهم يعودون الى الامتناع عنها
عندما يحرمون للحج .

واذا كان الطواف والسعي اللذان تما الآن لغرض الحج ، او العمرة مع الحج ،
فان الحاج لا يمكن ان يخلع ثياب الإحرام او يقص شعره الا عند اكمال مناسك
الحج في العاشر من ذي الحجة . والحجاج الذين احرموا للحج او للعمرة مع الحج لا
حاجة بهم الى السعي مرة اخرى . غير ان الحجاج الذين يحرمون للتمتع يسعون
مرة اخرى عند اكمال طواف الإفاضة .

واذا كان الحج قد بدأ أو اوشك ان يبدأ ، فان على الحاج في ختام السعي
ان يعود (أو تعود) الى مسكنه للاستراحة والتهيؤ لمشاق المناسك التالية .
وعليه ان يلبي على الدوام .

« (وفي فقه أهل البيت ، على المتمتع ان يحل بعد العمرة ويجــدد الإحرام
للحج ، والقارن والمفرد اللذان هما من اهل مكة وما جاورها يؤخران العمرة
على الحج) » .

الـحـج

(اللهُ نُورُ السَّمٰواتِ والأَرضِ ؛ مَثَلُ نُورِهِ كَمِشكاةٍ فِيهَا مِصباحٌ المِصباحُ فِي زُجاجَةٍ الزُّجاجَةُ كَأَنَّها كَوكَبٌ دُرِّيٌّ يُوقَدُ مِن شَجَرَةٍ مُبارَكَةٍ زَيتُونَةٍ لا شَرقِيَّةٍ ولا غَربِيَّةٍ يَكادُ زَيتُها يُضِيءُ ولَو لَم تَمسَسهُ نارٌ ؛ نُورٌ عَلىٰ نُورٍ ، يَهدِي اللهُ لِنُورِهِ مَن يَشاءُ ويَضرِبُ اللهُ الأَمثالَ لِلنّاسِ واللهُ بِكُلِّ شَيءٍ عَلِيمٌ) .

(سورة النور ، ٣٥)

يتغير الحج فجأة في الايام السادسة والسابعة والثامنة من شهر ذي الحجة . فان المطوفين يرسلون وكلاءهم وخدمهم آنذاك لكي يهيئوا الخيام والمعدات لآلاف الحجاج . ويكون الرعاة البدو قد جاؤوا شيئاً فشيئاً بالاعداد الكبيرة من المواشي من اعـالي الوديان الى شرق مكة لكي تذبح كأضاح . وهؤلاء ينتظرون في عرفات ومنى في الصحراء ، في الوقت الذي تكون فيه البلدة المقدسة غاصة بوسائط النقل التي تروح وتغدو ، مع قوافل الجمال ، في الشوارع الملأى بالغبار ، كأن القيامة قد قامت ـ فان الحجاج ووسائط نقلهم يتهيأون لمناسك الحج في وادي عرفات ، على بعد حوالي ٢٢ كيلومتراً .

وعلى الحجاج الذين يريدون ان يتأسوا بنبيهم محمد صلى الله عليه وسلم في حجة الوداع قبل وفاته ، ان يتركوا مكة قبل ان تزول الشمس في اليوم الثامن من ذي الحجة . ويحسن ان لا تجري هذه المحاولة خلال السنين التي يجري فيها الحج في الاشهر الحارة ، وعلى الحجاج الذين يمشون على اقدامهم ان لا يغفلوا هـذا التحذير . والأفضل بدلاً عن ذلك ترك مكة بعـد غياب الشمس . ان الله لا يريد من البشر ان يضحوا بأنفسهم ، وهناك الكفـاية من دون ان يحاول الحجاج الموت قصداً . ان السيل المتجه نحو عرفات يبدأ حتى عندما يدخل الحجاج الذين وصلوا مكة من جدة متأخرين ، ويسارعون الى القيام بطوافهم الاول وسعيهم .

وتهتز مكة وتخرج في غبارها المتجمع كل سكانها الى الصحراء ، حتى أصحاب الحوانيت فيها مع بضاعتهم وسلاحهم سائرين في طريق الحجاج .

وفي خلال اوقات الحر الشديد يجري هذا الزحف في الليل . وبين كل آونة واخرى يضيء البرق الصيفي الموقع ، فيشع ضياؤه في السحب الكثيفة من الغبار الذي يخيم على الارض التي لم يغير «الدهر» فيها الا بمقدار تغييره للبحر . وتمر هذه الجموع العظيمة في صفوف غير منظمة ــ وقد يبلغ عددها نصف مليون من البشر ــ من أرض قاحلة جرداء ، وتقطع «الوادي» وهو محل يختنق الانفاس من شدة حرارته ليلا ونهاراً في جميع المواسم . وتراب هذا الطريق واحجاره كأنها رماد أتون . وفي السنة التي ولد فيها النبي (صلى الله عليه وسلم) صرح «أبرهة الأشرم» الحبشي انه سيدمر مكة ويهدم الكعبة ، وزحف على البلدة المقدسة في حملة عسكرية كبيرة كان فيها فيلة حرب . وفي هذا الوادي هلك جيشه عن آخره ، وقد اصيب بصورة غامضة بحصباء صغار امطرتها عليه الطيور الكثيرة ، (وقد أول هذا المثل بوباء الجدري) وعندما يقوم الحجاج بزحفهم هذا عليهم ان يلبوا على الدوام .

توقف النبي في حجة الوداع في التاسع من ذي الحجــــة ، في منى وهو في طريقه الى عرفات . ولقد كان اول اعتراف علني بمحمد صلى الله عليه وسلم في منى حيث آمن به (١٢) شخصاً ، وفي السنة التالية (٢٠) شخصاً ، وفي صباح اليوم التاسع بعد الشروق غادر المكان الصغير المؤذي بحرارة شمسه واستمر في طريقه.

وهنا ايضاً نعيد القول بأنه لا يصح للحجاج في أشهر الحر ان يفعلوا ما فعل النبي صلى الله عليه وسلم ، بل يكملون سيرهم الى «عرفات» في الليل ، (ويستحب عند التوجه الى منى ان يقول :

« أَللّٰهُمَّ إِيَّاكَ أَرْجُو وَإِيَّاكَ أَدْعُو فَبَلِّغْنِي أَمَلِي وَأَصْلِحْ لِي عَمَلِي » .

وإِذَا وَصَلَ إِلَى مِنَى فَلْيَقُلْ :

« اَلْحَمْدُ لِلّٰهِ الَّذِي أَقْدَمَنِيهَا صَالِحاً فِي عَافِيَةٍ ، وَبَلَّغَنِي

هٰذا اَلْمَكَانِ » .

ثُمَّ يَقُولُ : « أَللّٰهُمَّ هٰذِهِ مِنًى وَهِيَ مِمَّا مَنَنْتَ بِهَا عَلَيْنَا مِنَ اَلْمَنَاسِكِ فَأَسْأَلُكَ أَنْ تَمُنَّ عَلَيَّ بِمَا مَنَنْتَ بِهِ عَلَى أَنْبِيَائِكَ فَإِنَّما أَنَا عَبْدُكَ وَفِي قَبْضَتِكَ » .

أَوْ يَقُولُ عِنْدَ اَلْخُرُوجِ مِنْ مِنًى إلى عَرَفَاتٍ : « أَللّٰهُمَّ إِلَيْكَ تَوَجَّهْتُ وَإِلَى وَجْهِكَ ٱلْكَرِيمِ أَرَدْتُ . فَاجْعَلْ ذَنْبِي مَغْفُوراً وَحَجِّي مَبْرُوراً . وَأَرْحَمْنِي وَلَا تُخَيِّبْنِي إِنَّكَ عَلَى كُلِّ شَيْءٍ قَدِيرٍ » أَوْ يَقْرَأُ :

« أَللّٰهُمَّ إِلَيْكَ صَمَدْتُ وَإِيَّاكَ ٱعْتَمَدْتُ وَوَجْهَكَ أَرَدْتُ ؛ أَسْأَلُكَ أَنْ تُبَارِكَ لِي فِي رِحْلَتِي وَأَنْ تَقْضِيَ لِي حَاجَتِي وَأَنْ تَجْعَلَنِي مِمَّنْ تُبَاهِي بِهِ ٱلْيَوْمَ مَنْ هُوَ أَفْضَلُ مِنِّي » .

ويلبي استحباباً حتى يصل الى عرفات) » .

عرفات

عند الدخول الى وادي (عرفات) يقف الحجاج في المسجد المنعزل المسمى «مسجد نمرة» وأولئك الذين يحجون حسب المتعارف يصلون الى هذه النقطة خلال ساعات الصباح ، والأفضل البقـــاء هنا حتى الظهر ومن ثم الاغتسال والتهيؤ لعرفات . وعلى الحجاج بعد الاغتسال ان يدخلوا المسجد أو يتقربوا اليه اذا سمح الزحام .

ويتبعون امامهم (استحباباً) لتأدية صلاة الظهر والعصر ، لكل منها ركعتان ثم يلبون ويذهبون الى جبل عرفات ، وهو بروز من الصخر العادي في قلب واد

عريض ماحل . « (وفي فقه اهل البيت يكره الصعود الى الجبـــل ويستحب الوقوف في السفح) » .

ويعرف الحجاج القادمون من مكة ليلا وادي عرفات من عشرات الألوف من النيران والمصابيح التي تضيء خلال المخيمات . وقد تضيء بين آونــة واخرى مصابيح النفط المعلقة في الفضاء على أعمدة في تلك المضارب الواسعة . ويلمع برق الصحراء على رؤوس الجبـــال . ويسمع للمواشي هناك ثغـاء ورغاء ، واصوات مختلفة ، وللرجال دوي في ترتيل القرآن وذكر الله .

هنا في هذا الموضع التقى آدم بحواء بعد ان طردا من الجنــة وتاها عصرين كاملين في متاهات العالم الغريب .

ويستحب للحاج عندما يشاهد عرفات لأول مرة ان يقول :

« أَللّٰهُمَّ اَغْفِرْ لِي ، وَتُبْ عَلَيَّ وَأَعْطِنِي سُؤْلِي ، وَوَجِّهْ لِيَ أَلْخَيْرَ أَيْنَمَا تَوَجَّهْتُ ؛ سُبْحَانَ أَللّٰهِ وَأَلْحَمْدُ لِلّٰهِ وَلَا إِلٰهَ إِلَّا أَللّٰهُ وَأَللّٰهُ أَكْبَرُ) .

ولبِّ على الدوام ! واذا ما وصلت الى سفح جبل عرفات فسبِّح !

وعلى جميع الحجاج ان يكونوا في عرفات ظهر التاسع من ذي الحجة ، واذا ما زالت الشمس فان فريضة « الوقوف» تبدأ ، وهذا هو الحج ، وهذه هي الساعات السامية .

ان الحاج الذي اهتزت روحه عند دخوله حرم مكة ورأى الكعبة والحجر الأسود لأول مرة ، يجد خشوعاً وسمواً ما هما الا مقدمة لما يجده في عرفات . فهنا ، من هذا الجبل ، يمر الحاج بما يجب ان يكون ـ من الناحية الروحية او العقلية ـ انبل ساعات الحياة . فعند ذلك تكون مخيات المؤمنين قـــد غطت الوادي المتموج الى اقصى ما ترى العين . ان هذا الاجتماع العظيم ومركزه الجبل المقدس القائم في وسطه لهو قلب الإسلام النابض ، وهو يوم الاخوة الصادقة ، وانه اليوم الذي يتجلى فيه الرب لعباده .

لقد وُعدنا ان يغفر الله لنا في هذه الساعات عند عرفــات ، ويرسل رحمته الى اولئك الذين يستحقونها والذين يوقنون به .

هذا هو الخضوع والخشوع ، ولكننا لم نتعلم منه بعدُ معنى الأخوة والاعتصام بها في مواطننا عندما نمارس اعمالنا في الجبال والوديان بعيدين عن عرفات .

هذا هو يوم الميعاد ، لضمان ما يجب ان يكون عليه الإسلام عندمـا يتوصل المسلمون في كل مكان الى الوحدة التي لا تعرف الا اليوم فقط في عرفات .

وبستحب لجميع الحجاج اذا ما واجهوا الجبل ان يقفوا على اقـدامهم ظهراً ويتوبوا الى الله ويطلبوا منه المغفرة . وهناك ادعية متعارفة اعدت لهذا الوقت ، ولكن لا يمكن لأي احد ان يعبر بالفاظ عما يكن في قلوب الآخرين .

فتحدث الى الله بلغتك اذا شئت بصوت عـال ، فان الصوت سيرتفع من الجماهير كالموسيقى العظيمة . فسبح بحمده وقدرته واخشع له .

وعلى اولئك الحجاج القادرين جسدياً ، ان يظلوا وقوفاً الى ان تميل الشمس عن الافق .

دعاء يوم عرفات المأثور

علّم النبي صلى الله عليه وآله وسلم علياً عليه السلام هذا الدعاء ، قائلا : هو دعاء من كان قبلي من الانبياء :

« (لا إِلهَ إِلَّا اللهُ وَحْدَهُ لَا شَرِيكَ لَهُ ، لَهُ الْمُلْكُ وَلَهُ الْحَمْدُ ، يُحْيِي وَيُمِيتُ (وَفِي نسخة يُمِيتُ وَيُحْيِي) وَهُوَ حَيٌّ لَا يَمُوتُ ، بِيَدِهِ الْخَيْرُ وَهُوَ عَلَى كُلِّ شَيْءٍ قَدِيرٌ ، أَللَّهُمَّ لَكَ الْحَمْدُ كَالَّذِي نَقُولُ وَخَيْراً مِمَّا نَقُولُ « وَفِي نسخة وَخَيْرَ مَا نَقُولُ الْقَائِلُونَ إِلَى أَللَّهُمَّ » وَفَوْقَ مَا يَقُولُ الْقَائِلُونَ ، أَللَّهُمَّ لَكَ صَلَاتِي وَنُسُكِي « وَفِي نسخة بَدَلَ وَنُسُكِي وَدِينِي » وَمَحْيَايَ وَمَمَاتِي وَلَكَ بَرَاءَتِي « وَفِي نسخة تُرَاثِي » وَبِكَ حَوْلِي وَمِنْكَ قُوَّتِي ؛

اَللّٰهُمَّ إِنِّي أَعُوذُ بِكَ مِنَ ٱلْفَقْرِ وَمِنْ وَسَاوِسِ ٱلصَّدْرِ وَمِنْ شَتَاتِ ٱلْأَمْرِ وَمِنْ عَذَابِ ٱلْقَبْرِ « وَفِي نسخة وَمِنْ عذابِ ٱلنَّارِ زِيَادَة » ؛ اَللّٰهُمَّ إِنِّي أَسْأَلُكَ خَيْرَ ٱلرِّيَاحِ « وَفِي نسخة مِنْ خَيْرِ مَا تَأْتِي بِهِ ٱلرِّيَاحُ » وَأَعُوذُ بِكَ مِنَ شَرِّ مَا تَجِيءُ بِهِ ٱلرِّيَاحِ « وَفِي نسخة بدل ما تَجِيءُ ما تَأْتِي » وَأَسْأَلُكَ خَيْرَ ٱللَّيْلِ وَخَيْرَ ٱلنَّهَارِ ؛ اَللّٰهُمَّ ٱجْعَلْ فِي قَلْبِي نُوراً وَفِي سَمْعِي نُوراً وَبَصَرِي نُوراً وَلَحْمِي وَدَمِي وَعِظَامِي وَعُرُوقِي وَمَقْعَدِي وَمَقَامِي وَمَدْخَلِي وَمُخْرَجِي نُوراً ، وَأَعْظِمْ لِيَ نُوراً يَا رَبِّ يَوْمَ أَلْقَاكَ ؛ إِنَّكَ عَلَى كُلِّ شَيْءٍ قَدِير) » .

أو تقول دعاء النبي صلى الله عليه وسلم الآخر : « اَللّٰهُمَّ لَكَ ٱلْحَمْدُ كَٱلَّذِي نَقُولُ ، وَخَيْراً مِمَّا نَقُولُ ؛ اَللّٰهُمَّ لَكَ صَلاتِي وَنُسُكِي وَمَحْيَايَ وَمَمَاتِي ، وَإِلَيْكَ مَآبِي وَلَكَ يَا رَبِّ تُرَاثِي ، اَللّٰهُمَّ إِنِّي أَعُوذُ بِكَ مِنْ عَذَابِ ٱلْقَبْرِ ، وَوَسْوَسَةِ ٱلصَّدْرِ وَشَتَاتِ ٱلْأَمْرِ ؛ اَللّٰهُمَّ إِنِّي أَعُوذُ بِكَ مِنْ شَرِّ مَا يَجِيءُ بِهِ ٱلرِّيحِ » .

وتقول أيضاً : « لَا إِلٰهَ إِلَّا ٱللهُ وَحْدَهُ لَا شَرِيكَ لَهُ ، لَهُ ٱلْمُلْكُ وَلَهُ ٱلْحَمْدُ يُحْيِي وَيُمِيتُ وَهُوَ حَيٌّ لَا يَمُوتُ ، بِيَدِهِ ٱلْخَيْرُ وَهُوَ عَلَى كُلِّ شَيْءٍ قَدِيرٌ ؛ اَللّٰهُمَّ ٱجْعَلْ فِي قَلْبِي نُوراً وَفِي سَمْعِي نُوراً وَفِي بَصَرِي نُوراً ؛ اَللّٰهُمَّ ٱشْرَحْ لِي صَدْرِي وَيَسِّرْ لِي أَمْرِي ؛ اَللّٰهُمَّ يَا رَفِيعَ ٱلدَّرَجَاتِ وَمُنْزِلَ ٱلْبَرَكَاتِ وَفَاطِرَ ٱلْأَرَضِينَ وَٱلسَّمَاوَاتِ ، ضَجَّتْ إِلَيْكَ ٱلْأَصْوَاتُ ، بِصُنُوفِ

اَللُّغَاتِ تَسْأَلُكَ اَلْحَاجَاتِ ، وَحَاجِي أَنْ لَا تَنْسَانِي فِي دَارِ ٱلْبَلَاءِ إِذَا نَسِيَنِي أَهْلُ ٱلدُّنْيَا ؛ اَللَّهُمَّ إِنَّكَ تَسْمَعُ كَلَامِي وَتَرَى مَكَانِي وَتَعْلَمُ سِرِّي وَعَلَانِيَتِي وَلَا يَخْفَى عَلَيْكَ شَيْءٌ مِنْ أَمْرِي ؛ أَنَا ٱلْبَائِسُ ٱلْفَقِيرُ ، ٱلْمُسْتَغِيثُ ٱلْمُسْتَجِيرُ ، الْوَجِلُ ٱلْمُشْفِقُ ٱلْمُعْتَرِفُ بِذَنْبِهِ ، أَسْأَلُكَ مَسْأَلَةَ ٱلْمِسْكِينِ ، وَأَبْتَهِلُ إِلَيْكَ ٱبْتِهَالَ ٱلْمُذْنِبِ ٱلذَّلِيلِ ، وَأَدْعُوكَ دُعَاءَ ٱلْخَائِفِ ٱلضَّرِيرِ ، مَنْ خَضَعَتْ لَكَ رَقَبَتُهُ ، وَفَاضَتْ لَكَ عَبْرَتُهُ ، وَذَلَّتْ لَكَ جَبْهَتُهُ ، وَرَغِمَ لَكَ أَنْفُهُ . اَللَّهُمَّ لَا تَجْعَلْنِي بِدُعَائِكَ رَبِّ شَقِيًّا ، وَكُنْ رَؤُوفاً رَحِيماً يَا خَيْرَ ٱلْمَسْؤُولِينَ وَأَكْرَمَ ٱلْمُعْطِينَ . اَللَّهُمَّ رَبَّنَا آتِنَا فِي ٱلدُّنْيَا حَسَنَةً وَفِي ٱلْآخِرَةِ حَسَنَةً وَقِنَا عَذَابَ ٱلنَّارِ . اَللَّهُمَّ إِنِّي ظَلَمْتُ نَفْسِي ظُلْماً كَثِيراً وَإِنَّهُ لَا يَغْفِرُ ٱلذُّنُوبَ إِلَّا أَنْتَ ، فَٱغْفِرْ لِي مَغْفِرَةً مِنْ عِنْدِكَ ، وَٱرْحَمْنِي ، إِنَّكَ أَنْتَ ٱلْغَفُورُ ٱلرَّحِيمُ ؛ اَللَّهُمَّ ٱغْفِرْ لِي مَغْفِرَةً تُصْلِحُ بِهَا شَأْنِي فِي ٱلدَّارَيْنِ ، وَٱرْحَمْنِي رَحْمَةً وَاسِعَةً أَسْعَدُ بِهَا فِي ٱلدَّارَيْنِ ، وَتُبْ عَلَيَّ تَوْبَةً نَصُوحاً لَا أَنْكُثُهَا أَبَداً ، وَأَلْزِمْنِي سَبِيلَ ٱلْاسْتِقَامَةِ لَا أَزِيغُ عَنْهَا أَبَداً . اَللَّهُمَّ ٱنْقُلْنِي مِنْ ذُلِّ ٱلْمَعْصِيَةِ إِلَى عِزِّ ٱلطَّاعَةِ ، وَٱكْفِنِي بِحَلَالِكَ عَنْ حَرَامِكَ ، وَأَغْنِنِي بِفَضْلِكَ عَمَّنْ سِوَاكَ ، وَنَوِّرْ قَلْبِي وَقَبْرِي ، وَٱهْدِنِي وَأَعِذْنِي مِنَ ٱلشَّرِّ كُلِّهِ ، وَٱجْمَعْ لِي ٱلْخَيْرَ كُلَّهُ ؛ اَللَّهُمَّ إِنِّي أَسْأَلُكَ ٱلْهُدَى وَٱلتُّقَى وَٱلْعَفَافَ وَٱلْغِنَى . اَللَّهُمَّ ٱرْزُقْنِي ٱلْيُسْرَى وَجَنِّبْنِي

ٱلْعُسْرَى ، وَٱرْزُقْنِي طَاعَتَكَ مَا أَبْقَيْتَنِي ؛ ٱسْتَوْدَعْتُكَ دِينِي وَأَمَانَتِي وَخَوَاتِيمَ عَمَلِي وَقَوْلِي وَبَدَنِي وَنَفْسِي وَأَهْلِي وَأَحِبَّائِي وَسَائِرَ ٱلْمُسْلِمِينَ وَجَمِيعَ مَا أَنْعَمْتَ بِهِ عَلَيَّ وَعَلَيْهِمْ مِنْ أُمُورِ ٱلدُّنْيَا وَٱلْآخِرَةِ . ٱللَّهُمَّ لَا تَجْعَلْهُ آخِرَ عَهْدِي بِهٰذَا ٱلْمَوْقِفِ ، وَٱرْزُقْنِيهِ مَا بَقِيتُ أَبَداً . وَٱجْعَلْنِي فِي هٰذَا ٱلْيَوْمِ مُسْتَجَاباً دُعَائِي ، مَغْفُورَةً ذُنُوبِي ، وَأَعْطِنِي مِنَ ٱلرِّضْوَانِ وَٱلرِّزْقِ ٱلْوَاسِعِ ٱلْحَلَالِ مَا تَقَرُّ بِهِ عَيْنِي ؛ وَبَارِكْ لِي فِي جَمِيعِ أُمُورِي وَفِي ٱلْأَهْلِ وَٱلْمَالِ وَٱلْوَلَدِ ، وَصَلَّى ٱللهُ عَلَى سَيِّدِنَا مُحَمَّدٍ وَعَلَى آلِهِ وَصَحْبِهِ وَسَلَّمَ » .

ادعية واذكار اخرى

وَرَدَ لِلْوُقُوفِ فِي عَرَفَاتٍ أَدْعِيَةٌ وَأَذْكَارٌ كَثِيرَةٌ ، أَهَمُّهَا دُعَاءٌ رُوِيَ عَنْ سِبْطِ الرَّسُولِ صلى الله عليه وآله وسلم الحُسَيْنِ بْنِ عَلِيٍّ عليهما السلام . وهو مُشْتَمِلٌ عَلَى شَرْحِ ما يُمْكِنُ مِنْ آثَارِ الْقُدْرَةِ الالهِيَّةِ والحِكَمِ الرَّبَّانِيَّةِ والتَّوْحِيدِ الإلهِي الخَالِصِ ، وهو طَوِيلٌ جِدّاً وبَعْدَهُ دُعَاءٌ رُوِيَ عَنْ زَيْنِ الْعَابِدِينَ وسَيِّدِ التَّابِعِينَ عَلِيِّ بْنِ الحُسَيْنِ عليهما السلام وهو يُشْبِهُ الدُّعَاءَ الأوَّلَ ؛ وَلِطُولِهِمَا لَمْ نَذْكُرْهُمَا فِي هذا المختصر ونَذْكُرُ مِنَ الأَدْعِيَةِ والاذكارِ القَصِيرَةِ المَأْثُورَةِ ما يَتَحَمَّلُهُ هذا الكتاب :

(١) حَمْدُ ٱللهِ تَعَالَى وَٱلثَّنَاءُ عَلَيْهِ وَتَمْجِيدُهُ وَتَهْلِيلُهُ .

(٢) ٱلْإِكْثَارُ مِنَ ٱلدُّعَاءِ وَٱلْبُكَاءِ فَإِنَّ ذٰلِكَ ٱلْيَوْمَ يَوْمُ دُعَاءٍ وَمَسْأَلَةٍ وَلَيْسَ مَوْطِنٌ أَحَبَّ إِلَى ٱلشَّيْطَانِ أَنْ يَذْهَلَ ٱلْعَبْدُ فِيهِ مِنْ ذٰلِكَ ٱلْمَوْطِنِ . وَٱلدُّعَاءُ أَفْضَلُ ٱلْأَعْمَالِ فِي ذَلِكَ ٱلْيَوْمِ .

(٣) اَلدُّعَاءُ لِنَفْسِهِ وَلِوَالِدَيْهِ وَلِإِخْوَانِهِ وَأَقَلُّهُمْ أَرْبَعُونَ .
فَعَنِ (اَلصَّادِقِ) عَلَيْهِ اَلسَّلَام : « مَنْ دَعَا لِأَخِيهِ بِظَهْرِ اَلْغَيْبِ
وَكَّلَ اَللهُ بِهِ مَلِكاً يَقُولُ : وَلَكَ مِثْلاه) . وَعَنِ (اَلْكَاظِمِ)
عَلَيْهِ اَلسَّلَام :(مَنْ دَعَا لِأَخِيهِ بِظَهْرِ اَلْغَيْبِ نُودِيَ مِنَ اَلْعَرْشِ:
وَلَكَ مِائَةُ أَلْفِ ضِعْفٍ مِثْلَه) .

(٤) أَنْ يُعَدِّدَ ذُنُوبَهُ وَيَتُوبَ إِلَى اَللهِ مِنْهَا وَيَسْتَغْفِرَهُ .

(٥) أَنْ يَسْتَعِيذَ بِاللهِ مِنَ اَلشَّيْطَانِ اَلرَّجِيمِ .

(٦) قَوْلُ : اَللهُ أَكْبَرُ (مِائَة) .

(٧) لَا إِلَهَ إِلَّا اَللهُ (مِائَة) .

(٨) اَلْحَمْدُ لِلهِ (مِائَة) .

(٩) سُبْحَانَ اَللهِ (مِائَة) .

(١٠) مَا شَاءَ اَللهُ وَلَا قُوَّةَ إِلَّا بِاللهِ (مِائَة) .

(١١) أَللَّهُمَّ صَلِّ عَلَى مُحَمَّدٍ وَآلِ مُحَمَّدٍ (مِائَة) .

(١٢) أَشْهَدُ أَنْ لَا إِلَهَ إِلَّا اَللهُ وَحْدَهُ لَا شَرِيكَ لَهُ ،
لَهُ اَلْمُلْكُ وَلَهُ اَلْحَمْدُ ، يُحْيِي وَيُمِيتُ وَيُمِيتُ وَيُحْيِي وَهُوَ حَيٌّ
لَا يَمُوتُ ؛ بِيَدِهِ اَلْخَيْرُ وَهُوَ عَلَى كُلِّ شَيْءٍ قَدِير (مِائَة) .

(١٣) قِرَاءَةُ عَشْرِ آيَاتٍ مِنْ أَوَّلِ اَلْبَقَرَةِ .

(١٤) قُلْ هُوَ اَللهُ أَحَد (ثَلَاثاً) .

(١٥) آيَةُ اَلْكُرْسِي (٢٠) إِنَّا أَنْزَلْنَاهُ .

(١٦) آيَةُ ٱلسُّخْرَةِ (وَهِيَ) :

(إِنَّ رَبَّكُمُ ٱللهُ ٱلَّذِي خَلَقَ ٱلسَّمٰوَاتِ وَٱلْأَرْضَ فِي سِتَّةِ أَيَّامٍ ثُمَّ ٱسْتَوَى عَلَى ٱلْعَرْشِ ، يُغْشِي ٱللَّيْلَ وَٱلنَّهَارَ يَطْلُبُهُ حَثِيثاً وَٱلشَّمْسَ وَٱلْقَمَرَ وَٱلنُّجُومَ مُسَخَّرَاتٍ بِأَمْرِهِ ، أَلَا لَهُ ٱلْخَلْقُ وَٱلْأَمْرُ، تَبَارَكَ ٱللهُ رَبُّ ٱلْعَالَمِينَ) . (سُورَةُ ٱلْأَعْرَافِ ، ٥٣)

(١٧) قُلْ أَعُوذُ بِرَبِّ ٱلْفَلَقِ .

(١٨) قُلْ أَعُوذُ بِرَبِّ ٱلنَّاسِ .

(١٩) ٱلْحَمْدُ لِلهِ عَلَى كُلِّ نِعْمَةٍ أَنْعَمَ بِهَا عَلَيَّ مِنَ ٱلْخَلْقِ وَٱلسَّمْعِ وَٱلْبَصَرِ وَٱلْأَهْلِ وَٱلْمَالِ . وَيُعَدِّدُ نِعَمَ ٱللهِ تَعَالَى عَلَيْهِ وَاحِدَةً وَاحِدَةً بِقَدْرِ ٱسْتِطَاعَتِهِ .

(٢٠) أَللّٰهُمَّ لَكَ ٱلْحَمْدُ عَلَى نَعْمَائِكَ ٱلَّتِي لَا تُحْصَى بِعَدَدٍ وَلَا تُكَافَأُ بِعَمَلٍ .

(٢١) ٱلْإِكْثَارُ مِنَ ٱلصَّلَاةِ عَلَى مُحَمَّدٍ وَآلِ مُحَمَّدٍ .

(٢٢) دُعَاءُ ٱللهِ بِأَسْمَائِهِ ٱلَّتِي فِي آخِرِ ٱلْحَشْرِ (فَيَقُولُ) :

(أَسْأَلُ ٱللهَ بِأَنَّهُ هُوَ ٱللهُ ٱلَّذِي لَا إِلٰهَ إِلَّا هُوَ ؛ عَالِمُ ٱلْغَيْبِ وَٱلشَّهَادَةِ ؛ هُوَ ٱلرَّحْمٰنُ ٱلرَّحِيمُ ؛ هُوَ ٱللهُ ٱلَّذِي لَا إِلٰهَ إِلَّا هُوَ ٱلْمَلِكُ ٱلْقُدُّوسُ ٱلسَّلَامُ ٱلْمُؤْمِنُ ٱلْمُهَيْمِنُ ٱلْعَزِيزُ ٱلْجَبَّارُ ٱلْمُتَكَبِّرُ ؛ سُبْحَانَ ٱللهِ عَمَّا يُشْرِكُونَ . هُوَ ٱللهُ ٱلْخَالِقُ ٱلْبَارِئُ ٱلْمُصَوِّرُ لَهُ ٱلْأَسْمَاءُ ٱلْحُسْنَى ؛ يُسَبِّحُ لَهُ مَا فِي ٱلسَّمٰوَاتِ وَٱلْأَرْضِ، وَهُوَ

ٱلْعَزِيزُ ٱلْحَكِيمُ .

(٢٣) أَسْأَلُكَ يَا ٱللهُ ، يَا رَحْمَنُ ، بِكُلِّ ٱسْمٍ هُوَ لَكَ ؛ وَأَسْأَلُكَ
بِقُوَّتِكَ وَقُدْرَتِكَ وَعِزَّتِكَ ، وَبِجَمِيعِ مَا أَحَاطَ بِهِ عِلْمُكَ ؛
وَبِجَمْعِكَ وَبِأَرْكَانِكَ كُلِّهَا ؛ وَبِحَقِّ رَسُولِكَ صَلَوَاتُ ٱللهِ عَلَيْهِ ؛
وَبِٱسْمِكَ ٱلْأَكْبَرِ وَبِٱسْمِكَ ٱلْعَظِيمِ ٱلَّذِي مَنْ دَعَاكَ بِهِ كَانَ حَقًّا
عَلَيْكَ أَنْ تُجِيبَهُ (أَنْ لَا تُخَيِّبَهُ) ؛ (نسخة بدل) وَبِٱسْمِكَ
ٱلْأَعْظَمِ ٱلْأَعْظَمِ ٱلْأَعْظَمِ ٱلَّذِي مَنْ دَعَاكَ بِهِ كَانَ حَقًّا عَلَيْكَ
أَنْ لَا تَرُدَّهُ ؛ وَأَنْ تُعْطِيَهُ مَا سَأَلَ : أَنْ تَغْفِرَ لِي جَمِيعَ ذُنُوبِي فِي
جَمِيعِ عِلْمِكَ فِيَّ) .

(وَيَسْأَلُ ٱللهَ تَعَالَى حَوَائِجَهُ كُلَّهَا مِنْ أَمْرِ ٱلْآخِرَةِ وَٱلدُّنْيَا) .

(٢٤) ٱللَّهُمَّ إِنِّي أَسْأَلُكَ ٱلْوِفَادَةَ إِلَيْكَ فِي كُلِّ عَـامٍ بَقِيَ
مِنْ عُمْرِي .

(٢٥) أَسْأَلُ ٱللهَ ٱلْجَنَّةَ (سبعين مرة) .

(٢٦) أَتُوبُ إِلَى ٱللهِ (سبعين مرة) .

(٢٧) ٱللَّهُمَّ إِنِّي عَبْدُكَ ، فَلَا تَجْعَلْنِي مِنْ أَخْيَبِ وَفْدِكَ ،
وَٱرْحَمْ مَسِيرِي إِلَيْكَ مِنَ ٱلْفَجِّ ٱلْعَمِيقِ. ٱللَّهُمَّ، رَبَّ ٱلْمَشَاعِرِ كُلِّهَا ،
فُكَّ رَقَبَتِي مِنَ ٱلنَّارِ ، وَأَوْسِعْ عَلَيَّ مِنْ رِزْقِكَ ٱلْحَلَالِ ، وَٱدْرَأْ
عَنِّي شَرَّ فَسَقَةِ ٱلْجِنِّ وَٱلْإِنْسِ ؛ ٱللَّهُمَّ لَا تَمْكُرْ بِي وَلَا تَخْدَعْنِي
وَلَا تَسْتَدْرِجْنِي ؛ ٱللَّهُمَّ إِنِّي أَسْأَلُكَ بِحَوْلِكَ وَجُودِكَ وَكَرَمِكَ

وَمِنْكَ وَفَضْلِكَ ، يَا أَسْمَعَ ٱلسَّامِعِـــينَ ، يَا أَبْصَرَ ٱلنَّاظِرِينَ ،
يَا أَسْرَعَ ٱلْحَاسِبِينَ ، يَا أَرْحَمَ ٱلرَّاحِمِينَ : أَنْ تُصَلِّيَ عَلَى مُحَمَّدٍ
وَآلِ مُحَمَّدٍ ، وَأَنْ ... (تَفْعَلَ بِي كَذَا وَكَذَا ... وَيَطْلُب
حَوَائِجَهُ) .

(٢٨) أَنْ يَرْفَعَ يَدَيْهِ نَحْوَ ٱلسَّمَاءِ (وَيَقُولُ) :

(أَللَّهُمَّ ، حَاجَتِي إِلَيْكَ ٱلَّتِي إِنْ أَعْطَيْتَنِيهَا لَمْ يَضُرَّنِي مَا مَنَعْتَنِي ،
وَإِنْ مَنَعْتَنِيهَا لَمْ يَنْفَعْنِي مَا أَعْطَيْتَنِي : خَلَاصَ رَقَبَتِي مِنَ ٱلنَّارِ .
أَللَّهُمَّ إِنِّي عَبْدُكَ ، وَمُلْكُ نَاصِيَتِي بِيَدِكَ ، وَأَجَلِي بِعِلْمِكَ ،
أَسْأَلُكَ أَنْ تُوَفِّقَنِي لِمَا يُرْضِيكَ عَنِّي ، وَأَنْ تَسَلَّمَ مَنَاسِكِي ٱلَّتِي
أَدَّيْتُهَا لِخَلِيلِكَ إِبْرَاهِيمَ ، صَلَوَاتُ ٱللهِ عَلَيْهِ ، وَدُلِلْتُ عَلَيْهَا بِنَبِيِّكَ
مُحَمَّدٍ صَلَّى ٱللهُ عَلَيْهِ وَآلِهِ ؛ أَللَّهُمَّ ٱجْعَلْنِي مِمَّنْ رَضِيتَ عَمَلَهُ وَأَطَلْتَ
عُمْرَهُ وَأَحْيَيْتَهُ بَعْدَ ٱلْمَوْتِ حَيَاةً طَيِّبَةً) .

(٢٩) (أَللَّهُمَّ فُكَّنِي مِنَ ٱلنَّارِ ، وَأَوْسِعْ عَلَيَّ مِنْ رِزْقِكَ
ٱلْحَلَالِ ٱلطَّيِّبِ ، وَٱدْرَأْ عَنِّي شَرَّ فَسَقَةِ ٱلْجِنِّ وَٱلْإِنْسِ ، وَشَرَّ
فَسَقَةِ ٱلْعَرَبِ وَٱلْعَجَمِ) .

(فَإِذَا) فَرَغَ مِنْ هَذِهِ الأَدْعِيَةِ قَبْلَ غُرُوبِ الشَّمْسِ فَلْيُكَرِّرْهَا
(٣٠) الأَدْعِيَةُ الْمَذْكُورَةُ فِي كُتُبِ الأَعْمَالِ ، خُصُوصًا دُعَاءَ الصَّحِيفَةِ الْكَامِلَةِ لِزَيْنِ
الْعَابِدِينَ (عَلَيْهِ السَّلَامُ) ، وَدُعَاءٌ آخَرُ لَهُ (عَلَيْهِ السَّلَامُ) ، وَدُعَاءَ الْحُسَيْنِ (عَلَيْهِ السَّلَامُ)،
الى غير ذلك . (٣١) زيارة الحسين عليه السلام .

(٣٢) فَإِذَا صَارَ قَرِيبَ غُرُوبِ الشَّمْسِ، فَلْيَقُلْ : « اللَّهُمَّ إِنِّي أَعُوذُ بِكَ مِنَ الْفَقْرِ وَمِنْ تَشَتُّتِ الْأَمْرِ وَمِنْ شَرِّ مَا يَحْدُثُ بِاللَّيْلِ وَالنَّهَارِ ؛ أَمْسَى ظُلْمِي مُسْتَجِيراً بِعَفْوِكَ ، وَأَمْسَى خَوْفِي مُسْتَجِيراً بِأَمَانِكَ ، وَأَمْسَى وَجْهِيَ الْفَانِي مُسْتَجِيراً بِوَجْهِكَ الْبَاقِي ؛ يَا خَيْرَ مَنْ سُئِلَ وَيَا أَجْوَدَ مَنْ أَعْطَى ؛ جَلِّلْنِي بِرَحْمَتِكَ وَأَلْبِسْنِي عَافِيَتَكَ ، وَاصْرِفْ عَنِّي شَرَّ جَمِيعِ خَلْقِكَ » . ثُمَّ يَقُولُ :

« يَا خَيْرَ مَنْ سُئِلَ وَيَا أَوْسَعَ مَنْ أَعْطَى وَيَا أَرْحَمَ مَنِ اسْتُرْحِمَ » ثُمَّ يَطْلُبُ حَاجَتَهُ .

(٣٣) فَإِذَا غَرَبَتِ الشَّمْسُ، فَلْيَقُلْ :

« اللَّهُمَّ لَا تَجْعَلْهُ آخِرَ الْعَهْدِ مِنْ هَذَا الْمَوْقِفِ ، وَارْزُقْنِيهِ مِنْ قَابِلٍ أَبَداً مَا أَبْقَيْتَنِي ، وَاقْبَلْنِي الْيَوْمَ مُفْلِحاً مُنْجَحاً مُسْتَجَاباً لِي ، مَرْحُوماً مَغْفُوراً لِي بِأَفْضَلِ مَا يَنْقَلِبُ فِيهِ الْيَوْمَ أَحَدٌ مِنْ وَفْدِكَ وَحُجَّاجِ بَيْتِكَ الْحَرَامِ ، وَاجْعَلْنِي الْيَوْمَ مِنْ أَكْرَمِ وَفْدِكَ عَلَيْكَ ؛ وَأَعْطِنِي أَفْضَلَ مَا أَعْطَيْتَ أَحَداً مِنْهُمْ مِنَ الْخَيْرِ وَالْبَرَكَةِ وَالرَّحْمَةِ وَالرِّضْوَانِ وَالْمَغْفِرَةِ ؛ وَبَارِكْ لِي فِيمَا أَرْجِعُ إِلَيْهِ مِنْ أَهْلٍ أَوْ مَالٍ أَوْ قَلِيلٍ أَوْ كَثِيرٍ ؛ وَبَارِكْ لَهُمْ فِيَّ » .

حجة الوداع

في السنة العاشرة من الهجرة تلقى النبي محمد صلى الله عليه وسلم وحياً بقرب وفاته فجمع أهله وأصحابه وأتباعه لما عُرف في الاخير بحجة الوداع . وكان محمد

صلى الله عليه وسلم قد تسمم في السنة السابعة من الهجرة ، عندما قاد الحملة ضد يهود خيبر ، وفي الواقع ان النبي صلى الله عليه وسلم لم يسترد صحته التامة منذ ذلك الحين .

أدى النبي مناسك الحج وقد تبعه اكثر من مائة الف من المؤمنين كلهم في ثياب الإحرام ، في مكة ثم زار عرفات . وعلى قمة الجبل الصخري القى نظرة على الجمع المحتشد ، وهو لا يزال على ظهر الجبل ، ثم خطب رافعاً طرفه الى السماء مبتدئاً خطبته بحمد الله ، ثم استمر في خطبته بتؤدة ، وردّد زنجي قوي الصوت ، جميل ، كلماتِه جملة جملة لكي يسمع الجميع .

وبعد انتهاء العبادة وجه النبي صلى الله عليه وسلم خطابه الى الآلاف المؤلفة على المنحدرات الصخرية في الوادي المحمل المحيط بالجبل ، وحمل صوت الزنجي كلماته مرة اخرى اليهم . فحرم على المسلمين الربا وقبول الفائض عن اي مبلغ يقترض كيفما كان نوعه . وعليهم ان يعفوا عمن اساء اليهم قبل الاسلام ، ويتركوا الثأر العربي ، وحضهم على صيانة حقوق نسائهم ، فالكل سواء في الإسلام . وعيّن الزمن على الاشهر القمرية منذ ذلك اليوم اثني عشر شهراً قمرياً حسب قوانين الارض والسماء .

وعندما اكمل النبي كلامه ، وبعد فترة صمت قال فجـأة وهو لم يزل على ظهر الجبل :

(أمّا بَعدُ ، أيُّهَا ٱلنَّاس ، أَسمَعُوا مِنِّي أُبَيِّن لَكُمْ ، فَإِنِّي لا أدري لَعَلِّي لا ألقَاكُمْ بَعدَ عَامِيَ هٰذا في مَوقِفي هٰذا) إلى قوله : (أيُّهَا ٱلنَّاسُ ، إنَّمَا ٱلمُؤمِنُونَ إخوَةٌ ، فَلا يَحِلُّ لِامرىء مَالُ أَخِيهِ إلّا عَن طِيبِ نَفسٍ مِنهُ ، ألا هَلْ بَلَّغتُ ؟ ألَلّهُمَّ آشهَدْ ! فَلا تَرجِعُنَّ بَعدِيَ كُفّاراً يَضرِب بَعضُكُمْ رِقَابَ بَعضٍ ، فَإِنِّي قَدْ تَرَكتُ فِيكُمْ ما إن أخَذتُمْ بِهِ لَن تَضِلُّوا بَعدَه : كِتَابَ ٱللهِ ، ألا هَلْ بَلَّغت ؟ ألَلّهُمَّ آشهَدْ . أيُّهَا ٱلنَّاس !

إنَّ رَبَّكُمْ واحِدٌ ، وإِنَّ أَباكُمْ واحِدٌ ، كُلُّكُمْ لِآدَمَ ، وآدَمُ مِنْ تُرابٍ ، إِنَّ أَكْرَمَكُمْ عِنْدَ اللهِ أَتْقاكُمْ ، وَلَيْسَ لِعَرَبِيٍّ عَلَى عَجَمِيٍّ فَضْلٌ إِلَّا بِالتَّقْوَى .

وأدار وجهه نحو السماء وقال :

أَلَا هَلْ بَلَّغْتُ ؟ أَللّهُمَّ أَشْهَدْ !

فصاح الحاضرون من آلاف الحجاج : « نَعَمْ . حَقًّا يا رَبّ » .

قال : « فَلْيُبَلِّغِ الشّاهِدُ الْغَائِبَ » .

فاهتز لهذه المظاهرة وصاح مرة اخرى وهو يشير نحو السماء : رَبِّ اسْمَعْ شَهادَتَهُمْ ! وقيل انه بعد ذلك بقليل ، حينما كان النبي باقياً في عرفات نزل الوحي الأخير بآخر آيات القرآن الكريم . وقد ذكر ان الوحي نزل من السماوات بقوة سماوية حتى ان جمل النبي برك . ثم بلغ النبي محمد صلى الله عليه وسلم رسالة الله ليسمعها الجميع فقال :

(اليَوْمَ أَكْمَلْتُ لَكُمْ دينَكُمْ وأَتْمَمْتُ عَلَيْكُمْ نِعْمَتِي وَرَضِيتُ لَكُمُ الْإِسلامَ دِيناً) .   « سورة المائدة ، ٤ »

وعم الفرح العظيم الحاضرين غير ان ابا بكر رضي الله عنه بكى ، فقد ادرك ان هذه آخر رسالة للنبي في الارض ، وان وفاة النبي صلى الله عليه وسلم قد أوشكت .

« (وله خطبة خطبها وهو قابض على عضادة باب الكعبة ذكرت ما يحدث في آخر الزمان من التطورات والحوادث وشيوع الفحشاء وانهيار الممالك الاسلامية وكل ما يجري في هذا الزمان ، وهي طويلة جـداً كأنه كان ينظار الى حوادث هذا العصر فينقلها كمؤرخ ، الا انه كان يخبر عما يحدث في المستقبل بعلم من الله) » .

المزدلفة

ويذهب الحاج من عرفات الى المزدلفة بعد أن تغيب الشمس ، وعند ذلك يترك الجميع مخيماتهم ويغادرون الجبل المقدس فوراً تاركين الوادي في سرعة كأنه جيش منهزم ، وهذا التدفق العظيم يسمى النفر او الإفاضة .

وتسارع جموع الحجاج وهي تلبي من اول القمة الى المزدلفة ، وهي تبعـد ثمانية كيلومترات ، حيث تنمو أشتات من الشوك على التلول المحترقة من الحرارة ، وحيث يجب على الجميع ان يصلوا المغرب والعشاء ويبحثوا في ظلام الصحراء عن (٤٩) حصاة اذا أرادوا ان يبقوا في منى ثلاثة ايام ، اما اذا ارادوا ان يبقوا اربعة ايام فلا بد من ان يلتقطوا (٧٠) حصاة يأخذونها الى منى لرمي الجمرات، وهي فريضة رمي الاعمدة الثلاثة التي ترمز الى الشيطان وغوايته .

ومن المستحب للحاج عندما يكون في المزدلفة أن يقف ليذكر الله في المسجد الذي لا سقف له ، ويسمى « المشعر الحرام » ويقول :

« أَللّٰهُ أَكْبَرُ اللّٰهُ أَكْبَرُ اللّٰهُ أَكْبَرُ ، لَا إِلٰهَ إِلَّا اللّٰهُ . اللّٰهُ أَكْبَرُ وَلِلّٰهِ ٱلْحَمْد .. أَللّٰهُمَّ كَمَا أَوْقَفْتَنَا فِيهِ وَأَرَيْتَنَا إِيَّاهُ فَوَفِّقْنَا لِذِكْرِكَ كَمَا هَدَيْتَنَا .. وَٱغْفِرْ لَنَا وَٱرْحَمْنَا كَمَا وَعَدْتَنَا بِقَوْلِكَ وَقَوْلُكَ ٱلْحَق :

« ... فَإِذَا أَفَضْتُمْ مِنْ عَرَفَاتٍ فَٱذْكُرُوا ٱللّٰهَ عِنْدَ ٱلْمَشْعَرِ ٱلْحَرَامِ وَٱذْكُرُوهُ كَمَا هَدَاكُمْ وَإِنْ كُنْتُمْ مِنْ قَبْلِهِ لَمِنَ ٱلضَّالِّينَ ، ثُمَّ أَفِيضُوا مِنْ حَيْثُ أَفَاضَ ٱلنَّاسُ وَٱسْتَغْفِرُوا ٱللّٰهَ ، إِنَّ ٱللّٰهَ غَفُورٌ رَحِيمٌ » . **(سورة البقرة ١٩٧ - ١٩٨)**

« أَللّٰهُمَّ إِنَّا نَسْأَلُكَ يَا غَفُورُ يَا رَحِيمُ أَنْ تَفْتَحَ لِأَعْيُنِنَا أَبْوَابَ ٱلْإِجَابَةِ ، يَا مَنْ إِذَا سَأَلَهُ ٱلْمُضْطَرُّ أَجَابَهُ ، يَا مَنْ يَقُولُ

لِلشَّيْءِ كُنْ فَيَكُونُ .. أَللَّهُمَّ إِنَّا جِئْنَاكَ بِجَمْعِنَا مُتَشَفِّعِينَ إِلَيْكَ فِي غُفْرَانِ ذُنُوبِنَا فَلَا تَرُدَّنَا خَائِبِينَ ، وَآتِنَا أَفْضَلَ مَا تُوتِي عِبَادَكَ الصَّالِحِينَ ، وَلَا تَصْرِفْنَا مِنْ هَذَا الْمَشْعَرِ الْعَظِيمِ إِلَّا فَائِزِينَ مُفْلِحِينَ ، غَيْرَ خَزَايَا وَلَا نَادِمِينَ ، لَا ضَالِّينَ وَلَا مُضِلِّينَ ، يَا أَرْحَمَ الرَّاحِمِينَ . أَللَّهُمَّ وَفِّقْنَا لِلْهُدَى ، وَأَعْصِمْنَا مِنْ أَسْبَابِ الْجَهْلِ وَالرَّدَى ، وَسَلِّمْنَا مِنْ آفَاتِ النُّفُوسِ ، فَإِنَّهَا شَرُّ الْعِدَى ، وَاجْعَلْنَا مِمَّنْ أَقْبَلْتَ عَلَيْهِ فَأَعْرَضَ عَمَّنْ سِوَاكَ ، وَخُذْ بِأَيْدِينَا إِلَيْكَ ، وَارْحَمْ تَضَرُّعَنَا بَيْنَ يَدَيْكَ . إِلَهَنَا ، قَوِّمْنَا إِذَا اعْوَجَجْنَا ، وَأَعِنَّا إِذَا اسْتَقَمْنَا ، وَكُنْ لَنَا وَلَا تَكُنْ عَلَيْنَا ، وَأَحْيِنَا فِي الدُّنْيَا مُؤْمِنِينَ طَائِعِينَ ، وَتَوَفَّنَا مُسْلِمِينَ تَائِبِينَ ، وَاجْعَلْنَا مِمَّنْ يَأْخُذُ كِتَابَهُ بِالْيَمِينِ ، وَاجْعَلْنَا يَوْمَ الْفَزَعِ الْأَكْبَرِ مِنَ الْآمِنِينَ ، وَمَتِّعْنَا أَللَّهُمَّ بِالنَّظَرِ إِلَى وَجْهِكَ الْكَرِيمِ ، بِرَحْمَتِكَ يَا أَرْحَمَ الرَّاحِمِينَ » .

وَتُكْثِرُ بعد ذلك من الذكر ومن قوله تعالى :

« رَبَّنَا آتِنَا فِي الدُّنْيَا حَسَنَةً وَفِي الْآخِرَةِ حَسَنَةً وَقِنَا عَذَابَ النَّارِ » .

مستحبات الوقوف بالمشعر

« (ويستحب للمفيض من عرفات الى المشعر :

(١) السكينة والوقار والاستغفار والاقتصاد في المشي فلا يسرع ولا يبطىء والاكثار من قول :

« أَللَّهُمَّ أَعْتِقْ رَقَبَتِي مِنَ النَّارِ » .

(٢) ان يقول حين افاضته اليه :

« أَللَّهُمَّ إِنِّي أَعُوذُ بِكَ أَنْ أَظْلِمَ أَوْ أُظْلَمَ أَوْ أَقْطَعَ رَحِماً أَوْ أُوذِيَ جَاراً » .

(٣) اذا انتهى الى الكثيب الاحمر عن يمين الذاهب الى عرفات فليقل :

« أَللَّهُمَّ ارْحَمْ مَوْقِفِي ، وَزِدْ فِي عَمَلِي ، وَسَلِّمْ لِي دِينِي ، وَتَقَبَّلْ مَنَاسِكِي » .

ثم يقول :

« أَللَّهُمَّ لَا تَجْعَلْهُ آخِرَ الْعَهْدِ مِنْ هٰذَا الْمَوْقِفِ ، وَأَرْزُقْنِيهِ أَبَداً مَا أَبْقَيْتَنِي » .

(٤) فاذا وصل الى المشعر فليقل :

« أَللَّهُمَّ هٰذِهِ جَمْعٌ جَمَعَ أَللَّهُمَّ إِنِّي أَسْأَلُكَ أَنْ تَجْمَعَ لِيَ فِيهَا جَوَامِعَ الْخَيْرِ ، أَللَّهُمَّ لَا تُؤْيِسُنِي مِنَ الْخَيْرِ ، أَللَّهُمَّ لَا تُؤْيِسُنِي مِنَ الْخَيْرِ الَّذِي سَأَلْتُكَ أَنْ تَجْمَعَهُ لِيَ فِي قَلْبِي ، وَأَطْلُبُ إِلَيْكَ أَنْ تُعَرِّفَنِي مَا عَرَّفْتَ أَوْلِيَاءَكَ فِي مَنْزِلِي هٰذَا ، وَأَنْ تَقِيَنِي جَوَامِعَ الشَّرِّ » .

(٥) احياء تلك الليلة بالعبادة والذكر والدعاء لنفسه ولوالديه وولده واقاربه واخوانه فان ابواب السماء لا تغلق فيها بقول الله تعالى :

« أَنَا رَبُّكُمْ وَأَنْتُمْ عِبَادِي أَدَّيْتُمْ حَقِّي وَحَقٌّ عَلَيَّ أَنْ أَسْتَجِيبَ لَكُمْ » .

(٦) ويقف ان شاء قريباً من الجبل في سفحه وان شاء حيث يبيت ، فاذا وقف متوجهاً الى القبلة حمد الله عز وجل وأثنى عليه وذكر من آلائه وبلائه ما يقدر عليه وصلى على النبي (صلى الله عليه وآله وسلم) ودعا بالدعاء المأثور فاذا طلع الفجر فليصل وليقل :

(اَلْحَمْدُ لِلهِ وَاللهُ أَكْبَرُ وَالثَّنَاءُ اَلْجَمِيلُ لِلهِ ، أَشْهَدُ أَنْ لَا إِلهَ إِلَّا اللهُ وَأَنَّ مُحَمَّداً رَسُولُ اللهِ . اَللّهُمَّ صَلِّ عَلَى مُحَمَّدٍ وَآلِ مُحَمَّدٍ ، وَصَلِّ عَلَى عَلِيٍّ وَاَلْحَسَنِ وَاَلْحُسَيْنِ وَعَلَى اَبْنِ اَلْحُسَيْنِ وَمُحَمَّدِ بْنِ عَلِيٍّ وَجَعْفَرِ بْنِ مُحَمَّدٍ ، وَمُوسَى بْنِ جَعْفَرٍ ، وَعَلَى اَبْنِ مُوسَى وَمُحَمَّدِ بْنِ عَلِيٍّ وَعَلَى اَبْنِ مُحَمَّدٍ وَاَلْحَسَنِ بْنِ عَلِيٍّ وَمُحَمَّدِ بْنِ اَلْحَسَنِ ، عَلَيْهِمُ اَلسَّلَامُ . اَللّهُمَّ زِدْهُمْ شَرَفاً إِلَى شَرَفِهِمْ ، اَللّهُمَّ إِنِّي أَتَقَرَّبُ إِلَيْكَ بِمُوَالاتِهِمْ وَأَبْرَأُ إِلَيْكَ مِنْ أَعدائِهِمْ .

(ثم يقول) :

اَللّهُمَّ ، رَبَّ اَلْمَشْعَرِ اَلْحَرَامِ ، فُكَّ رَقَبَتِي مِنَ اَلنَّارِ ، وَأَوْسِعْ عَلَيَّ مِنْ رِزْقِكَ اَلْحَلالِ ، وَاَدْرَأْ عَنِّي شَرَّ فَسَقَةِ اَلْجِنِّ وَالْإِنْسِ ؛ اَللّهُمَّ أَنْتَ خَيْرُ مَطْلُوبٍ إِلَيْهِ ، وَخَيْرُ مَدْعُوٍّ ، وَخَيْرُ مَسْئُولٍ ، وَلِكُلِّ وَافِدٍ جَائِزَةٌ فَاجْعَلْ جَائِزَتِي فِي مَوْطِنِي هذا أَنْ تُقِيلَنِي مِنْ عَثْرَتِي وَتَقْبَلَ مَعْذِرَتِي وَأَنْ تُجَاوِزَ عَنْ خَطِيئَتِي ، ثُمَّ اَجْعَلِ اَلتَّقْوَى مِنَ اَلدُّنْيَا زَادِي ؛ وَتَقَبَّلْنِي مُفْلِحاً مُنْجَحاً مُسْتَجَاباً لِي بِأَفْضَلِ مَا يَرْجِعُ بِهِ أَحَدٌ مِنْ وَفْدِكَ وَزُوَّارِ بَيْتِكَ اَلْحَرَامِ : بِرَحْمَتِكَ يَا أَرْحَمَ اَلرَّاحِمِينَ .

(٧) وادع الله كثيراً لنفسك ولوالديك ولولدك واهلك ومالك وجميع المؤمنين والمؤمنات ثم يقول :

(أَللَّهُ أَكْبَرُ)(مائة) أَلْحَمْدُ لِلَّهِ (مائة) سُبْحَانَ أَللَّهِ (مائة)
لَا إِلٰهَ إِلَّا أَللَّهُ (مائة) ويقول : (اَللّٰهُمَّ اَهْدِنِي مِنَ أَلضَّلَالَةِ ،
وَأَنْقِذْنِي مِنَ أَلْجِهَالَةِ ، وَأَجْمِعْ لِي خَيْرَ أَلدُّنْيَا وَأَلْآخِرَةِ ، وَخُذْ
بِنَاصِيَتِي إِلَىٰ هُدَاكَ ، وَأَنْقُلْنِي إِلَىٰ رِضَاكَ ، فَقَدْ تَرَى مَقَامِي بِهٰذا
أَلْمَشْعَرِ أَلَّذِي أَنْخَفَضَ لَكَ فَرَفَعْتَهُ ، وَذَلَّ لَكَ فَأَكْرَمْتَهُ ، وَجَعَلْتَهُ
عَلَماً لِلنَّاسِ ، فَبَلِّغْنِي فِيهِ مُنَايَ ، وَنَيْلَ رَجَائِي . أَللّٰهُمَّ إِنِّي أَسْأَلُكَ
بِحَقِّ أَلْمَشْعَرِ أَلْحَرَامِ أَنْ تُحَرِّمَ شَعْرِي وَبَشَرِي عَلَى أَلنَّارِ ، وَأَنْ
تَرْزُقَنِي حَيَـاةً فِي طَاعَتِكَ وَبَصِيرَةً فِي دِينِكَ وَعَمَلاً بِفَرَائِضِكَ
وَأَتِّبَاعاً لِأَوَامِرِكَ وَخَيْرَ أَلدَّارَيْنِ ؛ وَأَنْ تَحْفَظَنِي فِي نَفْسِي وَوَالِدَيَّ
وَوَلَدِي وَأَهْلِي وَإِخْوَانِي وَجِيرَانِي بِرَحْمَتِكَ) (وليجتهد) في
الدعاء والمسألة والتفرغ الى الله سبحانه والابتهال له حتى تطلع
الشمس) .

(١٤) الاعتراف بخطاياه سبع مرات حين طلوع الشمس على جبل ثبير فيقول مثلاً :

(أَللّٰهُمَّ إِنِّي أَعْتَرِفُ لَكَ بِذُنُوبِي) (يقولها سبع مرات) ولا
يبعـد استحباب ذكر ما يعلمه منها بعينه وما لا يعلمه يعترف
به اجمالاً (ثم يقول) أَسْتَغْفِرُ أَللّٰهَ (سبع مرات) .

(١٥) ان يذكر الله تعالى حال افاضته من المشعر ويستغفره .

(١٦) أن يمشي على سكينة ووقار فاذا وصل الى وادي محسر أسرع في مشيه

ان كان ماشيًا ، وحرّك دابتـه ان كان راكبًا حتى يجوز وادي محسر ؛ ودون ذلك
في الفضل أن يسرع بقدر مائة ذراع ودونه الاسراع مائة خطوة بل يستحب له
اذا نسي ذلك ان يعود الى ذلك المكان ويسرع فيه حتى لو دخل مكة استحب
له العود .

(١٧) ان يقول حين الاسراع في وادي محسر :

« أللّٰهُمَّ سَلِّمْ عَهْدِي وَأَقْبَلْ تَوْبَتِي وَأَجِبْ دَعْوَتِي وَأَخْلِفْنِي
بِخَيْرٍ فِيمَا تَرَكْتُ بَعْدِي ، (وَلْيَقُلْ) « رَبِّ أَغْفِرْ وَأَرْحَمْ وَتَجَاوَزْ
عَمَّا تَعْلَمْ ، إِنَّكَ أَنتَ ٱلْأَعَزُّ ٱلْأَكْرَمُ » .

منى ـ مكان الذبح والنحر

كان «منى» ـ الذي مررنا به من قبل في سيرنا الخارجي من مكة الى عرفات ـ
محل تجمع القبائل البدوية قبل زمن النبي محمد (صلى الله عليه وسلم) بكثير . فهنا
النصب المصنوعة من الصخر والطين التي تشير الى حيث ظهر الشيطان لاسماعيل
ابن النبي ابراهيم وهو يحذره من أن يذبحه ابوه ويغريه بالهرب .

وان النبي ابراهيم رأى في منامه أنه قد أمر بأن يذبح ابنه قربانًا لله ، فقال
ابراهيم لابنه انها سيذهبان معًا لكي يجدا حطبًا للنار ، ولكن هناك تحت السماء
اعترف الاب الكسير القلب لابنه بما كان ينوي ، فرضي اسماعيل بالقدر ، واعد
نفسه لكي يطيع الامر الالهي ؛ فصعدا الى موضع الذبح كما رآه ابراهيم في منامه ،
وهو الموضع القاحل الآن الذي يشرف على الجمرات الثلاث في منى .

فظهر الشيطان ثلاث مرات لاسماعيل الذي كان يمشي وراء ابيـه ، وكانت
المرة الاولى حيث تقع (الجمرة الاولى) الآن ، وهو عمود سميك قصير ذو قمة مدورة
محاط بجدار مستدير ، ثم ظهر الشيطان مرة اخرى في موضع (الجمرة الوسطى) ،
وهي نصب مماثل للجمرتين في شارع القرية ، وكان ظهوره الثالث في الموضع
المعروف الآن بجمرة العقبة تحت السفح الذي كان على اسماعيل ان يموت
فيه ذبيحا .

وفي كل من هذه المرات حذر الشيطان اسماعيل من نية ابيه ، وكان الابن يرميه بحجر .

وعندما تم وثاق اسماعيل ونكس رأسه الى الاسفل استعداداً للذبح ، وضع النبي ابراهيم السكين على رقبة ابنه ، غير أن حدهـا انقلب على يده ممتنعاً عن اختراق جسده . وحاول ابراهيم ثلاث مرات ان يكمل الذبح ، وانقلبت السكين ثلاث مرات ، وفجأة ظهر الملك جبرائيل ومعه كبش وقال لابراهيم : ان الله قد قبل الذبح من دون ان تذبح اسماعيل ، وقدم له الكبش ليفديه به .

تقع قرية منى المتفتتة في واد عال بلغ من ضيقه انه اصبح كالمضيق ، مسخته قطع الصخور التي كثرت فيها الكهوف والمنحنيات في كلا الجانبين ، وهنا في خلال مراسيم الحج التي تجري في منى ، يخيم عشرات الالوف من الحجـاج البدو وهم يزحفون في الحفر والكهوف والشقوق في الصخور المحترقة ، لا تكاد اجسامهم ولا اعقاب ارجلهم تشعر بالالم ، وهم يحتمون بالأعالي المشتعلة في أتون الوادي .

ان منى مكان يموت فيه الكثيرون . وتكون الحرارة في الصيف فوق الطاقة ، ودرجة الحرارة ظهراً تتعدى الاربعين مئوية ، ومع ذلك فلا يكون ذلك غير اعتيادي . وهناك اربعة شوارع متوازية في القـرية يمتد اوسعها الى قمة الوادي ، وفي هذا الشارع الاعمدة الغريبة والنصب التي تشير الى المكان الذي ظهر فيـه الشيطان لابن النبي ابراهيم .

ويقع تحت منى « مسجد الخيف » وهو المسجد الذي صلى فيه النبي محمد صلى الله عليه وسلم . ويروى حديث أنه صلى في ذلك الموضع سبعون من انبياء الله . منهم موسى .

وعندما تقرب من القرية قل :

« اَلْحَمْدُ لِلّهِ ٱلَّذِي بَلَّغَنِيهَا سَالِماً مُعَافى ، أَللَّهُمَّ هذِهِ مُنى قَدْ أَتَيْنُها وَأَنا عَبْدُكَ وَٱبْنُ (أو اَبْنَةُ) عَبْدِكَ ، أَسْأَلُكَ أَنْ تَمُنَّ عَلَيَّ بِمَا مَنَنتَ بِهِ عَلَى أَوْلِيَائِكَ ؛ أَللّهُمَّ إِنِّي أَعُوذُ بكَ مِنَ ٱلْحِرْمان وَٱلْمُصِيبَةِ في دِيني وَدُنْيايَ ، يا أَرْحَمَ ٱلرَّاحِمينَ ، وَصَلَّى ٱللّهُ عَلَى سَيِّدِنا مُحَمَّدٍ وَعَلى آلِهِ وَصَحْبِهِ وَسَلَّمَ » .

وعندما تصل من المزدلفة الى منى في العاشر من شهر ذي الحجة وهو اليوم الذي يسمى عيد الاضحى (عيد النحر) او عيد القربان ، فإن سيل الحجاج يغمر الوادي الصخري بين الجبال . فيتموج السيل نحو جمرة العقبة وهو نصب صخري على علو ثلاثة امتار بني في سفح منخفض من قمة الوادي .

ويستطيع الحجاج الذين يشكون من اعياء الحر او أي ضعف آخر ان يتأخروا حتى يخف الضغط ؛ ولكن من المستحب الوصول الى جمرة العقبة قبل أن تزول الشمس .

ونحن الآن نوشك ان نقترب من نهاية الحج ، فيجب ان تبذل الجهود للقيام بالمناسك في ترتيبها الصحيح . ولكن لا تنس انه ليس علينا ان نتجاوز طاقتنا.

وفي جمرة العقبة عندما تصبح على بعد رمي الجمرات يجب على كل حاج ان يرمي سبع حصيات من التسعة والاربعين (٤٩) او من السبعين (٧٠) التي جمعها من المزدلفة ، ويجب ان ترمى واحدة واحدة .

وعند رمي الجمرات قل :

« بِسْمِ اللّهِ ، اللّهُ أَكْبَرُ ، رَجْماً لِلشَّيْطَانِ وَحِزْبِهِ ، أَللّهُمَّ أَجْعَلْهُ حَجّاً مَبْرُوراً وَذَنْباً مَغْفُوراً وَسَعْياً مَشْكُوراً وَعَمَلاً صَالِحاً مَقْبُولاً وَتِجَارَةً لَنْ تَبُورَ » .

ويقول ايضاً :

« بِسْمِ اللّهِ ، اللّهُ أَكْبَرُ ، صَدَقَ وَعْدَهُ ، وَنَصَرَ عَبْدَهُ ، وَأَعَزَّ جُنْدَهُ وَهَزَمَ ٱلْأَحْزَابَ وَحْدَهُ ، لَا إِلَهَ إِلَّا اللّهُ وَلَا نَعْبُدُ إِلَّا إِيَّاه ، مُخْلِصِينَ لَهُ ٱلدِّينَ وَلَوْ كَرِهَ ٱلْكَافِرُون ، وَصَلَّى ٱللّهُ عَلى سَيِّدِنَا مُحَمَّدٍ وعَلى آلِهِ وَصَحْبِهِ وَسَلَّم » .

وينبغي للمرء الا يقتصر على الأدعية المذكورة ، بل يدعو في كل مكان بما يحب ويكثر من ذكر الله تعالى ومن قراءة القرآن الكريم ، والصلاة والسلام على رسول الله صلى الله عليه وسلم ، ويكرر الادعية سالفة الذكر ويقول عقب كل دعاء :

« رَبَّنَا آتِنَا فِي ٱلدُّنْيَا حَسَنَةً وَفِي ٱلْآخِرَةِ حَسَنَةً وَقِنَا عَذَابَ ٱلنَّارِ » .

ويلاحظ أن يذكر عند كل جمرة ، وعليك أن تكثر من التهليل والتكبير والتسبيح والتمجيد والذكر العظيم ما استطعت في كل مكان ، وقبل وبعد كل دعاء مما مر ، لأن ذلك فرصة عظيمة والحصول عليها قليل . نسأل الله تعالى أن يجعلنا ممن كتبت لهم حجات عدة ، إنه على ما يشاء قدير .

« (ويستحب للرامي الطهارة من الحدث ، بل يكره بدونها بل والغسل وأخذ الحصى باليسرى والرمي باليمنى والدعاء ، بأن يقول والحصى بيــده والظاهر هي اليمنى .

« ٱللَّهُمَّ هـؤُلَاءِ حَصَيَاتِي فَأَحْصِهِنَّ لِي وَٱرْفَعْهُنَّ فِي عَمَلِي » .

ثم يرمي ويقول مع كل حصاة :

(ٱللهُ أَكْبَرُ ٱللَّهُمَّ ٱدْحَرْ عَنِّي ٱلشَّيْطَانَ ، ٱللَّهُمَّ تَصْدِيقاً بِكِتَابِكَ وَعَلَى سُنَّةِ نَبِيِّكَ صَلَّى ٱللهُ عَلَيْهِ وَآلِهِ وَسَلَّمَ . ٱللَّهُمَّ ٱجْعَلْهُ لِي حَجًّا مَبْرُوراً وَعَمَلاً مَقْبُولاً وَسَعْياً مَشْكُوراً وَذَنْباً مَغْفُوراً ! .

وليكن بينه وبين الجمرة قدر (عشرة أذرع أو خمسة عشر ذراعاً) فاذا أتى محله ورجع من الرمي فليقل :

(ٱللَّهُمَّ بِكَ وَثِقْتُ وَعَلَيْكَ تَوَكَّلْتُ فَنِعْمَ ٱلرَّبُّ وَنِعْمَ ٱلْمَوْلَى وَنِعْمَ ٱلنَّصِيرُ ! .

ويستحب الحذف (بالمعجمتين) في الرمي بأن يضع الحصاة على الابهام ويدفعها بظفر السبابة ، والرمي راجلاً ، بل يستحب المشي الى مرمى الجمار ، واستقبال جمرة العقبة على وجه يكون مستدبر القبلة بخلاف غيرها فإنه يستقبلها ويستقبل القبلة) » .

ومن هذه اللحظة فصاعداً ليس على الحاج ان يلبي فقد انقضى وقت التلبية . ويرمي الحاج في كل يوم من اليومـــين التاليين في منى كلا مــن الجمرات الثلاث ويرمي على كل جمرة منها سبع حصيات ، « (واذا بات في منى ليلـــة الثالث عشر وجب ان يرمي الجمرات في يومه ايضاً) » . وفي اليوم الاول من منى لا ترمى الحصيات الا على جمرة العقبة .

وبعد ذلك عند الرجوع من موقع جمرة العقبة يجب على جميع الحجاج القادرين ان يقدموا الهـــدي وينبغي ان يتم التصرف بلحوم الحيوانات المذبوحة بشكل معقول ، فإما ان تحفظ ليستفاد منها في الأكل بنى ، وامـا ان توزع للفقراء ، ويجب ان لا تترك فتتعفن وتسمم الجو ، ان الله غـير محتاج الى الهدي ذاته ، ولا ينبغي ان يكون الهدي اهلاكاً بلا فائدة .

« لَنْ يَنالَ اللَّهَ لُحُومُها ولا دِماؤُها ، وَلٰكِنْ يَنالُهُ التَّقْوَى مِنْكُمْ ؛ كَذٰلِكَ سَخَّرَها لَكُمْ لِتُكَبِّرُوا اللَّهَ عَلى ما هَداكُمْ وَبَشِّرِ الْمُحْسِنِينَ » .

(سورة الحج ، ٣٧)

« (وانما امر بالهدي لفوائد اقتصادية تعود على اهل البلاد الحجازية ، اذ ان سكانها يعتمدون في عيشهم على ما تدر عليهم موارد الحج ، فضلاناً لهذا المورد يعمل بالحكم الشرعي ، فإنه يعمد الى توازن العرض والطلب والمحافظة على الثمن ، لأن زيادة العرض على الطلب تقلل الثمن ، كما هو معروف في قوانين الاقتصاد عامة ، فلو فرض اهمال ذبح الهدي لبقيت المواشي مكدسة ، وبذلك يفقد اهل البلاد اهم مورد للثروة والمعيشة ، وتقل رغبتهم في تنميتها ، فالذبح واجب وان استلزم دفن المواشي او حرقها او اتلافها بعد الذبح ـ دفعاً لفساد الجو ورعاية لصحة الانسان . فاذا ذبحت الاضاحي وجب حفظها بوسائل مختلفة حذراً من الاسراف والتبذير المحرم شرعاً ، واذا لم يمكن حفظها وجب دفنها او استعمال العقاقير المانعة من التعفن اتقاء من ضررها الصحي . ولا يجوز ترك الذبح بتاتاً لأن الفوائد الاقتصادية والشعائر المطلوبة لا تحصل بترك الذبح) » .

وبعد رمي الجمرات والذبح يوم النحر (العاشر من ذي الحجة) على الحجاج ان

يقصروا من شعورهم ، وهذا مجرد ذكرى ، ففي وسعنا ان ننجز خصلة من شعر الرأس ، ولا يجوز للمرأة اكثر من ذلك ، والمستحب للرجال حلق الرأس .

وعند الانتهاء من هذه المناسك يجوز ان لا يبقى الحاج بعد ذلك في ثياب الاحرام .

ويمكنه خلعها لانتهاء وقتها ، وبلوغ الحج نهايته ، ولا تعود شعائر الإحرام ذات مغزى ، والحجاج الذين يأتون معهم بألبسة اخرى من مكة يستطيعون ان يغيروا ملابسهم ، ويظل آخرون في لباس الاحرام المكون من قطعتين ، غير ان عمل الاحرام يكون قد انتهى .

على ان محظورات الاحرام ، والكف عن الاتصال الجنسي واستعمال الطيب والروائح والحلى والزينة الشخصية لا يزول الا بعد طواف الافاضة ، وهو طواف الحج الثاني الذي يتم بأسرع ما يمكن بعد رمي جمرة العقبة وتقديم الهدي والانتهاء من الاحرام وتقصير الشعر .

« (وفي فقه اهل البيت يباح للمحرم بعد التقصير او الحلق جميع محظورات الاحرام الا الطيب فانه لا يباح الا بعد طواف الافاضة والا النساء فلا يحل وطيهن الا بعد طواف النساء) » .

وفي خلال السنوات التي يجري فيها الحج في اشد شهور السنة حراً يجدر بالحجاج ان يرموا جمرة العقبة ويقدموا الهدي مبكرين في الصباح لكي يعودوا مسرعين الى مكة قبل ان يزداد حر النهار للانتهاء من طواف الافاضة .

طواف الافاضة

ان هذا الطواف هو اول المناسك الواجب الانتهاء منها . والتهيؤ له وتطبيقه كالطواف السابق (أي طواف العمرة) . ويمكن تلاوة الادعية والاذكار والاوراد بدون تغيير ، أو تغير حسبما يريد الحاج ان يعبر عن عواطفه خير تعبير .

وفي خلال هذا الطواف يرى الحاج الاطمئنان اكثر من قبل ، ويجد السمو في التضرع ، ثم ان هناك نوعاً من الهدوء والسكينة . فالتهيج العــاطفي يقل ويزداد عمق الشعور والادراك .

ولا تنس ان تذكر وتدعو لأولئك الذين تحبهم ، الاحيــاء منهم والاموات ، والمسلمين الذين منعتهم حكوماتهم الملحدة من اداء فريضة الحج والذين يعيشون في

بؤس واستعباد ويموتون شهداء . واذا وقفت في حرم الكعبة المقدسة فادع ان
تشمل رحمة الله جميع المسلمين الذين وقعوا تحت سيطرة السوفييت الغاشمة اطلب
الى الله ان يرأف بجميع المسلمين مها كانت جنسياتهم وقومياتهم والوانهم فيحررهم
من ربقة الأجنبي ، وان تسقط الحكومات الظالمة وان تفتح جميع الطرق الى
مكة ، وادع لأرواح الابطال من الامم الاسلامية التي لم تشاهد مكة مرة اخرى ـ
كشعوب القرم التي ابادها السوفييت ـ والذين هلكوا ولم يتخلوا عن شخصيتهم
أو دينهم .

« كُتِبَ عَلَيْكُمُ ٱلْقِتَالُ وَهُوَ كُرْهٌ لَكُمْ ، وَعَسَى أَنْ تَكْرَهُوا
شَيْئاً وَهُوَ خَيْرٌ لَكُمْ ، وَعَسَى أَنْ تُحِبُّوا شَيْئاً وَهُوَ شَرٌّ لَكُمْ ،
وَٱللَّهُ يَعْلَمُ وَأَنْتُمْ لَا تَعْلَمُونَ . يَسْأَلُونَكَ عَنِ ٱلشَّهْرِ ٱلْحَرَامِ
قِتَالٍ فِيهِ ، قُلْ قِتَالٌ فِيهِ كَبِيرٌ وَصَدٌّ عَنْ سَبِيلِ ٱللَّهِ وَكُفْرٌ بِهِ
وَٱلْمَسْجِدِ ٱلْحَرَامِ وَإِخْرَاجُ أَهْلِهِ مِنْهُ أَكْبَرُ عِنْدَ ٱللَّهِ ، وَٱلْفِتْنَةُ أَكْبَرُ
مِنَ ٱلْقَتْلِ ، وَلَا يَزَالُونَ يُقَاتِلُونَكُمْ حَتَّى يَرُدُّوكُمْ عَنْ دِينِكُمْ
إِنِ ٱسْتَطَاعُوا ، » .

(سورة البقرة ، ٢١٥ ـ ٢١٦)

وليس من الواجب ان يتم طواف الافاضة يوم الوصول الى منى ، ولكنه يحل
الحاج من جميع ممنوعات الاحرام ، ثم انه يمثل نهاية الحج .

ويمكن تأجيل طواف الافاضة الى حين الانتهاء من مناسك منى كا كانت عادة
النبي صلى الله عليه وسلم . وعلى كل حال فإن على أولئك الحجاج الذين يسرعون
الى مكة لكي يتموا طواف الافاضة في نفس اليوم بعد رمي جمرة العقبة ، ان
يظلوا في مكة خلال ساعات الحر في ظل المسجد الحرام اذا رغبوا ، غير أن
على الجميع ان يعودوا الى منى قبل أن تغيب الشمس .

نبقى في وادي منى يومين او ثلاثة أيام بعد العاشر من ذي الحجة للدعاء
والتسبيح ، ولرمي الجمرات . ويفضل بعض الحجاج أن يقضوا اغلب ساعات

النهار في مكة ، ولا يعودون إلا للنوم في مِنى ولرمي الجمرات ، غير ان على الجميع ان يظلوا في الوادي ليلتين على الأقل بعد ليلة العاشر من ذي الحجة . وهـذه الأيام تسمى « أيام التشريق » اتباعًا للعادة القديمة . في تجفيف المواشي المذبوحة تحت الشمس .

« وَٱذْكُرُوا ٱللَّهَ فِي أَيَّامٍ مَعْدُودَاتٍ فَمَنْ تَعَجَّلَ فِي يَوْمَيْنِ فَلا إِثْمَ عَلَيْهِ وَمَنْ تَأَخَّرَ فَلا إِثْمَ عَلَيْهِ لِمَنِ ٱتَّقَى وَٱتَّقُوا ٱللَّهَ وَٱعْلَمُوا أَنَّكُمْ إِلَيْهِ تُحْشَرُون » .

(سورة البقرة ، ٢٠٢)

وفي خلال اليوم الثاني من الاقامة في مِنى يجب على جميع الحجاج ان يرموا الجمرات الثلاث ، في كل مرة سبع حصيـات ، فيكون المجموع (٢١) حصاة . وليكن اليوم الاول فإن رمي الشيطان لا يبدأ قبل ان تمر الشمس من الزوال .

ومناسك اليوم الثالث تشابه مناسك اليوم الثاني بحيث تنفد ذخيرة الحاج من الـ (٤٩) حصاة التي جاء بها من المزدلفة .

فاذا اضطر الحاج الذي يريد العودة الى مكة في الثاني عشر من ذي الحجة الى التأخر لأي سبب كان بعد المغيب فإن عليه ان يؤجل عودتـه الى اليوم التالي (الثالث عشر من ذي الحجة) ، حيث على الحـاج ان يقوم برمي اضافي للجمرات الثلاث ، ويجمع الـ (٢١) حصاة المطلوبة من مِنى نفسها ، وفي هـذه الحالة يمكن ان يجري الرمي في أي وقت بعد الفجر .

وعلى جميع الحجاج أن يغادروا مِنى ويعودوا الى مكة قبل مغيب اليوم الثالث عشر من ذي الحجة .

فاذا ما تركت مِنى وراءك وانتهى طواف الافاضة فان الحج يكون قد انتهى . « (وفي فقه أهل البيت يجب بعد طواف الافاضة طواف النساء وليس هو من أركان الحج الا ان النساء لا تباح للرجال اذا لم يطوفوا طواف النساء ، والرجال لا يباحون للنساء اذا لم يطفن ذلك الطواف) » .

— ٩٣ —

العمرة بعد الحج

لا حاجة للحجاج الذين جاءوا في الاصل الى مكة محرمين للعمرة مع التمتع أو للعمرة مع الحج ، أن يؤدوا العمرة بعد الانتهاء من مناسك الحج . غير أن على جميع الذين يدخلون مكة محرمين للحج فقط أن يؤدوا العمرة منفردة بعد ذلك . وأن يقوموا بذلك بعد الانتهاء من الحج مباشرة . وعلى اولئك الحجاج، او سوام من الاشخاص الذين يقطنون في مكة والذين يرغبون في تأدية العمرة في غير موسم الحج ، ان يذهبوا الى التنعيم وهو موضع يبعد خمسة كيلومترات عن مكة ، على طريق الجمال الى المدينة ، وهناك يرتدون ثياب الاحرام .

وعليهم ان يتلفظوا بالنية المعتادة ويعودوا الى مكة ويؤدوا الطواف والسعي كما شرح في اوائل هذا الكتاب ، وينتهوا بتقصير شعورهم .

« (وفي فقه اهل البيت لا تكون العمرة بعد الحج الا لأهل مكة ومن جاورها الى اثني عشر ميلاً ، ومن بعد عن ذلك فرضه التمتع وهو تقديم العمرة على الحج كما تقدم) » .

الحجة البدلية (النيابة)

لقد اجيز لنا ان نرسل الآخرين من محلنا اذا حال المرض او الكِبَر دون ان نقوم بالرحلة انفسنا . ولقد روي في الحديث ان رجلاً جاء الى النبي صلى الله عليه وسلم فقال :

> « يَا رَسُولَ اللهِ ، إنَّ أُخْتِي نَذَرَتْ أَنْ تَحِجَّ وَمَاتَتْ قَبْلَ أَنْ تَحِجَّ ، أَفَأَحِجُّ عَنْهَا ؟ » فقال صلوات الله عليه : « لَوْ كَانَ عَلَى أُخْتِكَ دَيْنٌ أَكُنْتَ قَاضِيه ؟ » قال : « نعم » .. قال : « فَاقْضُوا حَقَّ اللهِ فَهُوَ أَحَقُّ بِالْقَضَاءِ » .

وفي وسعنا ان نحج باسم اي شخص عزيز علينا يموت قبل ان يؤدي الفريضة

المقدسة . ومن الافضل في هـذه الحالة ان تكون نفقـة الحج من المال الذي تركه الميت .

طواف الوداع

لا يجري طواف الوداع او الصدر حول الكعبة الا قبيل مغادرة الحاج او الحاجة مكة الى بلاده او بلادها ، وهو يمكن ان يتم من جانب كل احـد من الناس في اي موسم كان عند ترك مكة لمدة غير معينـة . ولا ترتدى ثياب الاحرام ، ولا تسرع الخطى في الاشواط الثلاثة الاولى كما كنت تفعــل في الطوافات السابقة .

وبعد الانتهاء من الطواف حول الكعبة يستحب للحاج ان يذهب الى المكان المسمى المستجار (الملتزم) بين ابواب الكعبة الفضية والذهبية العالية وبين الحجر الاسود ، وهناك يقرأ الادعية كما فعل في طواف القـدوم (الزيارة) وطواف الافاضة ، ثم يصلي ركعتين في مقام ابراهيم ، ثم يقوم من صلاته الى الحجر الاسود فيقبله قبلة الوداع .

ويعود مرة اخرى الى المستجــار (الملتزم) فيضع يديه ووجهه على جدار الكعبة ويدعو :

(أَللّٰهُمَّ إِنِّي عَبْدُكَ وَأَبْنُ عَبْدِكَ وَأَبْنُ أَمَتِكَ ، حَمَلْتَنِي عَلَى دَاَبَّتِكَ وَسَيَّرْتَنِي فِي بِلَادِكَ حَتَّى أَدْخَلْتَنِي حَرَمَكَ وَأَمْنَكَ ، وَقَدْ رَجَوْتُ بِحُسْنِ ظَنِّي أَنْ تَكُونَ قَدْ غَفَرْتَ لِي ذَنْبِي ، فَلَكَ ٱلْحَمْدُ وَلَكَ ٱلشُّكْرُ . أَللّٰهُمَّ أَحْفَظْنِي مِنْ يَمِينِي وَمِنْ شِمَالِي وَمِنْ خَلْفِي وَمِنْ أَمَامِي وَمِنْ فَوْقِي وَمِنْ تَحْتِي حَتَّى تُقْدِمَنِي عَلَى أَهْلِي ، فَإِذَا أَقْدَمْتَنِي عَلَى أَهْلِي فَأَكْفِنِي مَؤُونَةَ عِيَالِي وَأَكْفِنِي مَؤُونَةَ خَلْقِكَ أَجْمَعِين) .

وبعد ذلك يذهب الى بئر زمزم ويشرب من مائه ، ثم يغادر المسجد المقدس عن طريق باب الوداع ويترك مكة ، والافضل ان يكون الخروج من طريق «كدا» . وعند المرور من باب «الوداع» ، يقول ما كان النبي صلى الله عليه وسلم يقوله اذا انصرف من حج او عمرة او غزو ، وهو :

(آيِبُونَ تَائِبُونَ عَابِدُونَ لِرَبِّنَا حَامِدُونَ ، صَدَقَ أَللّهُ وَعْدَهُ وَنَصَرَ عَبْدَهُ وَهَزَمَ ٱلْأَحْزَابَ وَحْدَه) .

المدينة

قرأنا في الحديث ان على المسلمين الذين يقومون بالرحلة المقدسة الى مكة ، ان يزوروا المدينة والمسجد الاقصى في القدس . وزيارة هـذين الاخيرين ليست واجبة ولكنها مستحبة استحباباً مؤكداً (والاخبار في زيارة النبي كثيرة عن ابن عمر وابن عدي والطبراني وعن انس وعطا وعن ابن عباس وغيرهم وفي صحيح مسلم امر النبي بزيارة القبور) . والمدينة هي البلدة المقدسة الثانية في الاسلام ، وتقع على بعد (٣٧٥) كيلومتراً تقريباً الى الشمال من مكة . وهناك مرقد النبي مع كثير من اصحابه .

وهناك طرق كثيرة تؤدي الى المدينة شمالاً من جـدة ومكة . والطريق الرئيسية بين مكة والمدينة هي طريق جمال ليس الا ولا تطرق الا قليلا ، غير ان الطريق الساحلية من جدة ورابغ تسير عليه السيارات واللوريات التي تحمل الحجاج الى المدينة تقطع الطريق الصحراوية في حوالي اثنتين وعشرين ساعـة . ومنظر الطريق مكرب وهي شاقة . وفي غير مناطق الماء ، حيث توجد بعض الاحيان بعض اشجار النخيل ، لا يوجد غير الرمال . وقد يمر عقاب او لقلق في الجو الخالي لولاه . وتختفي العقارب في ظل الصخور الصحراوية . وفي اشهر الصيف يعاني المسافر الحر الشديد وفي الشتاء تصيبه ضربات الرياح البـاردة كشفرات السكاكين . ويسكن بعض البدو قرب كل بئر يبيعون الماء والقهوة ، وقد يقدمون التمر والطعام للمارين .

وأول نقطة من الطريق الشمالي من جدة هي في ذهبان ، والثانية في قول ، والثالثة في رابغ . وذهبان وقول قريتان صغيرتان ، اما رابغ فانها ثغر صغير .

وفي رابغ ينشطر الطريق شطرين احدهما يستمر الى الشمال الغربي على طول الساحل الى « مستورة » ثم ينعطف داخلا الى « ابيار بن حصاني والشفية » «والمسيجيدية» و«الفريش» و « أبيار علي » وهي ذو الحليفة ميقات أهل المدينة ، ثم المدينة .

والطريق الاخرى المؤدية الى رابغ تنعطف داخلا على الفور الى بئر المبارك و«البستان» و« ام البراك » و« الحفة » و«المفرق» ثم يتصل بالطريق الآخر في «المسيجيدية» .

والحجاج الذين يأتون من الجنوب غير مصحوبين بالمطوف يقابلهم على العموم وكيله في أبواب المدينة ، وهو يدعى « المزور » ويتم انباؤه بكتاب او رسالة لاسلكية . فاذا لم يكن المزور موجوداً فان موظفي الحج في البلدة وهم الذين يستقبلون جميع وسائط النقل المقبلة على المدينة ، يستقدمونه ليصحب الحجاج الى الاماكن المعدة لهم .

والمدينة ، هي يثرب القديمة ، وهي واحة ذات حدائق كثيرة ، ولا تفضلها في القدسية غير مكة . وقد التجأ اليها محمد صلى الله عليه وسلم بعد هجرته من مكة . وهناك اوحي اليه كثير من القرآن والاحكام . ويقع جبل « احد » خارج المدينة مباشرة ، وهو الجبل الذي قاتل فيه النبي محمد واصحابه قريشاً في السنة الثالثة للهجرة ، وهناك في سفح الجبل قبور (٧٣) من اصحابه منهم الحمزة بن عبد المطلب عم النبي .

والى القرب من المدينة يقع موضع المعركة الحربية «الخندق» حيث هاجمت قريش المدينة بعشرة آلاف من الأحلاف ، ولكنهم ردوا بخندق حفره النبي إذ كان يتوقع ذلك الهجوم ، وكان ذلك في السنة الخامسة من الهجرة . وهناك سبعة جوامع وقبور لأصحاب النبي .

وتقع الى الخارج مباشرة قبور العباس ، وهو العم الآخر للنبي صلى الله عليه وسلم ، والحسن بن علي سبط النبي من ابنته فاطمة ، وزين العابدين علي بن الحسين عليه السلام ومحمد بن علي الباقر عليه السلام وجعفر بن محمد الصادق عليه السلام واسماعيل ابنه ، وهناك يرقد عثمان بن عفان صهر النبي محمد صلى الله عليه وسلم

والخليفة الثالث في الاسلام . والى القرب من ذلك قبور عدد من زوجات النبي صلى الله عليه وسلم ، وشهداء احد وحليمـــة السعدية والشهداء عند باب البقيع ونافع ، ومالك صاحب المذهب وعقيل بن ابي طالب وسيداتنا بنات النبي صلى الله عليه وسلم ومالك الانصاري البيرقي وعلي عريض ، كل ذلـــك في (البقيع) مقبرة المدينة .

« وأما قبر فاطمة بنت النبي عليها السلام فقد قيل انه في البقيع وقيل انه في حجرتها التي كانت ملاصقة لحجرة النبي ، وبعد توسيع المسجـــد صارت جزءاً منه ، فزرها في كلا المقامين وقل :

(السَّلامُ عَلَيْكِ يا بِنْتَ رَسُولِ اللهِ ، السَّلامُ عَلَيْكِ يا بِنْتَ نَبِيِّ اللهِ ، السَّلامُ عَلَيْكِ يا بِنْتَ حَبِيبِ اللهِ ، السَّلامُ عَلَيْكِ يا بِنْتَ خَلِيلِ اللهِ ، السَّلامُ عَلَيْكِ يا بِنْتَ صَفِيِّ اللهِ ، السَّلامُ عَلَيْكِ يا بِنْتَ أَمِينِ اللهِ ، السَّلامُ عَلَيْكِ يا بِنْتَ خَيْرِ خَلْقِ اللهِ ، السَّلامُ عَلَيْكِ يا بِنْتَ أَفْضَلِ أَنْبِيَاءِ اللهِ ، السَّلامُ عَلَيْكِ يا بِنْتَ خَيْرِ ٱلْبَرِيَّةِ ، السَّلامُ عَلَيْكِ يَا سَيِّدَةَ نِسَاءِ ٱلْعَالَمِينَ مِنَ ٱلْأَوَّلِينَ وَٱلْآخِرِينَ ، السَّلامُ عَلَيْكِ يا زَوْجَةَ وَلِيِّ اللهِ وَخَيْرِ ٱلْخَلْقِ بَعْدَ رَسُولِ اللهِ ، السَّلامُ عَلَيْكِ يا أُمَّ ٱلْحَسَنِ وَٱلْحُسَيْنِ ، سَيِّدَيْ شَبابِ أَهْلِ ٱلْجَنَّةِ ، السَّلامُ عَلَيْكِ أَيَّتُها ٱلصِّدِّيقَةُ ٱلشَّهِيدَةُ ، السَّلامُ عَلَيْكِ أَيَّتُها ٱلصَّادِقَةُ ٱلرَّشِيدَة ، السَّلامُ عَلَيْكِ أَيَّتُها ٱلرَّضِيَّةُ ٱلْمَرْضِيَّة ، السَّلامُ عَلَيْكِ أَيَّتُها ٱلْفاضِلَةُ ٱلزَّكِيَّة ، السَّلامُ عَلَيْكِ أَيَّتُها ٱلْحَوْراءُ ٱلْإِنْسِيَّة ، السَّلامُ عَلَيْكِ أَيَّتُها ٱلتَّقِيَّةُ ٱلنَّقِيَّة ، السَّلامُ عَلَيْكِ أَيَّتُها ٱلْمُحَدَّثَةُ ٱلْعَلِيمَة ، السَّلامُ عَلَيْكِ أَيَّتُها ٱلطَّاهِرَةُ ٱلْمُطَهَّرَة ، السَّلامُ عَلَيْكِ أَيَّتُها

ٱلْمَظْلُومَةُ ٱلْمَغْصُوبَةُ ، ٱلسَّلَامُ عَلَيْكِ أَيَّتُهَا ٱلْمُضْطَهَدَةُ ٱلْمَقْهُورَةُ ، ٱلسَّلَامُ عَلَيْكِ يا فَاطِمَةُ بِنْتَ رَسُولِ ٱللهِ ، وَرَحْمَةُ ٱللهِ وَبَرَكَاتُهُ ، صَلَّى ٱللهُ عَلَيْكِ وَعَلَى رُوحِكِ وَبَدَنِكِ ، أَشْهَدُ أَنَّكِ مَضَيْتِ عَلَى بَيِّنَةٍ مِنْ رَبِّكِ ، وَأَنَّ مَنْ سَرَّكِ فَقَدْ سَرَّ رَسُولَ ٱللهِ ، وَمَنْ جَفَاكِ فَقَدْ جَفَا رَسُولَ ٱللهِ ، وَمَنْ قَطَعَكِ فَقَدْ قَطَعَ رَسُولَ ٱللهِ ، لِأَنَّكِ بِضْعَةٌ مِنْهُ وَرُوحُهُ ٱلَّتِي بَيْنَ جَنْبَيْهِ ، أَشْهِدُ ٱللهَ وَرُسُلَهُ وَمَلائِكَتَهُ أَنِّي رَاضٍ عَمَّنْ رَضِيتِ عَنْهُ ، وَسَاخِطٌ عَلَى مَنْ سَخِطْتِ عَلَيْهِ ، مُتَبَرِّئٌ مِمَّنْ تَبَرَّأْتِ مِنْهُ ، مُوَالٍ لِمَنْ وَالَيْتِ مُعَادٍ لِمَنْ عَادَيْتِ مُبْغِضٌ لِمَنْ أَبْغَضْتِ مُحِبٌّ لِمَنْ أَحْبَبْتِ ؛ وَكَفَى بِٱللهِ شَهِيـــــداً وَحَسِيباً وَجَازِياً وَمُثِيباً وَصَلَّى ٱللهُ عَلَيْكِ وَعَلَى أَبِيكِ مُحَمَّدٍ رَسُولِ اللهِ ، وَعَلَى بَعْلِكِ أَمِيرِ ٱلْمُؤْمِنِينَ وَعَلَى أَبْنَائِكِ ٱلْأَئِمَّةِ ٱلطَّاهِرِينَ ، وَسَلَّمَ تَسْلِيماً كَثِيراً) .

« ثم تقول ما روي عن الباقر عليه السلام » :

يا مُمْتَحَنَةُ ٱمْتَحَنَكِ ٱللهُ ٱلَّذِي خَلَقَكِ قَبْلَ أَنْ يَخْلُقَكِ فَوَجَدَكِ لِمَا ٱمْتَحَنَكِ صَابِرَةً وَزَعَمْنَا أَنَّا أَوْلِيَاؤُكِ وَمُصَدِّقُونَ وَصَابِرُونَ لِكُلِّ مَا أَتَانا بِهِ أَبُوكِ وَأَتَانا بِهِ وَصِيُّهُ فَإِنَّا نَسْأَلُكِ إِنْ كُنَّا صَدَّقْنَاكِ أَلَا أَلْحَقْتِنَا بِتَصْدِيقِنَا لَهُمَا لِنُبَشِّرَ أَنْفُسَنَا بِأَنَّا قَدْ طَهُرْنَا بِوَلَايَتِكِ .

« ثم تقول » :

السَّلامُ عَلَيْكِ يا سَيِّدَةَ نِسَاءِ ٱلْعَالَمِين ، السَّلامُ عَلَيْكِ يا والِدَةَ الْحُجَجِ عَلى ٱلنَّاسِ أَجْمَعِين، السَّلامُ عَلَيْكِ أَيَّتُها ٱلْمَظْلُومَةُ ٱلْمَمْنُوعَةُ حَقَّها (السَّلامُ عَلَيْكِ أَيَّتُها ٱلصِّدِّيقَةُ ٱلطَّاهِرَةُ ٱلْمَظْلُومَةِ ، السَّلامُ عَلَيْكِ يا بِضْعَةَ ٱلنَّبِيِّ صَلَّى ٱللهُ عَلَيْهِ وَآلِهِ خ) .

ثم قل :

أَللّٰهُمَّ صَلِّ عَلى أَمَتِكَ وَٱبْنَةِ نَبِيِّكَ وَزَوْجَةِ وَصِيِّ نَبِيِّكَ صَلاةً تُزْلِفُها فَوْقَ زُلْفَى عِبَادِكَ ٱلْمُكَرَّمِينَ مِنْ أَهْلِ ٱلسَّمْوات وَٱلأَرَضِين) .

وبعد الوصول الى المدينة والاغتسال وتغيير الملابس يقصــد الى اول محل تستحب زيارته وهو مسجد الحرم النبوي ، ثاني مسجد بناه النبي محمد صلى الله عليه وسلم لأتباعه من المؤمنين بعد هجرته من مكة ، فقد كان المسجد الاول في «قبا» وهو يبعد بضعة كيلومترات عن المدينة على طريق الجبال من مكة . وقد اشتغل النبي شخصياً في بناء كلا المسجدين ، غير انه هنا في مسجد النبي محل قـبره الشريف ؛ والى جواره قبرا ابي بكر وعمر . وقـد بني المسجد الاصلي بالآجر المجفف بالشمس (اللبن) ، وكانت ارضه من التراب ، وسقفه من جذوع النخل المغطاة بالطين ودعائمه من الجذوع . اما اليوم فان الاعمــدة من المرمر اللماع ، وذلك لأن حرم النبي قد اعيد بناؤه وأضيف اليه كثير من قبل عـدة ملوك آخرهم السلطان عبد المجيد ، ولم يبق ثابتاً لا يتغير الا الإيمـان . (وجـدد بناءه صاحب الجلالة عبد العزيز آل سعود ملك المملكة العربية السعودية) . واذا ما بانت لك ابنية المدينة فقل :

(أَللّٰهُمَّ إِنَّ هٰذا حَرَمُ نَبِيِّكَ وَقَدْ حَرَّمْتَهُ عَلى لِسانِهِ صَلَّى ٱللهُ عَلَيْهِ وَسَلَّمَ فَٱجْعَلْهُ وِقايَةً لِي مِنَ ٱلنَّارِ ، وَأَماناً مِنْ سُوءِ ٱلْحِساب) .

وعند رؤيتك القبة الشريفة قل :

(أَللّٰهُمَّ إِنِّي أَسْأَلُكَ ٱلثَّبَاتَ فِي ٱلْأَمْرِ وَعَزِيمَةَ ٱلرُّشْدِ وَشُكْرَ ٱلنِّعْمَةِ وَحُسْنَ عِبَادَتِكَ ، وَأَسْأَلُكَ مِنْ خَيْرِ مَا تَعْلَمُ وَأَسْتَغْفِرُكَ مِمَّا تَعْلَمُ ، إِنَّكَ أَنْتَ عَلَّامُ ٱلْغُيُوبِ . وَصَلَّى ٱللّٰهُ عَلَى سَيِّدِنَا مُحَمَّدٍ وَعَلَى آلِهِ وَصَحْبِهِ وَسَلَّمَ) .

يدخل الحجاج المسجد بصحبة المطوف او المزور من «باب السلام» وهم يقولون :

(رَبِّ أَدْخِلْنِي مَدْخَلَ صِدْقٍ وَأَخْرِجْنِي مُخْرَجَ صِدْقٍ وَأَجْعَلْ لِي مِنْ لَدُنْكَ سُلْطَاناً نَصِيراً) أَللّٰهُمَّ صَلِّ عَلَى سَيِّدِنَا مُحَمَّدٍ وَعَلَى آلِهِ وَٱغْفِرْ لِي ذُنُوبِي وَٱفْتَحْ لِي أَبْوَابَ رَحْمَتِكَ وَأَدْخِلْنِي فِيهَا يَا أَرْحَمَ ٱلرَّاحِمِينَ) .

ويتبع ذلك نفس الكلمات التي يفوه بها الحجاج الداخلون الى المسجد في مكة ثم يقرأ :

(أَللّٰهُمَّ ٱفْتَحْ لِي أَبْوَابَ رَحْمَتِكَ وَمَغْفِرَتِكَ . وَأَدْخِلْنِي فِيهَا . بِٱسْمِ ٱللّٰهِ وَٱلْحَمْدُ لِلّٰهِ ، وَٱلصَّلَاةُ وَٱلسَّلَامُ عَلَى رَسُولِ ٱللّٰهِ صَلَّى ٱللّٰهُ عَلَيْهِ وَسَلَّمَ) .

وفي داخل المسجد الحالي حدود مسجد النبي ، وقد اثرت بقضبان من النحاس ، ويسمى هذا الموقع بالروضة ، ويقع على يمين القبة التي فيها قبر النبي محمد صلى الله عليه وسلم (وقد ورد فيها الحديث الشريف :

(مَا بَيْنَ بَيْتِي وَمِنْبَرِي رَوْضَةٌ مِنْ رِيَاضِ ٱلْجَنَّةِ) .

وطولها ٢٢ متراً وعرضها ١٥ متراً) .

فادخل الى المحل المسمى بالروضة وصلِّ ركعتين واقرأ الدعاء التالي :

(أَللّٰهُمَّ إِنَّ هٰذِهِ رَوْضَةٌ مِنْ رِياضِ ٱلْجَنَّةِ ، شَرَّفْتَها وَكَرَّمْتَها وَنَوَّرْتَها بِنُورِ نَبِيِّكَ وَحَبِيبِكَ مُحَمَّدٍ صَلَّى ٱللهُ عَلَيْهِ وَسَلَّمَ ، فَٱحْشُرْنا فِي زُمْرَتِهِ وَأَمِتْنا عَلى مَحَبَّتِهِ وَسُنَّتِهِ ، وَأَسْقِنا مِنْ حَوْضِهِ وَبِيَدِهِ ٱلشَّرِيفَةِ شُرْبَةً هَنِيئَةً لا نَظْمَأُ بَعْدَها أَبَداً ، إِنَّكَ عَلى كُلِّ شَيْءٍ قَدِير) .

ثم قم بعد ذلك في خشوع الى قبر النبي . وبرقد هناك في الحجرة محمد صلى الله عليه وسلم وابو بكر وعمر وقد غطيت الضرائح بالحرير الاخضر ، وقد كان ذلك الموقع في زمن النبي صلى الله عليه وسلم بيت زوجته عائشة ويبلغ طوله (١٦) متراً وعرضه (١٥) متراً فاذا وقفت هناك فزر النبي وقل :

(اَلسَّلامُ عَلَيْكَ أَيُّها ٱلسَّيِّدُ ٱلْكَرِيمُ وَٱلرَّسُولُ ٱلْعَظِيمُ وَٱلرَّؤُوفُ ٱلرَّحِيمُ وَرَحْمَةُ ٱللهِ وَبَرَكاتُهُ ، السَّلامُ عَلَيْكَ يا نَبِيَّ اللهِ ، السَّلامُ عَلَيْكَ يا صَفْوَةَ خَلْقِ اللهِ ، السَّلامُ عَلَيْكَ يا حَبِيبَ اللهِ ، أَشْهَدُ أَنْ لا إِلٰهَ إِلَّا ٱللهُ وَحْدَهُ لا شَرِيكَ لَهُ ، وَأَنَّكَ عَبْدُهُ وَرَسُولُهُ ، وَأَشْهَدُ أَنَّكَ بَلَّغْتَ ٱلرِّسالَةَ ، وَأَدَّيْتَ ٱلْأَمانَةَ ، وَنَصَحْتَ ٱلْأُمَّةَ ، وَجاهَدْتَ فِي سَبِيلِ اللهِ ، فَصَلَّى عَلَيْكَ ٱللهُ صَلاةً دائِمَةً إِلى يَوْمِ ٱلدِّينِ . رَبَّنا آتِنا فِي ٱلدُّنْيا حَسَنَةً وَفِي ٱلآخِرَةِ حَسَنَةً وَقِنا عَذابَ ٱلنَّارِ ، أَللّٰهُمَّ آتِهِ ٱلْوَسِيلَةَ وَٱلْفَضِيلَةَ وَٱلدَّرَجَةَ ٱلرَّفِيعَةَ ، وَٱبْعَثْهُ مَقاماً مَحْمُوداً ٱلَّذِي وَعَدْتَهُ ، إِنَّكَ لا تُخْلِفُ ٱلْمِيعادَ) .

ثم يبلّغ سلام من أوصاه تبليغه لرسول الله صلى الله عليه وسلم .
او قل ما روي عن الرضى عليه السلام في زيارة النبي وهو قوله :

« (السَّلامُ عَلى رَسُولِ الله ، السَّلامُ عَلَيْكَ وَرَحْمَةُ اللهِ وَبَرَكاتُه،
السَّلامُ عَلَيْكَ يا مُحَمَّدُ بْنُ عَبْدِ الله ، السَّلامُ عَلَيْكَ يا خِيرَةَ اللهِ خ »
السَّلامُ عَلَيْكَ يا حَبيبَ الله ، السَّلامُ عَلَيْكَ يا صُفوَةَ الله ، السَّلام
عَلَيْكَ يا أمينَ الله ، « السَّلامُ عَلَيْكَ يا حُجَّةَ الله ، أَشْهَدُ أَنَّكَ
رَسُولُ الله ، وَأَشْهَدُ أَنَّكَ مُحَمَّدُ بْنُ عَبْدِ الله خ » وَأَشْهَدُ أَنَّكَ
قَدْ نَصَحْتَ لِأُمَّتِكَ وَجاهَدْتَ في سَبيلِ رَبِّكَ وَعَبَدْتَهُ حَتّى أَتاكَ
الْيَقينِ ، فَجَزاكَ اللهُ أَفْضَلَ ما جَزَى نَبِيّاً عَنْ أُمَّتِهِ ؛ أَللَّهُمَّ صَلِّ
عَلى مُحَمَّدٍ وَ آلِ مُحَمَّدٍ أَفْضَلَ ما صَلَّيْتَ عَلى إِبْراهيمَ وَ آلِ إِبْراهيمَ؛
إِنَّكَ حَميدٌ مَجيد) . »

فاذا انتهى الزائر من ذلك يستطيع ان يسبح ويصلي ما يشاء ، وما يخطر
بباله ، ثم يذهب الى قبر ابي بكر رضي الله عنه ويقرأ التحية التالية :

السَّلامُ عَلَيْكَ يا خَليفَةَ رَسُولِ اللهِ ، السَّلامُ عَلَيْكَ يا صاحِبَ
رَسُولِ اللهِ في الْغارِ ، السَّلامُ عَلَيْكَ يا أمينَهُ عَلى الْأَسْرارِ ،
جَزاكَ اللهُ عَنّا أَفْضَلَ ما جَزَى إِماماً عَنْ أُمَّةِ نَبِيِّهِ ، فَلَقَدْ خَلَفْتَهُ
أَحْسَنَ الْخَلَفِ ، وَسَلَكْتَ طَريقَهُ وَمِنْهاجَهُ خَيْرَ سُلُوكٍ ، وَنَصَرْتَ
الْإِسْلامَ ، وَوَصَلْتَ الْأَرْحامَ ، وَلَمْ تَزَلْ قائِماً بِالْحَقِّ حَتّى
أَتاكَ الْيَقينَ . فَالسَّلامُ عَلَيْكَ وَرَحْمَةُ اللهِ وَبَرَكاتُه .

فاذا وصلت الى قبر عمر رضي الله عنه فاقرأ التحية التالية :

(اَلسَّلامُ عَلَيْكَ يا مُظْهِرَ اَلْإِسلام ، اَلسَّلامُ عَلَيْكَ يا فاروق ، اَلسَّلامُ عَلَيْكَ يا مَنْ نَطَقْتَ بِالصَّواب ، وَكَفِلْتَ اَلأَيتام ، وَوَصَلْتَ اَلأَرحام وَقَوِّيَ بِكَ اَلْإِسلام ، اَلسَّلامُ عَلَيْكَ وَرَحْمَةُ الله) .

وهنا يستطيع الزائر (او الزائرة) ان يدعو لنفسه او لغيره (او لغيرها) ولجميع المسلمين من الغائبين عن المدينة ، ولا سيما اولئك المؤمنين المحرومين من هذه الزيارة . ثم يصلي الزائر ركعتي الزيارة .

ويستحب بعد زيارة قبر النبي ومسجده ان يزور «البقيع» مقبرة المدينة ويدعو لأصحاب النبي وزوجاته واقربائه وأتباعه ويقرأ الزيارة التالية :

(اَلسَّلامُ عَلَيْكُمْ جَميعاً أَهلَ اَلْبَقيعِ ، أَهلَ اَلْجَنابِ اَلرَّفيعِ ، وَرَحْمَةُ اَللهِ وَبَرَكاتُه) .

وتقرأ الفاتحة وتدعو بما تشاء وتقرأ زيارة ائمة البقيع عليهم السلام :

« (اَلسَّلامُ عَلَيْكُمْ يا خزَّانَ عِلْمِ اَللهِ وَحَفَظَةَ سِرِّهِ وَتَرَاجِمَةَ وَحْيِهِ ، أَتَيْتُكُمْ يا بَني رَسُولِ اَللهِ عارِفاً بِحَقِّكُمْ ، مُسْتَبْصِراً بِشَأْنِكُمْ ، مُعادِياً لِأَعْدائِكُمْ مُوالِياً لِأَوْلِيائِكُمْ ، بِأَبي أَنْتُمْ وَأُمِّي ، صَلَّى اَللهُ عَلَى أَرْواحِكُمْ وَأَبْدانِكُمْ ؛ أَللّهُمَّ إِنِّي أَتَوَلَّى آخِرَهُمْ كَما تَوَلَّيْتُ أَوَّلَهُمْ وَأَبْرَأُ مِنْ كُلِّ وَليجَةٍ دُونَهُمْ ؛ آمَنْتُ بِاَللهِ وَكَفَرْتُ بِالجِبْتِ وَاَلطَّاغُوتِ وَاَللاتِ وَاَلعُزَّى ، وَكُلِّ نَدٍّ يُدْعَى مِنْ دُونِ اَللهِ) » .

ثم تزور العباس عمّ النبي صلى الله عليه وسلم فتقول :

« (اَلسَّلامُ عَلَيْكَ ياعَبَّاسُ بْنَ عَبْدِ اَلْمُطَّلِبِ ، اَلسَّلامُ عَلَيْكَ ياعَمَّ رَسُولِ اَللهِ ، اَلسَّلامُ عَلَيْكَ ياصاحِبَ اَلسِّقَايَةِ وَرَحْمَةُ اَللهِ وَبَرَكاتُه) » .

وتزور فاطمة بنت اسد بن هاشم ، امّ امير المؤمنين علي عليه السلام ، في مزارها المعروف بالبقيع ، وفي قبة ائمة البقيع ايضاً فتقول :

« (السَّلامُ عَلى فاطِمَةَ بِنْتِ أَسَدِ بْنِ هاشِمِ بْنِ عَبْدِ مَنافٍ ؛ السَّلامُ عَلَيْكِ يا أُمَّ سَيِّدِ ٱلْأَوْصِياءِ ؛ السَّلامُ عَلَيْكِ يا أُمَّ خَلِيفَةِ سَيِّدِ ٱلْأَنْبِياءِ ؛ السَّلامُ عَلَيْكِ يا أُمَّ أَمِيرِ ٱلْمُؤْمِنِينَ عَلِيِّ بْنِ أَبي طالِبٍ عَلَيْهِ ٱلسَّلامُ ؛ السَّلامُ عَلى مَنْ كانَتْ لِرَسُولِ ٱللهِ صَلَّى ٱللهُ عَلَيْهِ وَآلِهِ وَسَلَّمَ بِمَنْزِلَةِ ٱلْأُمِّ ؛ السَّلامُ عَلَيْكِ يا مَنِ أَضْطَجَعَ في قَبْرِها رَسُولُ ٱللهِ صَلَّى ٱللهُ عَلَيْهِ وَآلِهِ وَسَلَّمَ ، وَكَفَّنَها بِقَمِيصِهِ وَلَقَّنَها جَوابَ مُنْكَرٍ وَنَكِيرٍ ؛ السَّلامُ عَلَيْكِ وَعلى وَلَدِكِ أَمِيرِ ٱلْمُؤْمِنِينَ وَٱلْأَئِمَّةِ ٱلْمَيامِينَ مِنْ وَلَدِهِ وَرَحْمَةُ ٱللهِ وَبَرَكاتُهُ) » .

وتقول في زيارة ابراهيم ابن رسول الله صلى الله عليه وآله وسلم :

(السَّلامُ عَلى رَسُولِ ٱللهِ ، السَّلامُ عَلى جَمِيعِ أَنْبِياءِ ٱللهِ وَرُسُلِهِ ، السَّلامُ عَلى إِبْراهِيمَ ٱبْنِ رَسُولِ ٱللهِ ، السَّلامُ عَلَيْكَ أَيُّها ٱلنَّسَمَةُ ٱلزَّاكِيَةِ ، السَّلامُ عَلَيْكَ يا ٱبْنَ خَيْرِ ٱلْوَرَى ، السَّلامُ عَلَيْكَ يا مَنِ أَخْتارَهُ ٱللهُ إِلَيْهِ طاهِراً نَقِيًّا قَبْلَ أَنْ يَكْتُبَ عَلَيْهِ حَلالَهُ وَحَرامَهُ ، السَّلامُ عَلَيْكَ وَرَحْمَةُ ٱللهِ وَبَرَكاتُهُ) » .

وتزور عبدالله والد النبي صلى الله عليه وآله وسلم وتقول بهذه الزيارة :

« (السَّلامُ عَلَيْكَ يا صاحِبَ ٱلْمَجْدِ ٱلْأَثِيلِ ؛ السَّلامُ عَلَيْكَ يا خَيْرَ فَرْعٍ مِنْ دَوْحَةِ ٱلْخَلِيلِ ، السَّلامُ عَلَيْكَ يا ٱبْنَ ٱلذَّبِيحِ إِسْماعِيلَ ؛ السَّلامُ عَلَيْكَ يا سُلالَةَ ٱلْأَبْرارِ ؛ السَّلامُ عَلَيْكَ يا أَبا

ٱلنَّبِيِّ ٱلْمُخْتَارِ وَعَمِّ ٱلْوَصِيِّ ٱلْكَرَّارِ وَوَالِدِ ٱلْأَئِمَّةِ ٱلْأَطْهَارِ ؛
السَّلَامُ عَلَيْكَ يَا مَنْ أَضَاءَتْ بِنُورِ جَبِينِهِ عِنْدَ وِلَادَتِهِ أَطْرَافُ
ٱلسَّمَاءِ ؛ السَّلَامُ عَلَيْكَ يَا يُوسُفَ آلِ عَبْدِ مَنَافٍ ؛ السَّلَامُ عَلَيْكَ
يَا مَنْ سَلَكَ مَسْلَكَ جَدِّهِ إِسْمَاعِيلَ فَأَسْلَمَ لِأَبِيهِ لِيَذْبَحَهُ ؛ السَّلَامُ
عَلَيْكَ يَا مَنْ فَدَاهُ ٱللهُ بِمَا فَدَاهُ ، وَتَقَبَّلَهُ فَأَعْطَاهُ أُمَّهُ وَأَبَاهُ ؛
السَّلَامُ عَلَيْكَ يَا حَامِلَ نُورِ ٱلنُّبُوَّةِ ؛ السَّلَامُ عَلَيْكَ يَا أَشْرَفَ
ٱلنَّاسِ فِي ٱلْأُبُوَّةِ وَٱلْبُنُوَّةِ ؛ السَّلَامُ عَلَيْكَ يَا وَالِدَ خَاتَمِ ٱلنَّبِيِّينَ ؛
السَّلَامُ عَلَيْكَ يَا أَبَا ٱلطَّاهِرِينَ بَعْدَ ٱلطَّاهِرِينَ وَٱبْنَ ٱلطَّاهِرِينَ
وَرَحْمَةُ ٱللهِ وَبَرَكَاتُهُ) » .

ثم تزور الحمزة عم النبي صلى الله عليه وآله وسلم بأحُد فتقول :

« (السَّلَامُ عَلَيْكَ يَا عَمَّ رَسُولِ ٱللهِ وَخَيْرَ ٱلشُّهَدَاءِ ؛ السَّلَامُ
عَلَيْكَ يَا أَسَدَ ٱللهِ وَأَسَدَ رَسُولِهِ ؛ أَشْهَدُ أَنَّكَ جَاهَدْتَ فِي سَبِيلِ
ٱللهِ ، وَنَصَحْتَ لِرَسُولِ ٱللهِ صَلَّى ٱللهُ عَلَيْهِ وَآلِهِ وَسَلَّمَ ، وُجُدْتَ
بِنَفْسِكَ وَطَلَبْتَ مَا عِنْدَ ٱللهِ ، وَرَغِبْتَ فِيمَا وَعَدَ ٱللهُ) » .

ثم تزور شهداء أحُد فتقول :

« السَّلَامُ عَلَيْكُمْ يَا أَهْلَ ٱلدِّيَارِ ٱلْمُوحِشَةِ، أَنْتُمْ لَنَا فَرْطٌ وَإِنَّا
« ونحن خ ل » بِكُمْ لَاحِقُونَ ؛ السَّلَامُ عَلَيْكُمْ بِمَا صَبَرْتُمْ
فَنِعْمَ عُقْبَى ٱلدَّارِ » .

وتصلي عندهم ما احببت وتدعو الله تعالى بما شئت للدنيا والآخرة .
وليس هناك ما يجب اتباعه من مراسيم مخصوصة أو زيارة معينـــة او وقت

معين . فالناس لا يأتون المدينة لكي يعودوا الى اوطانهم فيقولوا انهم زاروا هذه الامكنة ولكن لكي يعبدوا الله ، حيث عبد النبي محمد صلى الله عليه وسلم ربه .

فزر « قبا » وهي قرية ذات حدائق خارج اسوار المدينة وحدود الموضع الاول للعبادة الذي عينه النبي واصحابه بعد هجرته من مكة الى المدينة . وهناك مسجد يسمى « مسجد التقوى » .

فقد جاء النبي صلى الله عليه وسلم وابو بكر بعد خروجها من مكة واجتيازها الصحراء الى « قبا » حيث استراحا مدة تزيد عن عشرة أيام . وفي خلال هذه المدة عين النبي موقع « مسجد التقوى » وصلى اول صلاة للجمعة ثم استمر في سيره الى المدينة .

وقد امرنا ان نصلي ركعتين ونقول :

« أَللّٰهُمَّ إِنَّ هٰذَا ٱلْمَسْجِدَ مَسْجِدُ قُبَاء ، وَمُصَلّى نَبِيّنَا وَحَبِيبِنَا وَسَيِّدِنَا مُحَمَّدٍ صَلَّى ٱللّٰهُ أَنَهُ عَلَيْهِ وَسَلَّمَ ؛ أَللّٰهُمَّ إِنَّكَ قُلْتَ وَقَوْلُكَ ٱلْحَقُّ فِي كِتَابِكَ ٱلْمُنَزَّلِ ، عَلى لِسَانِ نَبِيّكَ ٱلْمُرْسَلِ ، لَمَسْجِدٌ أُسِّسَ عَلى ٱلتَّقْوى مِنْ أَوَّلِ يَوْمٍ أَحَقُّ أَنْ تَقُومَ فِيهِ . فِيهِ رِجَالٌ يُحِبُّونَ أَنْ يَتَطَهَّرُوا ، وَٱللّٰهُ يُحِبُّ ٱلْمُتَطَهِّرِينَ . » . (التوبة،١٠٩)

(أَللّٰهُمَّ طَهِّرْ قُلُوبَنَا مِنَ ٱلنِّفَاقِ وَأَعْمَالَنَا مِنَ ٱلرِّيَاءِ ، وَفُرُوجَنَا مِنَ ٱلزِّنَا ، وَأَلْسِنَتَنَا مِنَ ٱلْكَذِبِ وَٱلْغِيبَةِ ، وَأَعْيُنَنَا مِنَ ٱلْخِيَانَةِ ، فَإِنَّكَ تَعْلَمُ خَائِنَةَ ٱلْأَعْيُنِ وَمَا تُخْفِي ٱلصُّدُورُ . رَبَّنَا ظَلَمْنَا أَنْفُسَنَا وَإِنْ لَمْ تَغْفِرْ لَنَا وَتَرْحَمْنَا لَنَكُونَنَّ مِنَ ٱلْخَاسِرِينَ) .

ويقع قرب مسجد التقوى مسجد « الخاتم » وكان يدعى في الازمنة السابقة « بئر العريش » فقد كان خاتم النبي في عهدة ابي بكر عند موته ثم اصبح عند عمر ، ثم عثمان . وقد روي ان عثمان جاء مرة الى البئر للوضوء ، فلما كان يأخذ الماء سقط خاتم النبي محمد صلى الله عليه وسلم من يد عثمان في البئر ولم يعثر

عليه قط .

ويستحب للزائر بعد ذلك ان يزور مسجد القبلتين . وذلك ان النبي عندما جاء الى المدينة كان هو وجميع المسلمين يتجهون في صلاتهم نحو القدس غير أنه هناك تلقى الوحي الالهي الذي اسس قبلة الصلاة الجديدة وهي الكعبة المكرمة في مكة :

« قَدْ نَرَى تَقَلُّبَ وَجْهِكَ فِي السَّمَاءِ فَلَنُوَلِّيَنَّكَ قِبْلَةً تَرْضَاهَا فَوَلِّ وَجْهَكَ شَطْرَ الْمَسْجِدِ الْحَرَامِ ، وَحَيْثُ مَا كُنْتُمْ فَوَلُّوا وُجُوهَكُمْ شَطْرَهُ ، وَإِنَّ الَّذِينَ أُوتُوا الْكِتَابَ لَيَعْلَمُونَ أَنَّهُ الْحَقُّ مِنْ رَبِّهِمْ ، وَمَا اللهُ بِغَافِلٍ عَمَّا يَعْمَلُونَ » .

(سورة البقرة ، ١٤٤)

وصلِّ ركعتين في مسجد القبلتين ثم اتل الدعاء التالي :

(أَللّٰهُمَّ إِنَّ هٰذَا مَسْجِدُ الْقِبْلَتَيْنِ ، وَمُصَلَّى النَّبِيِّ سَيِّدِنَا مُحَمَّدٍ عَلَيْهِ الصَّلَاةُ وَالسَّلَامُ . أَللّٰهُمَّ كَمَا وَفَّقْتَنَا لِزِيَارَتِهِ وَمَنْ فِيهِ فِي هٰذِهِ الدُّنْيَا فَلَا تَحْرِمْنَا شَفَاعَتَهُ فِي الْآخِرَةِ) .

ويستحب بعد ذلك ان يذهب الى مسجد الاحزاب وهو مسجد الفتح في الخندق ، ويصلي ركعتين ويسبح ويدعو ثم يزور جبل احد حيث يرقد ثلاثة وسبعون من اصحاب النبي . « (ويستحب اتيان المشاهد كلها بالمدينة كمسجد الفضيخ ومسجد امير المؤمنين علي عليه السلام ومسجد سلمان) » . وقبل مغادرة المدينة يقوم الحاج بزيارة وداع لقبر النبي ويقول :

« اَلْحَمْدُ لِلَّهِ وَالصَّلَاةُ وَالسَّلَامُ عَلَى سَيِّدِنَا رَسُولِ اللهِ ؛ أَللّٰهُمَّ إِنَّا نَسْأَلُكَ فِي سَفَرِنَا هٰذَا الْبِرَّ وَالتَّقْوَى ، وَمِنَ الْعَمَلِ مَا تَرْضَى ؛ أَللّٰهُمَّ لَا تَجْعَلْ هٰذَا آخِرَ الْعَهْدِ بِرَسُولِكَ ، وَيَسِّرْ لَنَا

ٱلْعَوْدَ إِلَى ٱلْحَرَمَيْنِ ٱلشَّرِيفَيْنِ ، وَٱجْعَلْهُ سَبِيلاً سَهْلاً وَٱرْزُقْنَا ٱلْعَفْوَ وَٱلْعَافِيَةَ فِي ٱلدِّينِ وَٱلدُّنْيَا وَٱلْآخِرَةِ ، وَرُدَّنَا سَالِمِينَ ظَافِرِينَ غَانِمِينَ تَائِبِينَ عَابِدِينَ سَائِحِينَ رَاكِعِينَ سَاجِدِينَ ؛ ٱللَّهُمَّ بَارِكْ لَنَا فِيمَا وَهَبْتَ وَوَفِّقْنَا لِحَمْدِكَ وَشُكْرِكَ ؛ ٱللَّهُمَّ أَعِنِّي وَٱرْزُقْنِي وَأَدْخِلْنِي بِرَحْمَتِكَ فِي عِبَادِكَ ٱلصَّالِحِينَ ، وَصَلَّى ٱللهُ عَلَى سَيِّدِنَا مُحَمَّدٍ ٱلنَّبِيِّ ٱلْأُمِّيِّ وَعَلَى آلِهِ وَصَحْبِهِ وَسَلَّمَ » .

أو قل :

« (ٱلسَّلَامُ عَلَيْكَ يَا رَسُولَ ٱللهِ ؛ ٱلسَّلَامُ عَلَيْكَ أَيُّهَا ٱلْبَشِيرُ ٱلنَّذِيرُ ، ٱلسَّلَامُ عَلَيْكَ أَيُّهَا ٱلسِّرَاجُ ٱلْمُنِيرُ ؛ ٱلسَّلَامُ عَلَيْكَ أَيُّهَا ٱلسَّفِيرُ بَيْنَ ٱللهِ وَبَيْنَ خَلْقِهِ ؛ أَشْهَدُ يَا رَسُولَ ٱللهِ أَنَّكَ كُنْتَ نُوراً فِي ٱلْأَصْلَابِ ٱلشَّامِخَةِ وَٱلْأَرْحَامِ ٱلْمُطَهَّرَةِ ، لَمْ تُنَجِّسْكَ ٱلْجَاهِلِيَّةُ بِأَنْجَاسِهَا ، وَلَمْ تُلْبِسْكَ مِنْ مُدْلَهِمَّاتِ ثِيَابِهَا ، وَأَشْهَدُ يَا رَسُولَ ٱللهِ أَنِّي مُؤْمِنٌ بِكَ وَبِٱلْأَئِمَّةِ مِنْ أَهْلِ بَيْتِكَ أَعْلَامِ ٱلْهُدَى وَٱلْعُرْوَةِ ٱلْوُثْقَى وَٱلْحُجَّةِ عَلَى أَهْلِ ٱلدُّنْيَا ؛ ٱللَّهُمَّ لَا تَجْعَلْهُ آخِرَ ٱلْعَهْدِ مِنْ زِيَارَةِ نَبِيِّكَ عَلَيْهِ ٱلسَّلَامُ ، وَإِنْ تَوَفَّيْتَنِي فَإِنِّي أَشْهَدُ فِي مَمَاتِي عَلَى مَا أَشْهَدُ عَلَيْهِ فِي حَيَاتِي أَنَّكَ أَنْتَ ٱللهُ لَا إِلَهَ إِلَّا أَنْتَ وَحْدَكَ لَا شَرِيكَ لَكَ وَأَنَّ مُحَمَّداً عَبْدُكَ وَرَسُولُكَ وَأَنَّ ٱلْأَئِمَّةَ مِنْ أَهْلِ بَيْتِهِ أَوْلِيَاؤُكَ وَأَنْصَارُكَ وَحُجَجُكَ عَلَى خَلْقِكَ وَخُلَفَاؤُكَ فِي عِبَادِكَ وَأَعْلَامُكَ فِي بِلَادِكَ وَخُزَّانُ عِلْمِكَ

وَحَفَظَةُ سِرِّكَ وَتَرَاجِمَةُ وَحْيِكَ ؛ أَللّٰهُمَّ صَلِّ عَلـى مُحَمَّدٍ وَآلِ مُحَمَّدٍ وَبَلِّغْ رُوحَ نَبِيِّكَ مُحَمَّدٍ وَآلِهِ فِي سَاعَتِي هٰذِهِ وَفِي كُلِّ سَاعَةٍ تَحِيَّةً مِنِّي وَسَلَاماً ؛ السَّلامُ عَلَيْكَ يَا رَسُولَ اللهِ وَرَحْمَةُ اللهِ وَبَرَكَاتُهُ . (ثم تقول) أَللّٰهُمَّ لَا تَجْعَلْهُ آخِرَ الْعَهْدِ مِـنْ زِيَارَةِ نَبِيِّكَ ، فَإِنْ تَوَفَّيْتَنِي قَبْلَ ذٰلِكَ فَإِنِّي أَشْهَدُ فِي مَمَاتِي عَلـى مَا أَشْهَدُ عَلَيْهِ فِي حَيَاتِي أَنْ لَا إِلٰهَ إِلَّا أَنْتَ ، وَأَنَّ مُحَمَّداً عَبْدُكَ وَرَسُولُكَ ، وَأَنَّكَ قَدِ اخْتَرْتَهُ مِنْ خَلْقِكَ ثُمَّ اخْتَرْتَ مِنْ أَهْلِ بَيْتِهِ الْأَئِمَّةَ الطَّاهِرِينَ الَّذِينَ أَذْهَبْتَ عَنْهُمُ الرِّجْسَ وَطَهَّرْتَهُمْ تَطْهِيراً فَاحْشُرْنَا مَعَهُمْ وَفِي زُمْرَتِهِمْ وَتَحْتَ لِوَائِهِمْ وَلَا تُفَرِّقْ بَيْنَنَا وَبَيْنَهُمْ فِي الدُّنْيَا وَالْآخِرَةِ يَا أَرْحَمَ الرَّاحِمِينَ . السَّلامُ عَلَيْكَ لَا جَعَلَهُ اللهُ آخِرَ تَسْلِيمِي عَلَيْكَ) .

زيارات في مكة

« (وقبل ان ننتقل الى بيت المقدس رأينا من المناسب ان نثبت بعض الزيارات المستحبة للاماكن المشرفة بمكة لتتم بذلك الفائدة) » .

زيارة عبد مناف جد النبي (ص)

(السَّلامُ عَلَيْكَ أَيُّها السَّيِّدُ النَّبِيلُ ، السَّلامُ عَلَيْكَ أَيُّها الْغُصْنُ الْمُنِيرُ مِنْ شَجَرَةِ إِبْرَاهِيمَ الْخَلِيلِ ؛ السَّلامُ عَلَيْكَ يَا جَدَّ خَيْرِ

ٱلوَرَى ، ٱلسَّلَامُ عَلَيْكَ يَا ٱبْنَ ٱلْأَنْبِيَاءِ ٱلْأَصْفِيَاءِ ؛ ٱلسَّلَامُ عَلَيْكَ
يَا ٱبْنَ ٱلْأَوْصِيَاءِ ٱلْأَوْلِيَاءِ ؛ ٱلسَّلَامُ عَلَيْكَ يَاسَيِّدَ ٱلْحَرَمِ ؛ ٱلسَّلَامُ
عَلَيْكَ يَا وَارِثَ مَقَامِ إِبْرَاهِيمَ ، ٱلسَّلَامُ عَلَيْكَ يَا صَاحِبَ بَيْتِ ٱللهِ
ٱلْعَظِيمِ ؛ ٱلسَّلَامُ عَلَيْكَ وَعَلَى آبَائِكَ وَأَبْنَائِكَ الطَّاهِرِينَ وَرَحْمَةُ اللهِ
وَبَرَكَاتُه) .

زيارة عبد المطلب جد النبي (ص)

(ٱلسَّلَامُ عَلَيْكَ يَا سَيِّدَ ٱلْبَطْحَاءِ ، ٱلسَّلَامُ عَلَيْكَ يَا مَنْ نَادَاهُ
هَاتِفُ ٱلْغَيْبِ بِأَكْرَمِ نِدَاءٍ ، ٱلسَّلَامُ عَلَيْكَ يَا ٱبْنَ إِبْرَاهِيمَ ٱلْخَلِيلِ ،
ٱلسَّلَامُ عَلَيْكَ يَا وَارِثَ الذَّبِيحِ إِسْمَاعِيلَ ، ٱلسَّلَامُ عَلَيْكَ
يَا مَنْ أَهْلَكَ ٱللهُ بِدُعَائِهِ أَصْحَابَ ٱلْفِيلِ ، وَجَعَلَ كَيْدَهُـمْ فِي
تَضْلِيلٍ ، وَأَرْسَلَ عَلَيْهِمْ طَيْراً أَبَابِيلَ ، تَرْمِيهِم بِحِجَارَةٍ مِنْ سِجِّيلٍ ،
فَجَعَلَهُمْ كَعَصْفٍ مَأْكُولٍ ؛ ٱلسَّلَامُ عَلَيْكَ يَا مَنْ تَضَرَّعَ فِي حَاجَاتِهِ
إِلَى ٱللهِ ، وَتَوَسَّلَ فِي دُعَائِهِ بِنُورِ رَسُولِ ٱللهِ ، صَلَّى اللهُ عَلَيْهِ وَآلِهِ
وَسَلَّمَ . ٱلسَّلَامُ عَلَيْكَ يَا مَنِ ٱسْتَجَابَ ٱللهُ دُعَاءَهُ وَنُودِيَ فِي ٱلْكَعْبَةِ
وَبُشِّرَ بِٱلْإِجَابَةِ فِي دُعَائِهِ ، وَأَسْجَدَ ٱللهُ ٱلْفِيلَ إِكْرَاماً وَإِعْظَاماً لَهُ ؛
ٱلسَّلَامُ عَلَيْكَ يَا مَنْ أَنْبَعَ ٱللهُ لَهُ أَلْمَاءَ حَتَّى شَرِبَ وَأَرْوَى فِي ٱلْأَرْضِ
ٱلْقَفْرَاءِ ؛ ٱلسَّلَامُ عَلَيْكَ يَا ٱبْنَ الذَّبِيحِ وَأَبَا الذَّبِيحِ ؛ ٱلسَّلَامُ

عَلَيْكَ يَا سَاقِيَ الْحَجِيجِ وَحَافِرَ زَمْزَمَ ، السَّلَامُ عَلَيْكَ يَا مَنْ جَعَلَ اللهُ
مِنْ نَسْلِهِ سَيِّدَ الْمُرْسَلِينَ ، وَخَيْرَ أَهْلِ السَّمٰوَاتِ وَالْأَرَضِينَ ، السَّلَامُ
عَلَيْكَ يَا مَنْ طَافَ حَوْلَ الْكَعْبَةِ وَجَعَلَهُ سَبْعَةَ أَشْوَاطٍ ؛ السَّلَامُ
عَلَيْكَ يَا مَنْ رَأَى فِي الْمَنَامِ سِلْسِلَةَ النُّورِ ، وَعَلِمَ أَنَّهُ مِنْ أَهْلِ
الْجَنَّةِ ؛ السَّلَامُ عَلَيْكَ يَا شَيْبَةَ الْحَمْدِ ، السَّلَامُ عَلَيْكَ وَعَلَى آبَائِكَ
وَأَجْدَادِكَ وَأَبْنَائِكَ جَمِيعاً وَرَحْمَةُ اللهِ وَبَرَكَاتُه) .

زيارة ابي طالب عم النبي (ص)

(السَّلَامُ عَلَيْكَ يَا سَيِّدَ الْبَطْحَاءِ وَابْنَ رَئِيسِهَا ، السَّلَامُ عَلَيْكَ
يَا وَارِثَ الْكَعْبَةِ بَعْدَ تَأْسِيسِهَا ، السَّلَامُ عَلَيْكَ يَا كَافِلَ الرَّسُولِ
وَنَاصِرَه ، السَّلَامُ عَلَيْكَ يَا عَمَّ الْمُصْطَفَى وَأَبَا الْمُرْتَضَى ، السَّلَامُ
عَلَيْكَ يَا بَيْضَةَ الْبَلَدِ ، السَّلَامُ عَلَيْكَ أَيُّهَا الذَّابُّ عَنِ الدِّينِ ،
وَالْبَاذِلُ نَفْسَهُ فِي نُصْرَةِ سَيِّدِ الْمُرْسَلِينَ ، عَلَيْكَ وَعَلَى وَلَدِكَ أَمِيرِ
الْمُؤْمِنِينَ وَرَحْمَةُ اللهِ وَبَرَكَاتُه .

زيارة آمنة بنت وهب ام النبي (ص)

(السَّلَامُ عَلَيْكِ أَيَّتُهَا الطَّاهِرَةُ الْمُطَهَّرَة ، السَّلَامُ عَلَيْكِ يَا
مَنْ خَصَّهَا اللهُ بِأَعْلَى الشَّرَفِ ، السَّلَامُ عَلَيْكِ يَا مَنْ سَطَعَ مِنْ

جَبِينِهَا نُورُ سَيِّدِ ٱلْأَنْبِيَاءِ فَأَضَاءَتْ بِهِ ٱلْأَرْضُ وَٱلسَّمَاءُ ، ٱلسَّلَامُ عَلَيْكِ يَا مَنْ نَزَلَتْ لِأَجْلِهَا ٱلْمَلَائِكَةُ وَضُرِبَتْ لَهَا حُجُبُ ٱلْجَنَّةِ ، ٱلسَّلَامُ عَلَيْكِ يَا مَنْ نَزَلَتْ لِخِدْمَتِهَا ٱلْحُورُ ٱلْعِينُ، وَسَقَيْنَهَا مِنْ شَرَابِ ٱلْجَنَّةِ ، وَبَشَّرْنَهَا بِوِلَادَةِ خَيْرِ ٱلْأَنْبِيَاءِ ، ٱلسَّلَامُ عَلَيْكِ يَا أُمَّ رَسُولِ ٱللهِ ، ٱلسَّلَامُ عَلَيْكِ يَا أُمَّ حَبِيبِ ٱللهِ ، فَهَنِيئًا لَكِ بِمَا آتَاكِ ٱللهُ مِنْ فَضْلٍ وَٱلسَّلَامُ عَلَيْكِ وَعَلَى رَسُولِ ٱللهِ صَلَّى ٱللهُ عَلَيْهِ وَآلِهِ وَسَلَّمَ وَرَحْمَةُ ٱللهِ وَبَرَكَاتُهُ) .

زيارة خديجة بنت خويلد ام المؤمنين

وقبرها بالحجون في سفح الجبل ، وهو معروف ، فتقول :

(ٱلسَّلَامُ عَلَيْكِ يَا أُمَّ ٱلْمُؤْمِنِينَ ، ٱلسَّلَامُ عَلَيْكِ يَا زَوْجَةَ سَيِّدِ ٱلْمُرْسَلِينَ ، ٱلسَّلَامُ عَلَيْكِ يَا أُمَّ فَاطِمَةَ ٱلزَّهْرَاءِ سَيِّدَةِ نِسَاءِ ٱلْعَالَمِينَ ، ٱلسَّلَامُ عَلَيْكِ يَا أَوَّلَ ٱلْمُؤْمِنَاتِ ، ٱلسَّلَامُ عَلَيْكِ يَا مَنْ أَنْفَقَتْ مَالَهَا فِي نُصْرَةِ سَيِّدِ ٱلْأَنْبِيَاءِ وَنَصَرَتْهُ مَا ٱسْتَطَاعَتْ وَدَافَعَتْ عَنْهُ ٱلْأَعْدَاءَ ، ٱلسَّلَامُ عَلَيْكِ يَا مَنْ سَلَّمَ عَلَيْهَا جِبْرَائِيلُ وَبَلَّغَهَا ٱلسَّلَامَ مِنَ ٱللهِ ٱلْجَلِيلِ ، فَهَنِيئًا لَكِ بِمَا أَوْلَاكِ ٱللهُ مِنْ فَضْلٍ وَٱلسَّلَامُ عَلَيْكِ وَرَحْمَةُ ٱللهِ وَبَرَكَاتُهُ) .

بيت المقدس

ان بيت المقدس ، وبالأحرى الحرم الشريف وفيه قبـة الصخرة والمسجد الأقصى — هو ثالث محل مقدس في الاسلام .

ويقع المسجد الحالي والبنايات المحيطة به في موضع المعبد الذي بنـاه النبي سليمان عليه السلام قبل ثلاثة آلاف سنة ، واستولى عليه بعد خمسمائة سنة نبوخذ نصر واعاد بناءه في ذلك العصر (عزرا) و (نحميا) ، واعاده الى الوثنية انطونيو كوس ابيفانس أحد خلفاء الاسكندر ، ثم اعاد بنـاءه هيرود في ايام النبي عيسى عليه السلام . وبعد مرور سبعين عاماً على ذلك هـدم الامبراطور طايطوس المسجد من اساسه للمرة الثانية في تاريخه ، واخيراً اعاد بنـاءه عبد الملك بن مروان في موقعه الحالي . وذلك بعد اكثر من نصف قرن بقليل من وفاة النبي محمد ﷺ .

وقد قيل ان النبي ﷺ وقف هنا بعد اسرائه ليلا قبل أن يتشرف في خلوة الملأ الأعلى لكي يتسلم الاوامر الإلهية الخاصة بأحكام الصلاة واوقاتها .

والإسراء (او المعراج) تما في ليلة ٢٧ رجب في السنة التي تقدمت هجرة النبي من مكة . ويعتقد بعض المسلمين ان الاسراء من مكة الى بيت المقدس والمعراج من بيت المقدس الى السماء ، والعودة الى مكة ، حصلا بالجسد ، ويعتقد الآخرون انه حصل في حلم (بالروح) رآه النبي محمد ﷺ في منامه .

(وهذا الاعتقاد الثاني لم يعرف الا عن نفر قليل من المسلمين ومن عدام يحكمون بكفر من يعتقد بذلك لانه تكذيب للنبي الذي اخبر انه عرج بجسده الشريف ، والقرآن نطق بذلك . وقد اوضح العلماء المعراج الجساني حتى صار كأنه محسوس ، وليرجع الى كتاب (اسرار المعراج) بالعربية او كتاب (معراج خير الأنام آيينه اسلام) بالفارسية يرى المعراج محسوساً) . وكيفما كان فان المعراج واقع .

(سُبْحَانَ ٱلَّذِى أَسْرَىٰ بِعَبْدِهِ لَيْلاً مِنَ ٱلْمَسْجِدِ ٱلْحَرَامِ إِلَى ٱلْمَسْجِدِ ٱلْأَقْصَى ٱلَّذِى بَارَكْنَا حَوْلَهُ لِنُرِيَهُ مِنْ آيَاتِنَا إِنَّهُ ٱلسَّمِيعُ ٱلْبَصِيرُ) .
(سورة أسرى ، ١)

وقد روي ان الملك جبرائيل ظهر للنبي محمد صلى الله عليه وسلم عندما كان نائماً في الكعبة المكرمة . فغسل النبي بحوض ذهبي في ماء الايمان ثم ركب البراق الذي حمله الى بيت المقدس بسرعة الضوء ، فـكانت خطواته تطوي الفضاء بمقدار مدى الرؤية .

وفي بيت المقدس ترجل النبي في الموقع القديم لمعبد سليمان ، وهناك أم في صلاته جماعة الانبياء الذين سبقوه على الارض ، ومنهم ابراهيم وسليـمان وموسى وداود وعيسى عليهم السلام ، ثم ركب النبي محمـــد صلى الله عليه وسلم مرة اخرى الى السماء على براقه المجنح ، ووقف عند سدرة المنتهى موضع الملك جبرائيل السماوي الذي يقع تحت العرش المحيط بجميع المخلوقات .

وهنا تلقى النبي محمد صلى الله عليـــه وسلم الأمر الالهي بأن يؤدي جميــــع المسلمين الصلوات الخمس يومياً :

« لَيْسَ ٱلْبِرَّ أَنْ تُوَلُّوا وُجُوهَكُمْ قِبَلَ ٱلْمَشْرِقِ وَٱلْمَغْرِبِ ، وَلَـٰكِنَّ ٱلْبِرَّ مَنْ آمَنَ بِاللهِ وَٱلْيَوْمِ ٱلْآخِرِ وَٱلْمَلَائِكَةِ وَٱلْكِتَابِ وَٱلنَّبِيِّينَ ، وَآتَى ٱلْمَالَ عَلَى حُبِّهِ ذَوِي ٱلْقُرْبَى وَٱلْيَتَامَى وَٱلْمَسَاكِينَ وَٱبْنَ ٱلسَّبِيلِ وَٱلسَّائِلِينَ وَفِي ٱلرِّقَابِ ، وَأَقَامَ ٱلصَّلَاةَ وَآتَى ٱلزَّكَاةَ وَٱلْمُوفُونَ بِعَهْدِهِمْ إِذَا عَاهَدُوا ، وَٱلصَّابِرِينَ فِي ٱلْبَأْسَاءِ وَٱلضَّرَّاءِ وَحِينَ ٱلْبَأْسِ ، أُولَـٰئِكَ ٱلَّذِينَ صَدَقُوا وَأُولَـٰئِكَ هُمُ ٱلْمُتَّقُونَ » .
(سورة البقرة ، ١٧٦)

الحاج احمد كمال